Plutocratic
Insurgency Reader

Front Cover Image: *The Bosses of the Senate,* 1889 lithograph by Joseph Keppler (colored by J. Ottmann Lith. Co.). Published in *Puck,* January 23, 1889. ClassicStock/Alamy Stock Photo (Used by permission).

US Senate Description: This frequently reproduced cartoon, long a staple of textbooks and studies of Congress, depicts corporate interests—from steel, copper, oil, iron, sugar, tin, and coal to paper bags, envelopes, and salt—as giant money bags looming over the tiny senators at their desks in the Chamber. Joseph Keppler drew the cartoon, which appeared in *Puck* on January 23, 1889, showing a door to the gallery, the "people's entrance," bolted and barred. The galleries stand empty while the special interests have floor privileges, operating below the motto: "This is the Senate of the Monopolists by the Monopolists and for the Monopolists!" Keppler's cartoon reflected the phenomenal growth of American industry in the 1880s, but also the disturbing trend toward concentration of industry to the point of monopoly, and its undue influence on politics. This popular perception contributed to Congress's passage of the Sherman Anti-Trust Act in 1890. Source: https://www.senate.gov/artandhistory/art/artifact/Ga_Cartoon/ Ga_cartoon_38_00392.htm.

Plutocratic Insurgency Reader

Robert J. Bunker and
Pamela Ligouri Bunker, Editors

A *Small Wars Journal* Book

To order additional copies of this book, contact:
Xlibris
1-888-795-4274
www.Xlibris.com
Orders@Xlibris.com
788028

CONTENTS

ABOUT SMALL WARS JOURNAL
AND FOUNDATION

Small Wars Journal facilitates the exchange of information among practitioners, thought leaders, and students of Small Wars, in order to advance knowledge and capabilities in the field. We hope this, in turn, advances the practice and effectiveness of those forces prosecuting Small Wars in the interest of self-determination, freedom, and prosperity for the population in the area of operations.

We believe that Small Wars are an enduring feature of modern politics. We do not believe that true effectiveness in Small Wars is a 'lesser included capability' of a force tailored for major theater war. And we *never* believed that 'bypass built-up areas' was a tenable position warranting the doctrinal primacy it has held for too long—this site is an evolution of the MOUT Homepage, Urban Operations Journal, and urbanoperations.com, all formerly run by the *Small Wars Journal's* Editor-in-Chief.

The characteristics of Small Wars have evolved since the Banana Wars and Gunboat Diplomacy. War is never purely military, but today's

Small Wars are even less pure with the greater inter-connectedness of the 21st century. Their conduct typically involves the projection and employment of the full spectrum of national and coalition power by a broad community of practitioners. The military is still generally the biggest part of the pack, but there are a lot of other wolves. The strength of the pack is the wolf, and the strength of the wolf is the pack.

The *Small Wars Journal's* founders come from the Marine Corps. Like Marines deserve to be, we are very proud of this; we are also conscious and cautious of it. This site seeks to transcend any viewpoint that is single service, and any that is purely military or naively U.S.-centric. We pursue a comprehensive approach to Small Wars, integrating the full joint, allied, and coalition military with their governments' federal or national agencies, non-governmental agencies, and private organizations. Small Wars are big undertakings, demanding a coordinated effort from a huge community of interest.

We thank our contributors for sharing their knowledge and experience, and hope you will continue to join us as we build a resource for our community of interest to engage in a professional dialog on this painfully relevant topic. Share your thoughts, ideas, successes, and mistakes; make us all stronger.

"…I know it when I see it."

"Small Wars" is an imperfect term used to describe a broad spectrum of spirited continuation of politics by other means, falling somewhere in the middle bit of the continuum between feisty diplomatic words and global thermonuclear war. The *Small Wars Journal* embraces that imperfection.

Just as friendly fire isn't, there isn't necessarily anything small about a Small War.

The term "Small War" either encompasses or overlaps with a number of familiar terms such as counterinsurgency, foreign internal defense, support and stability operations, peacemaking, peacekeeping, and many flavors of intervention. Operations such as noncombatant evacuation, disaster relief, and humanitarian assistance will often either be a part of a Small War, or have a Small Wars feel to them. Small Wars involve a wide spectrum of specialized tactical, technical, social, and cultural skills and expertise, requiring great ingenuity from their practitioners. The *Small Wars Manual* (a wonderful resource, unfortunately more often referred to than read) notes that:

> *Small Wars demand the highest type of leadership directed by intelligence, resourcefulness, and ingenuity. Small Wars are conceived in uncertainty, are conducted often with precarious responsibility and doubtful authority, under indeterminate orders lacking specific instructions.*

The "three block war" construct employed by General Krulak is exceptionally useful in describing the tactical and operational challenges of a Small War and of many urban operations. Its only shortcoming is that is so useful that it is often mistaken as a definition or as a type of operation.

We'd like to deploy a primer on Small Wars that provides more depth than this brief section. Your suggestions and contributions of content are welcome.

Who Are Those Guys?

Small Wars Journal is NOT a government, official, or big corporate site. It is run by <u>Small Wars Foundation</u>, a non-profit corporation, for the benefit of the Small Wars community of interest. The site principals are Dave Dilegge (Editor-in-Chief) and Bill Nagle (Publisher), and it would not be possible without the support of myriad volunteers as well as authors who care about this field and contribute their original works to the community. We do this in our spare time, because we want to. McDonald's pays more. But we'd rather work to advance our noble profession than watch TV, try to super-size your order, or interest you in a delicious hot apple pie. If and when you're not flipping burgers, please join us.

Contributors

Editors

Dr. Robert J. Bunker is a Senior Fellow, Small Wars Journal—El Centro and an Instructor, Safe Communities Institute, Sol Price School of Public Policy at USC. He is also an Adjunct Research Professor, Strategic Studies Institute, US Army War College. Past positions include Minerva Chair, Office of the Secretary of Defense and Futurist in Residence, Behavioral Science Unit, FBI Academy. He holds a BA in history, BS in anthropology-geography and social science, and BA in behavioral science from California State Polytechnic University Pomona, and a MA in government and a PhD in political science from the Claremont Graduate University. He is the author of hundreds of publications including over twenty-five co-authored and edited books—including *Studies in Gangs and Cartels* and *Global Criminal and Sovereign Free Economies and the Demise of the Western Democracies*—and has given numerous presentations including US Congressional testimony.

Pamela Ligouri Bunker is an Associate, Small Wars Journal—El Centro and a Non-Resident Fellow in Terrorism & Counter-Terrorism, TRENDS Research and Advisory, Abu Dhabi. She holds a BS in anthropology-geography and a BS in social science from California State Polytechnic University Pomona, a MA in public policy from the Claremont Graduate University, and a MLitt in terrorism studies from the University of St. Andrews. She is a past senior officer of the Counter-OPFOR Corporation and has professional experience in research and program coordination in university, non-governmental organization (NGO), and city government settings. She is co-author of *Radical Islamist English-Language Online Magazines: Research Guide, Strategic Insights, and Policy Response* and co-editor of *Global Criminal and Sovereign Free Economies and the Demise of the Western Democracies.*

Contributors

Bryan T. Baker is an intelligence officer in the US Army Reserve. He also teaches Humane Letters—with an emphasis on American history and literature—at a classical preparatory academy in the Phoenix area. He holds a BA in political science and history from the University of Arizona and is currently completing a MA in international security through the same institution.

Rich Couch is a retired physical scientist. At his blog he writes essays combining reviews and opinions of books and articles on politics and current affairs (http://letstalkbooksandpolitics.blogspot.com).

Carlos Fazio is a Uruguayan journalist based in Mexico. He writes for the newspaper *La Jornada* and collaborates with the weekly *Brecha* of Uruguay.

Naimisha Forest is the pen-name of a retired career economist at an international financial institution, currently an independent scholar and blogger at the *Naimisha Forest* blog (https://naimisha_forest.silvrback.com).

Dr. Nils Gilman is Vice President for Programs at the Berggruen Institute, Los Angeles, California. He is a former Associate Chancellor and Chief of Staff, UC Berkeley and Director of Research, Monitor 360. He holds a BA in history, MA in history, and PhD in American History from UC Berkeley. He is the author of *Mandarins of the Future: Modernization Theory in Cold War America* and numerous other publications on history, politics, and technology.

Dr. Jesse Goldhammer is a Managing Director at Deloitte (of the Deloitte Touche Tohmatsu Limited group) focusing on cyber security and risk practice. He is a past Associate Dean of Business Development and Strategy, UC Berkeley School of Information. He holds a BA in social science from UC Berkeley as well as an MA and PhD in political science from New York University and UC Berkeley, respectively. He is an accomplished analyst, author and speaker on diverse topics, including scenario planning, social impact of technology, open innovation, cyber security and illicit globalization.

Dr. Alma Keshavarz is an Associate with Small Wars Journal—El Centro and a past Non-Resident Fellow in Terrorism and Security Studies, TRENDS Research & Advisory, Abu Dhabi. She holds a BA in political science and english from University of California, Davis, an MPP from Pepperdine's School of Public Policy, and a MA and PhD in political science from the Claremont Graduate University. She is the author of numerous articles and reports and a co-editor of *Iranian and Hezbollah Hybrid Warfare Activities* and *Blood and Concrete: 21st Century Conflict in Urban Centers and Megacities*. She is fluent in Spanish and Farsi.

Dr. Steven Metz is Director of Research at the Strategic Studies Institute, US Army War College. He has been with SSI since 1993, previously serving as Henry L. Stimson Professor of Military Studies, Chairman of the Regional Strategy Department, research director for the Joint Strategic Landpower Task Force, and co-director of SSI's Future of American Strategy Project. He holds a BA and a MA in international relations and affairs from the University of South Carolina and a PhD in political science from the Johns Hopkins University. His research has taken him to 30 countries, including Iraq immediately after the collapse of the Hussein regime. He writes a weekly column on security and defense for *World Politics Review* and is an Adjunct Scholar at the US Military Academy's Modern War Institute. He has published numerous reports and articles and is the author of *Iraq and the Evolution of American Strategy*.

John Robb is a highly regarded analyst and futurist, with a focus on the intersection of terrorism, infrastructure, technology, and markets. His expertise includes work in social software, military theory, and resilient communities. Previous experience includes service in a tier one counterterrorist unit that worked closely with Delta and Seal Team 6. In that role, he participated in global operations as a mission commander, pilot, and mission planner (El Salvador, Panama, Colombia, Egypt, etc.). He holds a BS in astronautical engineering from the US Air Force Academy and a Masters in public and private management (MPPM) from Yale University. He is the author of *Brave New War: The Next Stage of Terrorism and the End of Globalization*, a number of other publications, and runs the blog *Global Guerrillas* (https:// globalguerrillas.typepad.com).

Paul Rosenberg is a California-based activist turned journalist who's written for the *Christian Science Monitor*, *LA Times*, *Denver Post*, *Al Jazeera English*, *Salon.com* and dozens of others. He's been editor or senior editor at *Random Lengths News*, an alternative biweekly, since 2002, and has written over 300 book reviews. He shared in Project Censored #1 story for 2004 on the neocon origins of the Iraq War. He combines an interest in cognitive, social and physical sciences with a social justice perspective handed down from his immigrant grandparent's generation.

Dr. John P. Sullivan is a Senior Fellow, Small Wars Journal—El Centro and an Instructor, Safe Communities Institute, Sol Price School of Public Policy at USC. He is a retired Lieutenant, Los Angeles Sheriffs Department; specializing in emergency operations, transit policing, counterterrorism, and intelligence. He holds a BA in government from the College of William and Mary, a MA in urban affairs and policy analysis from the New School for Social Research, and a PhD in information and knowledge society from the Open University of Catalonia where he studied under Manuel Castells. He has published hundreds of articles and reports and is the co-editor of numerous anthologies including *The Rise of the Narcostate (Mafia States)*, *Mexico's Criminal Insurgency*, and *Crime Wars and Narco Terrorism in the Americas*.

George Thomas goes by the pen name Quintus Curtius at the *Fortress of the Mind* blog (https://qcurtius.com). He is a Managing Partner of Phillips & Thomas, LLC; a Kansas City area law firm that focuses its practice in the areas of criminal defense and bankruptcy. He is a former Missouri State Prosecutor and Major in the United States Marine Corps where he led intelligence task forces in Japan, Korea, and Bosnia at the national and multi-national level. He holds a BS in political science from the Massachusetts Institute of Technology and a JD from the University of Missouri-Kansas City School of Law. He is the author of seven books, including *On Moral Ends* and *Pantheon*, composed of annotated translations and essay collections and is fluent in Portuguese.

Dr. Steven Weber is a Professor, UC Berkeley School of Information and Department of Political Science. He holds a PhD and MD from Stanford University and a BA from Washington University. He works at the intersection of technology markets, intellectual property regimes, and international politics. Over the last 20 years Weber has advised multinational companies, government agencies, and non-profit organizations on risk analysis, strategy, and business forecasting in the areas of international political risk, technology, and global economic change, in part through The Glover Park Group in Washington DC. His books include *The Success of Open Source* and most recently *The End of Arrogance: America in the Global Competition of Ideas* (with Bruce Jentleson) and *Deviant Globalization: Black Market Economy in the 21st Century* (with Jesse Goldhammer and Nils Gilman).

The views expressed in this reader are those of the author(s) and do not necessarily reflect the official policy or position of the Department of the Army, the Department of Defense, the Federal Bureau of Investigation, the Department of Justice, or the US Government, or any other US armed service, intelligence or law enforcement agency, or local or state government.

Preface

The Twilight of Social Modernism

Nils Gilman

The Polo Lounge, Beverly Hills, CA

February 2019

We are reaching the end of the Westphalian-modernist system. This system is of more recent vintage than is usually acknowledged. Prior to the mid-20th century, a variety of more-or-less legitimate means of govern1ance existed, including not just sovereign states, but empires, colonies, dominions, mandates, trusteeships, condominia, protectorates, etc. The sorts of perceived obligations between rulers and ruled varied dramatically from one place to another. When the era of decolonization began in earnest in the wake of World War II, however, the formally sovereign state rapidly become hegemonic—or, rather, to be more precise, all other forms of governance lost their legitimacy.

The specific form of the sovereign state which reached its ideological apogee during the political period of decolonization was the state as modernization-and-welfare-providing entity. I have elsewhere referred to this ideological and institutional formation as "social modernism."[1] Inside that general social modernist rubric, there were of course vast debates, not least the Cold War era-defining struggle between authoritarian communism and democratic capitalism. But what both poles of the Cold War (and virtually all positions staked out in between or apart from them) had in common during this period was *the ideal that every person should live as a citizen within a sovereign state whose avowed objective was to create economic growth in the name of improved collective welfare.* Since the end of the Cold War, however, this social modernist ideal has been under sustained assault by what this volume refers to as the plutocratic insurgency.

The ideological underpinnings of this insurgency are worthy of brief consideration. On the one hand, the idea of the state as provider has been under sharp attack for two generations. From the 1970s through the early 21st century, the West experienced increasing ideological contestation of the idea that the state should be the leading economic institution (the ruler of "the commanding heights," in Lenin's phrase), taking direct responsibility for ensuring the social welfare of all citizens, and endowed with the authority to draw on national resources in order to achieve this goal. By the 1990s it had become a mainstream center-right opinion that for-profit entities could more efficiently supply "welfare"-like goods than could the state. While the center-left offered fitful resistance, the collapse of the far left threat with the end of the Cold War emboldened those whose goal was the systematic privatization of one public good after another.

On the other hand, the idea of the state as the primary locus of political identity and loyalty was (until recently at least) more quietly eroding. On a legal level, the idea that the rights of individuals depended uniquely and specifically on the state within which they happened to reside became increasingly contested, with promoters of human rights and supranational institutions like the European Union each in their own way challenging the unique privileges of the state. At the level of identity, various group and communal conceptions have increasingly challenged the hegemony of the national, including identities related to gender, religion, race and profession. Most pertinently to this volume, the identity as "global citizen" (a term which scarcely existed before the 1980s) came to be increasingly favored by the ultra-rich who saw themselves as above (often quite literally, in their private jets) any particular national identity—carrying multiple passports, and always happy to pick up another if it opened a useful set of doors.[2]

If criminal insurgencies are in part a subaltern reaction to the failures of state-led modernization,[3] then the plutocratic insurgency is what capitalist elites join when they no longer see themselves as organically connected or politically subordinated to a geographically-circumscribed state project.[4] These elites identify more with what Robert Bunker describes in these pages as "a supra-national globalized form of predatory capitalism that is attempting to move beyond the confines of mere sovereign states." The dimensions of this plutocratic insurgency are well documented in this timely volume, including first and foremost the war of the rich against progressive tax-paying; corporations' use of offshore tax havens to shelter profits from the national taxman; individual plutocrats' use of the corporate form to shelter personal income; the ongoing loss of stable middle class employment opportunities in the face of the Fourth Industrial Revolution's combination of artificial intelligence, robotics, and new models of "flexible" labor management; and the increase in precarity as pension systems and other forms of state-backed social security are downsized.[5] The lifestyles of plutocratic insurgents also receive due attention, from the creation of privatized residential enclaves, to the use of private transportation systems, internets, health care, education, and so on and so on. Increasingly, plutocratic insurgents maintain property and assets in multiple jurisdictions as a hedge against what is euphemistically called "political risk."[6]

But what is the political risk, exactly, that plutocratic insurgents face? Put another way: What are the alternatives to the political hegemony of plutocrats? So far, in much of the West, there have been two broad varietals, each of which promises something new and distinctly 21st century, but which also echo something old and very 19th century: socialism and nationalism. Both socialism and nationalism were ideas that emerged from the crucible of nineteenth century industrialism as alternative visions for how to deal with the loss of *Gemeinschaftliche* forms of mutual obligation and responsibility. Both offered alternative takes on who constituted "the circle of the 'we'" of a political community. Today, heritors of each of these traditions promise to take on the plutocratic insurgency, albeit in very different ways.

On the one hand, there are neo-socialists (or, as they style themselves in the United States, "democratic socialists") who point to the growing wealth disparities that are the result of the plutocratic insurgency and propose policies designed to abrogate the financial and political power of the rich. Proposals include raising top marginal income tax rates, imposing wealth and inheritance taxes, dissolving tax havens, re-empowering organized labor, and reinvigorating the state as a provider of public goods, for example through the formulation of a "Green New Deal."[7] On the other hand, even more prominently, are resurgent forms of authoritarian nationalism that aim to rebuild the communal solidarity through the exclusion of "outsiders," most commonly immigrants but sometimes also sexual, religious, or ethnic minorities. While the sponsors of these political movements (often mislabeled as "populists") express ritual disgust with "globalist elites," few if any of them have proposed concrete policies to designed to puncture plutocratic privileges—which may explain why Davos has gingerly embraced them.[8] It is unclear whether either of these movements will have the power to seriously restrain the plutocratic insurgency.

With the modernist social contract rewritten under the guise of privatization, de-pooling of collective risk, acceptance of massive economic inequality, and the rejection of traditional racial and gender hierarchies, the central question of our time is what sorts of moral and institutional bases can ground burden-sharing and collective action—especially in the face of the dramatic challenges of the 21st century, most of all climate change and the mass population migrations that will all but inevitably ensue. Whatever form this collection active should take, there is no question that, in this effort to imagine a new kind of politics suitable to addressing the challenges of our time, plutocratic insurgents and their hired help are a malignant adversary force. Should they continue to win, they will amplify the vicious cycle whereby, as the crises of our time get worse, more and more people will be tempted to eschew collective solutions in favor of immuring themselves within private enclaves of temporary security. In the end, however, as the

Romans, the Ming, and everyone else who has tried to hold back the tide has discovered, a wall is only a stay; if the threats the walls are designed to stop remain unaddressed, the walls merely ensure that the day of reckoning, when it comes, will be that much more dramatic.

Notes

1. Nils Gilman, *Mandarins of the Future: Modernization Theory in Cold War America*. Baltimore, MD: Johns Hopkins University Press, 2004. If the 19th century was where "the Social Question" emerged, and the 20th century is where the answer to that question was provided in the form of the disciplining welfare state, then the 21st century represents the collapse of that latter paradigm, whose manifestation is the twin insurgency of criminals and plutocrats. For 19th century worldly philosophers, "the social question" turned on what to do with the large populations of pre-industrial workers whose traditional forms of social support, like guilds, were being rendered obsolete by advancing technologies of production, producing visible and rapid decline in the quality of life of the mass of the population. Observing the social unrest and political upheaval that was the inevitable by-product of this, the German professor and politician Karl Biedermann observed that "the social peace depended on social justice for the working class." This observation would become the point of departure for Germany's construction, beginning in the late 19th century, of the institutions today regarded as the cornerstones of the welfare state, including public pensions, as well as disability and health insurance. By the middle of the twentieth century (after a great deal of political contestation), it had become conventional wisdom in the core industrial states of the North Atlantic that "taxes are what we pay for civilized society" (Oliver Wendell Holmes) and that welfare states were the cornerstone of social peace and political stability. On that latter point, see Charles S. Maier, "The Two Postwar Eras and the Conditions for Stability in Twentieth-Century Western Europe," *The American Historical Review*, 1981: 327-352.
2. Atossa Araxia Abrahamian, *The Cosmopolites: The Coming of the Global Citizen*. New York: Columbia Global Reports, 2015.
3. John P. Sullivan and Robert J. Bunker, "Rethinking insurgency: criminality, spirituality, and societal warfare in the Americas," *Small Wars & Insurgencies* 22:5, 2011: 742-763.
4. Many of the trends toward plutocratic insurgency are at their most intense in countries that were once standard-bearers of modernizing dreams, places like Nigeria, Mexico, Brazil, and India. In this sense, plutocratic insurgency can be seen as backfilling the vacuum created by the ideological and administrative

retreat of state-managed development. For so long Westerners, and Americans in particular, indulged themselves with the narcissistic pleasure of Marx's infamous dictum that "the more developed country only shows to the less developed ones the image of its own future"; if Americans wish to see their own future today, however, they might do well to spend less time listening to Silicon Valley dreamers and more time looking at how countries in the Global South are dealing with intense environmental stress under conditions of growing inequality. Conversely, it is no coincidence that the problem of plutocratic insurgency barely exists in places where the state as a modernizing force (for better or worse) retains a certain political purchase. This applies to places as otherwise different as Japan with its continued belief in industrial policy, China with its regional infrastructure planning, the petro-kleptocracy of Russia, or the old-style central planning regimes of a country like North Korea. In all these places, there may be corruption and oligarchy aplenty, but the beneficiaries remain under the thumb of the state. It is also notable that the places where the plutocratic insurgency has been suppressed—that is, where the prerogatives of the wealthy remain subordinated to the priorities of the state—are also not places where "populist" politics of either the anti-globalist variety or the neo-socialist variety have gotten much traction.

5. The austerity driven downsizing of social support is happening everywhere. Italy: https://www.thelocal.it/20190118/italian-government-approves-overhaul-of-welfare-and-pensions. Brazil: https://www.reuters.com/article/us-brazil-pensions-idUSKCN1PU250. Nicaragua: https://www.nbcnews.com/news/latino/nicaragua-steep-pension-cuts-tax-increases-could-plunge-country-recession-n970261. Russia: https://foreignpolicy.com/2019/02/11/russians-lower-their-standards/. The United States: https://www.forbes.com/sites/dianeoakley/2018/10/30/the-predictable-consequence-of-cutting-public-safety-pensions/#f9ef7951135e. And the list goes on.

6. Evan Osnos, "Doomsday Prep for the Super-Rich," *The New Yorker*, 30 January 2017, https://www.newyorker.com/magazine/2017/01/30/doomsday-prep-for-the-super-rich.

7. The U.S. Democratic primary in 2020 seems set to play out around the question of how far to go with this respect. Unfortunately, those proposing high marginal tax rates as a way to curb the wealth and power of ultra high net worth individuals do not seem to have a clear understanding of the way that globalized and corporatized finance has rendered personal income tax and even wealth taxes largely irrelevant to the super rich. In fact, serious plutocrats typically have very little "income," but rather control corporations or other wealth-generating assets through a complex web of offshore holdings that ultimately roll up into holding companies sitting in low- or no-tax jurisdictions. Abrogating these sites of arbitrage opportunity and/or limiting the mobility of capital is an essential

precondition for any effective effort to limit the prerogatives of the superwealthy.

8. Mark Bendeich, "Brazil's Bolsonaro uses Davos speech to appeal to big business," *Reuters,* 22 January 2019, https://www.reuters.com/article/us-davos-meeting-bolsonaro-business/brazils-bolsonaro-uses-davos-speech-to-appeal-to-big-business-idUSKCN1PG1SE.

Introduction

Plutocratic Insurgency Reader

Robert J. Bunker and Pamela Ligouri Bunker

Claremont, CA

June 2019

Plutocratic insurgency represents an emerging form of insurgency not seen since the late 19th century Gilded Age. It is being conducted by high net worth globalized elites allowing them to remove themselves from public spaces and obligations—including taxation—and to maximize their ability to generate profits transnationally. It utilizes 'lawyers & lobbyists' and corruption, rather than armed struggle—though mercenaries may be employed—to create shadow governance in pursuit of plutocratic policy objectives. Ultimately, this form of insurgency is representative of the challenge of 21st century predatory and sovereign-free capitalism to 20th century state moderated capitalism and its ensuing public welfare programs and middle class social structures. It can be viewed as a component of 'Dark Globalization' that, along with the emergence of criminal insurgency, is now actively threatening the public institutions and citizenry of the Westphalian state form.

The preceding abstract appeared in the initial plutocratic insurgency notes (No. 1 and No. 2 published in February 2017) to provide historical context to the readership of *Small Wars Journal* concerning a new, and potentially controversial, form of insurgency that is emerging as a component of 21st century dark (i.e. deviant) globalization. This insurgency form re-conceptualizes modern perceptions of how an insurgency is defined and who is waging it. Yet, in many ways, the need for a new interpretation of insurgency is no different than the need for the recognition of new warfare forms developing around state and non-state actor use of weaponized social media and other currently unrestricted processes of conflict.[1] Hence, the process of conflict (and its definition) may have drastically changed but the outcome of conflict [i.e. achieving *de facto* political power that translates into control over the allocation of great wealth and resources; be they state-(publicly) or family dynastic-(privately) based] has not.

Both elements signify the increasing erosion of the Westphalian nation-state's monopoly on warfare and the ongoing diminution of sovereign rights and prerogative. In the case of the ultra-wealthy, the fruits of their ongoing, yet relatively unrecognized, multi-decade insurgency have allowed them to increasingly transcend the confines and duties of sovereign state based citizenship. Numerous examples of plutocratic class (i.e. extra-sovereign; sovereign free) rights, privileges, and economic gains for the 1% and the MNCs (multinational corporations) they own blatantly exist. Some recent data points gleaned from global news media are as follows:

- *Multinational corporations paying little to no corporate taxes*; Special tax credits and other benefits allowed Amazon for a second year in a row to again pay no federal corporate taxes—this year on $11 billion in profits.[2] In 2017, Google moved $22.7 billion in foreign profits by means of a Dutch shell company to Bermuda for tax reduction (i.e. avoidance) purposes by what is known as the "Double Irish, Dutch Sandwich," effectively allowing it to pay far lower corporate taxes.[3]

- *The Internal Revenue Service's (IRS) inability to stop tax evasion by ultra-wealthy individuals*; The IRS is unable to collect billions of dollars owed by multi-billionaire plutocrats due to their strategy of US Congressional lobbying to obtain 'special considerations' and deploying battalions of high-priced legal and accounting 'hit teams' to fend off and ultimately exhaust IRS lawyers and auditors (personnel within the Global High Wealth Industry Group formed in 2009) in multiyear engagements.[4]

- *Rewriting the US tax code to benefit the ultra-wealthy and their corporations;* The Tax Cuts and Jobs Act of 2017 has resulted in some very specific winners—essentially the rich—and losers—essentially everyone else. Some of the greatest benefactors are heirs of the estates of the very rich, with estate taxes not being trigged for inheriting wealth until a total of $11 million for individuals and $22 million for couples is reached. Additionally, those in the $308,000 to $733,000 income range are greatly benefiting via income tax cuts as are corporations with a permanent tax cut from 35% to 21%; at least those corporations still actually paying taxes. Earners in high tax states (typically more liberal ones such as New York and California) will suffer as a result of the changes to the tax code as will the mass of the US populace (the middle class and below) as governmental revenues are further cut, federal institutions are hollowed out, and the provision of public goods and services increasingly curtailed.[5]

- *Half of the property in England is owned by less than 1% of its population*; Roughly 25,000 landowners—mostly members of the aristocracy (i.e. old school plutocrats with titles) and corporations—own 50% of England's land. Determining such ownership has been extremely difficult to ascertain as its been shrouded in secrecy. About 30% of ownership can be directly tied to aristocratic families and about 18% to English and foreign corporations. Land ownership in Scotland may be even more concentrated within a small cadre of elite families and their corporate entities.[6]

- *Giving bonuses to the top executives of bankrupt corporations to the detriment of all others*; Sears, Roebuck and Company the archetypical 'brick and mortar' department store has been slowing sinking under the weight of additional debt stemming from its inability, due to inefficiency and mismanagement, to compete in the new online economy that has emerged. As part of the bankruptcy process, its top executives are being paid $25.3 million *in additional compensation* to retain them during the restricting process. This amounts to a 'looting party' of a sinking company by those senior executives and managers that were responsible for the initial bankruptcy itself.[7]

- *Building special 'non-public' airport terminals at major airports only for plutocratic class use*; Los Angeles World Airport (LAX) in May 2017, in a first of its kind development in the United States, opened up an entire terminal known "Private Suite" only for the use of the 1%—corporate executive officers (CEOs), celebrities, and other moneyed class individuals. Clients receive discreet armed guard gate entry, individualized TSA (Transportation Security Administration) screening, chauffeured arrival and departures directly to the plane, and customs and immigrations desk fast-tracking (with tasty chocolates to boot).[8] Similar private terminals already exist in London, Munich, Frankfurt, and Dubai for these global elites.[9]

- *The emergence of a two-tier system of university housing—one for the children of the rich and another for everyone else;* Luxury-style housing is now being built at Northeastern University by a private company in what is one of the first local university and developer partnerships. This 'free-market' dorm commoditization lowers initial university risk and increases their cash flow. A dorm targeting the children of affluent parents was earlier completed last year at the University of Massachusetts Boston. A similar shift is taking place with more stratified university dorm pricing, resulting in pockets of affluence on some campuses mimicking growing levels of societal inequality.[10]

With these sobering data points related to growing economic inequality and middle-class erosion in mind, the introduction to this work is divided into three sections concerning insurgency theory and its new linkages to plutocracy, the interrelationship of plutocracy, criminality, and authoritarianism (a brief sketch of this emerging field of study), and an overview of the plutocratic insurgency reader itself.

Insurgency Theory

Western perceptions of insurgency have gone through two distinct periods of thought per Dr. Steven Metz, a leading insurgency scholar and current director of research at Strategic Studies Institute, US Army War College, who has been theorizing and writing on this subject matter off-and-on since the late 1980s. The initial period of thought is considered that of the *orthodox conceptualization*, dominant from the 1940s through 1990s, and focuses on political based insurgencies.[11] It represents the traditional view of insurgency via the lens of the Cold War. It is dominated by leftist (Marxist) revolutionary type insurgencies of the Mao Zedong (*On Guerrilla Warfare*), Vo Nguyen Giap (*People's War, People's Army*), and Che Guevara (*Guerrilla Warfare*) variety linked into the 'People's War' and later urban guerrilla approach of Carlos Marighella (*Mini-Manual of the Urban Guerrilla*).[12]

The second period of thought is considered the *counter-orthodox conceptualization* and developed from 1993 onward.[13] It shifts our perceptions from who is engaging in an insurgency (what organization; as in the case of the earlier leftist revolutionaries) to thinking of it "… as a *type of strategy* that can be used in many types of conflicts by many types of organizations."[14] This results in three strategic dimensions of insurgency being utilized by groups engaging in it: 1) functional focus, 2) organizational coherence, and 3) objective.[15] At the same time Metz's earlier articulation of the commercial and spiritual insurgency forms exist during the same period as this conceptualization. This means they *de facto* have to be considered to exist within it and/or were a stepping stone on the path to a more strategic rather than group focused insurgency construct.[16] During this time period, non-political groups have dominated in insurgent activities including warlords, cartels, and radical Islamists. This can be partially seen with the emergence of online publications such as *Inspire, Dabiq*, and *Rumiyah* promoting 'open source jihad' (OSJ) and 'just terror' (JT) approaches to insurgent and terrorist activities. Where this conceptualization greatly differs from the earlier one is that in People's War, the goal end state is victory while within the *counter-orthodox conceptualization* often the goal is to prolong conflict as long as possible—hence ongoing conflict becomes an end state in itself.

The theoretical debate now taking place is whether a third period of thought—the *dark (deviant) globalization conceptualization*—maybe valid as an insurgency construct. This conceptualization relates to the plutocratic insurgency model first articulated in 2011 and its interaction with earlier criminal insurgency model identified via the *counter-orthodox conceptualization*.[17] Dr. Metz, in correspondence with one of the authors (outside his official Department of Defense duties) is "not fully convinced insurgency is the right concept" for the plutocratic insurgency construct, although he agrees with most of the analysis related to the subject matter.[18] Dr. Nils Gilman (lead editor of the book *Deviant Globalization*) and Dr. John P. Sullivan (developer of the criminal insurgency construct), however, see the conceptualization as fitting within the broader parameters of insurgency. Dr. David Kilcullen (respected insurgency scholar and author of *Out of the Mountains*) has as of yet taken no position on this debate as it resides outside of his core work related to radical Islamist insurgency.

The major differences in the assumptions defining these three insurgency conceptualizations can be viewed in Table 1. The initial conceptualization (the *orthodox* one) is primarily drawn straight from Dr. Metz's work from 2012 with some additional cell attribute additions, with the intent of keeping it as close to his original analysis and intent as feasible. The follow-on conceptualization (the *counter-orthodox* one) represents a 'work-a-round' approach because his strategic dimensions approach is qualitatively different (much like apples vs. oranges) from an attributes perspective to his earlier one. For this reason, its time period components—such as spoils system seeking, weak authoritarianism, and patron-client interactions— essentially non-western derived—have been merged with his commercial (criminal) and spiritual insurgency forms so that it can be qualitatively compared cell-by-cell to the *orthodox* conceptualization attributes.[19]

Table 1.0 Insurgency Conceptualization Assumptions

	ORTHODOX CONCEPTUAL-IZATION	COUNTER-ORTHODOX CONCEPTUAL-IZATION	*DARK (DEVIANT) GLOBALIZATION CONCEPTUAL-IZATION*
INSURGENCY TYPE	Political (Form of Traditional War)	*Commercial (Criminal) & Spiritual*	*Commercial (Plutocratic)*
ACTORS	Chinese, Vietnamese, Algerians (Anti-Colonial; Leftists)	*African Warlords, Drug Cartels, Radical Islamists*	*1% (Global Elites) & Multinational Corporations (MNCs)*
TIME PERIOD	1940s-1990s	*1993-Current*	*2011-Current*
END STATE	Become the State; Split Off Piece of Nation and Become a State (Conflict Termination Sought; Victory)	*Become the New Elites; Perpetuate Spoils System for Own Power Structure (Ongoing Conflict Preferable)*	*Move Beyond the State; Privatize & Commoditize All Public Goods (Level of Conflict Irrelevant)*
MORALITY-CHARACTER	Immoral; Bad People (Communists)	*Immoral & Amoral; Criminals, Radicals, Cultists*	*Greedy; Hyper-Rational (Predatory Capitalist)*
POPULAR SUPPORT	Required (Insurgents Weak); Public Utilizes 'Rational Choice' to Obtain Best Deal	*Not Required (Armed Factional/Tribal Support Only); Oppressive (Parasitic) Rule*	*Not Required; Still Populism & Social Media Campaigns Utilized (For Public Office Capture)*

LEGITIMACY	Market Logic Based (Social Contract; Citizens & State)	*Derived from the Barrel of a Gun (Coercive); Minimal Goods & Services Provided to the Populace*	*Irrelevant (Masses Typically Ignored); Family Wealth & Societal Status (As Globalization's Winners)*
ECONOMY	Formal (Licit); State Taxable	*Informal (Barter) Criminal (Illicit)*	*Sovereign Free*
COERCIVE FORCES	Armies (Late Stage), Guerrillas, Insurgents, Terrorists	*Armed Militias, Armies (Late Stage), Cartel Enforcers, Guerrillas, Insurgents, Terrorists*	*Lawyers, Lobbyists, Mercenaries, Private Security*
PEOPLE ARE	Politically Salient; Side Getting Most Support Wins (Like in an Election)	*Politically Unimportant; To be Exploited as a Resource (Commodity)*	*Politically Unimportant; To be Treated as a Consumer (Purchaser of Goods & Services)*
NARRATIVE	Modernist (Western-Ethnocentric; Liberal Democratic); Colonial Model	*Pre-Modernist (Non-Western; Weak Authoritarianism); Patron-Client Model*	*Post-Modernist (Post-Western; Plutocratic) Global Elitist Model*
SOLUTION	State Becomes More Developed (More Western-Like)	*None; Pathological (Limited Capacity) States*	*Subordinate Plutocrats to State Authority*

Sources (Normal Text): Steven Metz, "Chapter 3: Rethinking Insurgency." Paul B. Rich and Isabelle Duyvesteyn, Eds., *The Routledge Handbook of Insurgency and Counterinsurgency*. London: Routledge, 2012: 32-44. Sources (*Italics Text*): Ibid, Steven Metz, *The Future of Insurgency*. Carlisle: Strategic Studies Institute, US Army War College, 10 December 1993, https://ssi.armywarcollege.edu/pubs/display.cfm?pubID=344, and Robert J. Bunker, *Old and New Insurgency Forms*. Carlisle: Strategic Studies Institute, US Army War College, March 2016, https://ssi.armywarcollege.edu/pubs/display.cfm?pubID=1313.

The third conceptualization—*dark (deviant) globalization*—exists outside of Dr. Metz's two initial conceptualizations. Further, it promotes the plutocratic insurgency form which here is argued to exist within Metz's commercial insurgency construct as a book end to the criminal insurgency one; though Metz, as earlier mentioned, is not fully convinced it represents a form of insurgency (based on a military definition). This 'out of paradigm' conceptualization (vis-à-vis the modern era) is alien to military thinking related to prior insurgency constructs because its end states are extra-sovereign in nature and include moving beyond the state (instead of taking it or a piece of it over) and not seeking to gain popular support or legitimacy. This reader represents an attempt to articulate this new conceptualization of privatized post-modern insurgency as a component of epochal warfare (and deviant globalization) theory.

Plutocracy, Criminality, and Authoritarianism

> "When plunder becomes a way of life for a group of men in a society, over the course of time they create for themselves a legal system that authorizes it and a moral code that glorifies it."
>
> – Frédéric Bastiat, 19th Century French Economist

The plutocratic insurgency conceptualization exists even further outside the modernist paradigm when incorporated into the twin (dual) insurgency writings of Dr. Nils Gilman. This represents a deeper expression of *the dark (deviant) globalization conceptualization* as a facet of fourth epochal warfare (also known as epochal change) theory.[20] This theory was the driving force behind the 2014 book *Global Criminal and Sovereign Free Economies and the Demise of the Western Democracies: Dark Renaissance* produced by the editors of this reader and their forthcoming Strategic Studies Institute, US Army War College monograph *Rising Inequality in the United States: Armed Forces Implications and Governmental Policy Response,* accepted for publication in the Fall of 2018.

The 2014 Gilman 'Twin Insurgency' essay (Reading 4 in this work) portrays the raw power of the criminal and plutocratic insurgency forms that achieve a vice-like compression grip on the Goldilocks Zone that the Liberal Democratic state inhabits.

This carefully moderated zone is one characterized by a vibrant middle class, legitimate economy, conventional warfare, and sovereign rights and is representative of the state deinstitutionalization process portraying the shift from the modern to post-modern eras in global human civilization. A Western state can be subjected solely to a criminal insurgency from below (at the criminal and illicit economic levels), subjected solely to a plutocratic insurgency from above (at the plutocratic and extra-sovereign economic level), or eventually face a combined twin insurgency from both below and above. Mexico initially was viewed as only facing a criminal insurgency but, with the publication of the book *The Rise of the Narcostate (Mafia States)*—the sixth *Small Wars Journal— El Centro* anthology—in August 2018 by Dr. Robert J. Bunker and Dr. John P. Sullivan (Eds.), our perceptions are shifting. When Mexico was a one party state—with 70 years of iron fisted PRI rule—the political families and plutocratic classes greatly profited as drug trafficking profits drastically increased from the 1980s onward. With a multi-party electoral system now in place since 2000, the plutocratic element has to some extent been cut out of this equation, with the result that many of them are now seeking direct alliances with the narcos outside of current (and still fragile) democratic state institutions. Hence, uncoordinated, as well as semi-coordinated, criminal and plutocratic twin-insurgency potentials now exist in Mexico.

Further, it is foreseen that entrepreneurial narco (mafia) states, once established, if allowed to flourish will over time—re-institutionalized their functional elements and transition into authoritarian states just as Medieval warlords (and other strongmen and criminal band leaders) evolved into dynastic political entities gaining the mantel of legitimacy over generational time spans. Full scale 'crime making' thus results in 'state making' and can be viewed as de-institutionalized 21st century warfare waged by non-state entities.[21] Of additional consternation is the re-positioning of Russia (long under former KGB officer Vladimir Putin) and China (now under former Communist Party leader Xi Jiping). This re-positioning suggests that these states are learning to prosper from the predatory nature of globalized capitalism with their own authoritarian variants. Their regimes are natural allies of both the plutocratic classes and criminal elements. Concern now exists that an authoritarian form of insurgency may at some future point be promoted to further inhibit the global spread and integrity of Western forms of governance.[22] Visually conceptualizing these commercial insurgency (and variant) forms and the challenges (and, in some instances, direct threats) they pose—as singular, synergistic, and fused processes—for liberal-democratic states can be viewed in Figure 1 below:

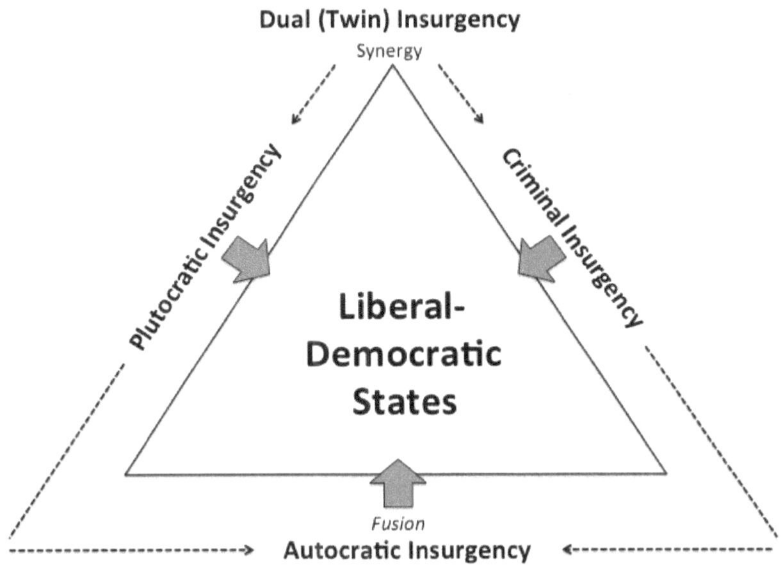

Figure 1. Commercial Insurgency Forms and Liberal-Democratic States [23]

The Plutocratic Insurgency Reader

The reader has been divided into an initial contributor biographies section—with fifteen short contributor biographies provided—followed by a preface written by Dr. Nils Gilman who is presently Vice President for Programs, Berggruen Institute, Los Angeles which is actively addressing programs related to the future of capitalism and the future of democracy. This preface provides insights into perceptions related to the end of the Westphalian-modernist system as well as the interrelationship between criminal and plutocratic insurgencies. He concludes with how the modernist social contract, formerly between the state and its citizens, is being rewritten by plutocrats (a malignant adversary force) who only have their own dynastic economic and security interests at heart.

This introduction—with its emphasis on insurgency theory; plutocracy, criminality and authoritarianism interrelationships; and an overview of the selected readings contained in this work—precedes the readings section which represents the bulk of the book. Twenty-seven readings are showcased, spanning September 2012 through February 2019. Readings number 1 and 2 dating to September 2012 concern the exchange beginning in 2011 between Dr. Robert J. Bunker and Dr. Nils Gilman regarding the 'plutocratic insurgency' construct and how to periodize its inception in the West. The initial query was a private exchange that carried its way over to *Small Precautions Blog* and then *Small Wars Journal*. The third reading, published by Dr. Bunker in February 2014 with the Strategic Studies Institute, US Army War College as a strategic insights essay highlights the generational shift in insurgency forms from Maoist based People's War to new 21st century forms derived from criminal, spiritual, and plutocratic motivations. Reading 4 is a reprint of Dr. Nils Gilman's powerful and persuasive 'Twin Insurgency' essay that details the interrelationship of the criminal and plutocratic insurgency forms and the challenge the disruptive synergy they produce represents to the Western liberal-democratic order. The fifth reading—once again written by Dr. Bunker and meant as a companion piece to the 'Twin Insurgency' essay— explains the predatory capitalism inherent in plutocratic insurgent activities and discusses the multinational corporations (MNCs) and increasingly stateless (i.e extra-sovereign) global elites that perpetrate it. Both of these two essays were initially meant for publication in later 2014, with the 'Twin Insurgency' piece pre-released online some months prior to the publication of the book *Global Criminal and Sovereign Free Economies and the Demise of the Western Democracies* (Routledge).

The sixth reading, dating from July 2014, is written by Rich Couch—a retired physical scientist—who provided commentary on the 'Twin Insurgency' essay at his *Let's Talk Books and Politics* blog.

He initially discusses the changing role of government in society in the 1970s and 1980s, excerpts some of Dr. Gilman's analysis, and then provides insights between the Gilman essay and Daniel Rodgers' book *Age of Fracture* (Belknap Press, 2011) which chronicles how social debate (and the categories of social reality that underpin them) within American society has devolved and fractured due to economic changes within an increasingly globalized world. This reading ends where the seventh one begins with the perceived takeover of the Republican party by plutocratic elements. Paul Rosenberg—a journalist and former California-based social justice activist—sets his verbal gunsights on Donald Trump, whom he characterizes as 'half plutocrat, half criminal and entirely ruthless.' He pulls in interview commentary by Dr. Gilman related to the 'Twin Insurgency' essay and how Donald Trump would be characterized via its lens in this October 2016 *Salon* online magazine article. Reading 8 represents the first of eleven *Small Wars Journal* plutocratic insurgency notes written between February 2017 and February 2019. In the initial note, written by Robert Bunker and Pamela Ligouri Bunker, key information and analysis is provided relating to the fact that eight individuals are now as wealthy as the poorest half of the world.

The ninth reading—representing the 2nd in the plutocratic insurgency note series—was penned by the same two authors with Pamela Ligouri Bunker as lead. That reading, also originating from February 2017, highlights how 69% of the US population have less than $1,000 in savings to their name and are just one illness or other major economic setback from financial disaster. The tenth and final reading published back in February 2017 was also written by the Bunker team for *Small Wars Journal.* This 3rd plutocratic insurgency note focuses on the concept of 'no shoring' as opposed to 'offshoring' or 'onshoring' jobs. No shoring concerns lost (offshored) jobs that do not come back to the US (onshored) because artificial intelligence and robotics systems are utilized in heavily automated factories when production facilities are brought back to our country. This growing trend further imperils our middle class structure and the upward social mobility of the American lower classes. The 11th reading by the Bunkers addresses the gradual extinction of tenure in American universities that *de facto* leads to silencing the middle class concerning debates related to income inequality and other social ills brought on by the plutocratic insurgency. This reading represents the 4th writing in plutocratic insurgency series of notes. The 12th reading by George Thomas—a former Marine officer, intellectual and moral classicist, and managing partner of a Midwest law firm—provides a link to a 28:15 minute podcast he created in March 2017. The podcast residing at the *Fortress of the Mind* blog offers his reading of and articulate commentary to the first four plutocratic insurgency notes published at *Small Wars Journal* (readings No. 8-11 in this work).

The 13th reading represents another plutocratic insurgency note produced by Robert Bunker and Pamela Ligouri Bunker. Initially published in July 2017 at *Small Wars Journal*, it focuses on what are called the techno-palaces of the global elite. The note was initially inspired by a trip Dr. Bunker took to downtown New York earlier that year for a DHS (Department of Homeland Security) speaking engagement. Many tall post-modernist structures—primarily known as 'needle towers'—have sprung up in the city with exorbitant individual condominium price tags only the plutocratic class can afford. This reading discusses the origins of these residential towers, how they have spread to other major global cities, and their implications. Reading fourteen is a reprint of the sixth *SWJ* plutocratic insurgency note first published in August 2017. Co-authored by Dr. John P. Sullivan and Dr. Bunker, the reading focuses on what are known as privately owned public spaces (POPS) that have intruded into major urban centers such as London, New York, San Francisco, and even China in such cities as in Shenzhen and Shanghai. These 'pseudo-public spaces' are reminiscent of feudal enclaves and reinforce plutocratic and corporate elite urban territorial control to the detriment of the lower socio-economic classes. Reading 15 offers another podcast link produced by George Thomas at his *Fortress of the Mind* blog site. The 26:50 minute podcast created in August 2017 focuses on his reading of and commentary on the 5th and 6th plutocratic insurgency notes chronicled earlier (Readings No. 13-14 in this work).

The 16th reading contained in the work represents an English to Spanish language translation of a *La Jornada* article written in December 2017 by Carlos Fazio—a Uruguayan journalist—concerning the Law of Internal Security (LSI) linked to Mexican President Enrique Peña Nieto. The author links the war on drugs in Mexico to plutocratic interests and is concerned a new phase may be beginning in which the government will suppress protests and other forms of anti-plutocratic demonstrations. The actual translation itself was undertaken by Dr. Alma Keshavarz, a then associate with *Small Wars Journal—El Centro*. Reading No. 17 brings us back to the plutocratic insurgency note series with the 8th note (published a few days prior to the 7th note due to a *SWJ* publishing snafu) once again written by Pamela Ligouri Bunker and Robert J. Bunker. This reading from January 2018 focuses on Apple, Inc.—the computer, iPhone, and technology company—which manifests a split Dr. Jekyll and Mr. Hyde persona as it claims to be an American company during the day when it sells its products to our citizens but at night claims to be a foreign company to escape the tax bill. Its strategy of using lawyers and lobbyists (hired legal and political guns) is right out of the plutocratic insurgency playbook and results in very little of its profits going back into the public US coffers for the benefit of the American citizenry. George Thomas was so struck by this reading that he dedicated a *Fortress of the Mind* blog article specifically to it (see reading 18) a few days after its publication. He focuses on Apple's relentless tax avoidance schemes, how it is attempting to become an extra-sovereign entity free of state taxation, and the collusion of Western democratic leaders to the detriment of the American public.

Reading 19 is composed of the 7th plutocratic insurgency note published at *SWJ*—also in January 2018 a few days after the 8th one. It is written by the editors and focuses on the fascinating, and in many ways diabolical, use of artificial intelligence (AI) pricing software by plutocratic elite controlled MNCs to optimize profit by means of online dynamic pricing and big data analysis that predicts how much a consumer will pay for a good or service. The use of such AI software allows MNCs to effectively control "The Invisible Hand" of capitalism and stack buying and selling transactions with the consumer increasingly in favor of big business. The 20th and 21st readings both provide overviews and commentary on the 8th plutocratic insurgency note and were initially published a few days after it came out at *Small Wars Journal*. The 20th reading is from a *Fortress of the Mind* blog post by George Thomas and reiterates the 'subtle e-market strong arming' and 'targeted shakedowns' related to turning AI software against unsuspecting online consumers. The 21st reading originates from the *Naimisha Forest* blog. The author of the short essay is a retired career economist at an international financial institution who writes under a pen-name for the purposes of anonymity. The essay discusses how the note—from an economist's perspective— pertains to the subject of 'perfect' or 'first-degree price discrimination.' This allows for the monopolist (the seller) to drain off consumer surplus and provide additional profits for the monopolist 'stakeholders.'

The 22nd reading, first published in January 2018, is significant and the only *SWJ* plutocratic insurgency to date with four authors; Robert Bunker, Nils Gilman, John Sullivan, and Pamela Ligouri Bunker who decided to provide a united 'intellectual front' in its writing. It concerns the *Tax Cuts and Jobs Act* of FY 2018 that is viewed by the authors collectively as a class warfare 'red line' having been crossed by the US government with regard to the governed. The Act's provisions ultimately result in a massive tax relief scheme for the plutocratic class at the expense of the middle and lower socio-economic rungs of American society. Its passage reflects the co-option of the Republican Party by the present presidential administration, which gained electoral currency through a 'pluto-populist' strategy. The 23rd reading provides a retrospective concerning the plutocratic insurgency construct. It was published by Dr. Bunker in March 2018 at *Small Wars Journal* and provides a research guide for readers on what he terms 'the Gilded Age Redux.' The guide provides theoretical and qualitative modeling insights into the plutocratic insurgency construct, a short abstract of the initial nine plutocratic insurgency notes, and links to two podcasts at the *Fortress of the Mind* blog which pertain to the first six of them. The guide achieved some minor notoriety being republished at *RealClearDefense (RCD)* soon after its posting at *SWJ*.

Reading 24 pertains to the thinking of Henry David Thoreau as it can be applied against the plutocratic insurgency. It was written by Bryan T. Baker—a reserve intelligence officer in the US Army and teacher at a classical preparatory academy—and published in March 2018 at *SWJ*. He argues in this essay that the middle and working classes in America have fallen asleep on their watch and are neglecting to *keep the republic*. He then goes on to draw upon moral insights provided by Thoreau related to rejecting materialism, embracing classical education, and cultivating philosophers in American society as a prelude to change that requires helping to awaken the mass of the American public from their slumber. The 25th reading represents another article translated from Spanish into English by Dr. Keshavarz. It references a November 2018 *Mira* piece once again written by Carlos Fazio (whose earlier essay can be found in Reading 16). This piece pertains to the cancelation of the Texcoco airport by president-elect Andrés Manuel López Obrador (AMLO) and how it sets him and his administration up for a direct conflict with plutocratic insurgent elements in Mexico.

The 26th reading dates to January 2019 and was the 10th plutocratic insurgency note published at *SWJ*. The reading—written by Pamela Ligouri Bunker and Robert Bunker—provides a plutocratic trifecta concerning the increasing wealth concentration of the world's billionaires, a record number of private (multi-million dollar+) jets arriving at the recent Davos meeting in Switzerland, and the demise of the American dream. The latter refers to how most US citizens no longer see hard work as a pathway to success in our country, resulting in the demise of the Horatio Alger mythos of that 'hard work and integrity will result in your success.' The 27th and final reading showcases another plutocratic insurgency note—the 11th one published in February 2019. Here, its authors Pamela Ligouri Bunker and Robert Bunker focus on the rise of the 'gig economy' as a permanent and involuntary low-paid and part-time labor model. Such a labor model maximizes income for the plutocratic classes while further compromising the incomes of the middle and lower classes who additionally are not allowed to work enough hours to secure health insurance benefits or obtain employer social security tax contributions.

A postscript written by George Thomas—a frequent contributor to the reader—is then provided. The postscript delves into historical comparisons of wealth and power concentrations in the hands of the few related to ancient Greece, Rome, and Renaissance Italy vis-à-vis our modern predicament. Our nation and society is in a dangerous place and will require the reforms of bold individuals seeking to reestablish balance and equality within a social structure increasingly represented by haves and have nots. Dr. John P. Sullivan—who has written many works on criminal insurgency and has co-authored some of the plutocratic insurgency notes contained within this reader—then provides an afterword. His afterword addresses the contemporary crisis of liberal democracy and the rise of authoritarian states with insights gleaned from scholars such as Manuel Castells, Thomas Picketty, and Paul Krugman.

Four appendices are situated towards the end of the book. They are meant to provide insurgency theory and strategic level state (and global economic change) contextualization. The initial appendix, containing a writing by Dr. Steven Metz, provides commercial insurgency excerpts from his 1993 Strategic Studies Institute, US Army War College monograph *The Future of Insurgency*. The second appendix, highlighting a writing by John Robb—author of the 2008 book *Brave New War* and developer of the open source warfare construct—discusses his 'hollow state' concept in which a financial crisis triggers a plutocratic and corporate feeding frenzy which results in the looting of marginally functioning state, economically gutting it. The third appendix is taken from the introduction and conclusion of the 2011 edited work *Deviant Globalization* by Dr. Nils Gilman, Dr. Jesse Goldhammer, and Dr. Steven Weber. It provides an overview of the deviant globalization construct and how it challenges the modern state and liberal (read liberal-democratic) perspectives on globalization—ones that were primarily optimistic in nature. The fourth and final appendix, written by one of the co-editors of the reader, represents excerpts from the 2016 Strategic Studies Institute, US Army War College monograph *Old and New Insurgency Forms*. Short passages related to the commercial, twin, and plutocratic forms are provided within it. The book then finishes with a curated bibliography of key plutocracy readings provided for those individuals who seek to do additional research and contemplation on this subject matter.

The editors wish to thank the many contributors to this work which importantly focuses on the plutocratic insurgency (and ensuing twin insurgency) construct. While a growing number of works related to economic inequality, the rise of a new plutocratic class, the demise of the American (and European) middle classes, and Western state corruption (and dysfunction) exist, very few specifically analyze these areas of concern from a national security—and its insurgency subfield—perspective. It is unknown if 'airing the dirty laundry' of post-modern and globalized capitalism with its criminal, predatory, and sovereign free components will make any meaningful difference to the fate of the modern Western state, its peoples, and the democratic principles it founded upon. Still, given the ongoing struggle with criminality (including governmental corruption) and authoritarianism both external, and now increasingly internal, to the United States, we would be remiss not to do our small part to help educate our fellow Americans about the challenges our nation is now facing.

Notes

1. See, for instance, David Patrikarakos, *War in 140 Characters: How Social Media Is Reshaping Conflict in the Twenty-First Century*. New York: Basic Books, 2017; P.W. Singer and Emerson T. Brooking, *LikeWar: The Weaponization of Social Media*. Boston: Eamon Dolan, 2018; and Qiao Liang and Wang Xiangsui, *Unrestricted Warfare: China's Master Plan to Destroy America*. Brattleboro: Echo Point Books and Media, 2015 (Originally published in 1999 in Chinese; FBIS Translation).
2. Tim Sticklings, "REVEALED: Amazon pays NOTHING in federal corporate taxes for the second year running despite doubling its profits to more than $11billion." *Daily Mail*. 14 February 2019, https://www.dailymail.co.uk/news/article-6703757/Amazon-pays-federal-corporate-taxes.html.
3. "Google shifted $23 billion to tax haven Bermuda in 2017: filing." *Reuters*. 3 January 2019, https://www.reuters.com/article/us-google-taxes-netherlands/google-shifted-23-billion-to-tax-haven-bermuda-in-2017-filing-idUSKCN1OX1G9.

4. Jesse Eisinger and Paul Kiel, "The IRS Tried to Take on the Ultrawealthy. It Didn't Go Well." *ProPublica*. 5 April 2019, https://www.propublica.org/article/ultrawealthy-taxes-irs-internal-revenue-service-global-high-wealth-audits. See also Jesse Eisinger and Paul Kiel, "How the IRS Was Gutted." *ProPublica*. 11 December 2018, https://www.propublica.org/article/how-the-irs-was-gutted. Even the slightly less affluent bringing much smaller incomes benefited from such strategies. In Australia "…in 2011-2012, 75 individuals who earning more than $1 million in pre-tax, gross income paid no tax." Malcolm Farr, "Franking Credits: The investment helping millionaires live tax free." *News.com.au*. 23 February 2019, https://www.news.com.au/finance/work/the-investment-helping-millionaires-live-tax-free/news-story/4e7331df69303caad86a5b3776e86ad9.

5. While many other income tax filers are said to be getting a slight tax break the actual benefits are ethereal with a 2025 sunset clause though investors and some small business owners will benefit. Zachary B. Wolf, "Here's who's winning under Trump's tax law." *CNN*. 13 April 2019, https://www.cnn.com/2019/04/13/politics/tax-reform-winners-and-losers/index.html and Aimee Picchi, "The tax law is 1 year old—here are the winners and losers." *CBS News*. 21 December 2018, https://www.cbsnews.com/news/the-tax-bill-is-one-year-old-here-are-the-winners-and-losers/.

6. Rob Evans, "Half of England is owned by less than 1% of the population." *The Guardian*. 17 April 2019, https://www.theguardian.com/money/2019/apr/17/who-owns-england-...r?CMP=twt_gu&utm_medium=&utm_source=Twitter#Echobox=1555530987. Also see Guy Shrubsole, *Who Owns England?* New York: William Collins, 2019 (Forthcoming).

7. Britanny De Lea, "Bankrupt Sears gets OK to pay executives millions in bonuses." *Fox Business*. 17 December 2018, https://www.foxbusiness.com/retail/bankrupt-sears-gets-ok-to-pay-executives-millions-in-bonuses. This is a product of the overall trend of corporate looting by CEOs. See Steven Clifford, *The CEO Pay Machine*. New York: Blue Rider Press, 2017.

8. Rory Carroll, "At LAX's new private terminal, the rich are pampered while normal people suffer." *The Guardian*. 12 May 2017, https://www.theguardian.com/world/2017/may/12/lax-private-terminal-rich-people-celebrities.

9. Tanza Loudenback, "I visited the private terminal at LAX where rich people pay upwards of $4,500 to skip the lines and pull up to their planes in BMWs, and it made me feel like a billionaire." *Business Insider*. 29 December 2018, https://www.businessinsider.com/private-suite-lax-terminal-wealthy-travelers-photos-tour-2018-10.

10. Deirdre Fernandes, "Pricey campus housing triggers a debate in Boston." *The Boston Globe*. 6 January 2019, https://www.bostonglobe.com/metro/2019/01/05/campus-divide-pricey-student-housing-triggers-debate-over-income-inequality/

oGSCZ0q4nMkgu5nNMRs5tK/story.html and Jon Marcus, "The business decision segregating college students by income and race." The Hechinger Report. 26 September 2016, https://hechingerreport.org/business-decision-segregating-college-students-income-race/.

11. Steven Metz, "Chapter 3: Rethinking Insurgency." In Paul B. Rich and Isabelle Duyvestyn (Eds.): *The Routledge Handbook of Insurgency and Counterinsurgency.* New York: Routledge, 2012: 32-36.

12. For insurgency form conceptualizations, see Robert J. Bunker, *Old and New Insurgency Forms.* Carlisle, PA: Strategic Studies Institute, US Army War College, 15 March 2016: 1-110, https://ssi.armywarcollege.edu/pubs/display.cfm?pubID=1313.

13. The origins of this conceptualization can be tied to Steve Metz's work *The Future of Insurgency.* Carlisle, PA: Strategic Studies Institute, US Army War College, 10 December 1993, https://ssi.armywarcollege.edu/pubs/display.cfm?pubID=344. Relevant excerpts appear in Appendix 1 of the reader.

14. Steven Metz, "Chapter 3: Rethinking Insurgency": 37-38.

15. Ibid: 41.

16. Steve Metz's work *The Future of Insurgency.* See also, John P. Sullivan and Robert J. Bunker, "Rethinking insurgency: criminality, spirituality and societal warfare in the Americas." Robert J. Bunker, (Ed.), *Criminal Insurgencies in Mexico and the Americas: The Gangs and Cartels Wage War.* London: Routledge, 2012: 742-762.

17. For the origins of this construct, see Nils Gilman, "Plutocratic Insurgency." *Small Precautions Blog.* 5 September 2012, http://smallprecautions.blogspot.com/2012/09/plutocratic-insurgency.html (Reading 1 in the reader) and Robert J. Bunker, "Plutocratic Insurgency." *Small Wars Journal.* 6 September 2012, https://smallwarsjournal.com/blog/plutocratic-insurgency (Reading 2 in the reader). Dark globalization is a component of epochal change theory while the term deviant globalization is derived from the following book; Nils Gilman, Jesse Goldhammer, and Steven Weber (Eds.), *Deviant Globalization: Black Market Economy in the 21ˢᵗ Century.* New York: Continuum, 2011.

18. Robert J. Bunker email correspondence with Steven Metz, 13 March 2019.

19. Steven Metz, "Chapter 3: Rethinking Insurgency": 32-44.

20. This theory has existed since the late 1980s. Components of it have been published in numerous works including Robert J. Bunker, "Epochal Change: War Over Political and Social Organization." *Parameters.* Vol. 27, No. 2, 1997: 15-25, http://strategicstudiesinstitute.army.mil/pubs/parameters/Articles/97summer/bunker.htm; Robert J. Bunker, "Grand strategic overview: Epochal change and new realities for the United States." *Small Wars & Insurgencies.* Vol. 22, No. 5, December 2011:728-741; Pamela Ligouri Bunker and Robert J. Bunker, "BREXIT and Epochal Change—Implications for the United Kingdom and

Beyond." *The Impact of Brexit for the GCC and the World*. TRENDS Working Paper 07/2016. Abu Dhabi: TRENDS Research and Advisory, 2016: 9-19, http://trendsinstitution.org/wp-content/uploads/2016/11/The-Impact-of-Brexit-for-the-GCC-and-the-World-final1.pdf.

21. Charles Tilly, "War Making and State Making as Organized Crime." Peter B. Evans, Dietrich Rueschemeyer, and Theda Skocpol (Eds.), *Bringing the State Back In*. Cambridge: Cambridge University Press, 1985: 169-191. See also, Vanda Felbab-Brown, "Foreword: Crime and State-making." John P. Sullivan and Robert J. Bunker (Eds.), *The Rise of the Narcostate (Mafia States)*. A Small Wars Journal—El Centro Anthology. Bloomington: Xlibris, 2018: xxxvii-xliii.

22. "Introduction." John P. Sullivan and Robert J. Bunker (Eds.), *The Rise of the Narcostate (Mafia States)*: xlv-lii. See also "Autocratic Insurgency" section of Robert J. Bunker and Pamela Ligouri Bunker, *Rising Inequality in the United States: Armed Forces Implications and Governmental Policy Response*. Carlisle: Strategic Studies Institute, US Army War College, Forthcoming.

23. "Figure 1: Commercial Insurgency Forms and Liberal-Democratic States." Robert J. Bunker and Pamela Ligouri Bunker, *Rising Inequality in the United States: Armed Forces Implications and Governmental Policy Response*.

Reading 1

Plutocratic Insurgency

Nils Gilman

First Published 5 September 2012 in Small Precautions Blog [1]
Reprinted with permission.

I recently engaged in a private exchange with leading 4GW thinker Robert Bunker on the question of how to periodize what he calls "plutocratic insurgency." Here are a few notes I took in the course of that exchange. The point of departure for this sort of an inquiry is to ask what the JohnGaltification of society would actually look like in practice—what would it seriously mean for the wealthy to opt out of participation in the collective institutions that make up society?

This is not an abstract exercise. One of the most important global trends of the last few decades has been the tendency of wealthy elites to hole themselves up in walled off enclaves. These islands of elitism are designed to be largely self-sufficient in their ability to deliver health care, food, security, education, entertainment, etc. to their residents, even as they sit amid seas of social misery. (Mike Davis has spent a good portion of his career chronicling this sort of thing, starting in Los Angeles with *City of Quartz,* and examining it as a global phenomenon in collections like *Dead Cities* and *Evil Paradises.)* From the point of view of the denizens of such communities, the primary function of the wider society is to serve as a source of cheap, servile labor, and as a well of resources to be looted. Gated communities, in turn, are merely an example of a broader pattern, in which economic, social, or political enclaves are carved out of a national state and enabled to play by a fundamentally different set of rules from the surrounding territory.

In themselves the creation of such enclaves do not amount to a plutocratic insurgency. Rather, plutocratic insurgency arises wherever you see financial and economic elites using such enclaves *as staging areas for making war on public goods*. This is what I take to be the defining political-economic feature of plutocratic insurgency: the attempt on the part of the rich to defund the provisioning of public goods, in order to defang a state which they see as a threat to their prerogatives. (Conceptually, plutocratic insurgencies thus need to be separated from kleptocracies—the latter involve the using the institutions of state to loot the population, whereas the former wish to neutralize those institutions in order to facilitate private sector looting. In practice these may overlap or co-mingle.)

Before discussing the periodization of this phenomenon, it's worth noting that the idea of plutocratic insurgency on its face is paradoxical, perhaps even oxymoronic: shouldn't plutocrats be the folks most invested in the perpetuation of a system which has them at the top? Why would the system's biggest beneficiaries want to make war on the system? The answer lies in part in the rise of an ideology—or perhaps more accurately, a narrative—that has allowed society's winners to imagine their success not as being the result of either the luck or the skill to *work the system* for their maximum personal benefit, but on the contrary as having been arrived at by pure dint of their own *rebellion against the system*. So when did this weird phenomenon begin to take hold?

While the ideological origins of the plutocratic insurgency can be traced to the foundation of the Mont Pelerin Society, it really starts to gain cultural visibility with the corporate raiders of the 1980s, guys who thought of themselves not as the leading lights of the empire, but rather as "barbarians at the gates" (a term Henry Kravis had no problem embracing at the time). These guys didn't see themselves as the system's ultimate winners, but rather as iconoclasts who were being rightfully rewarded for destroying entrenched, unproductive rent-seekers. What began to surface in the 1980s has only gained momentum with the growing financialization of the US economy.

On the one hand, then, an ideology of rebellion and success through the undermining of "the takers." The flip side is a material point: the very wealthy today are so rich that they can effectively afford to buy for themselves the sorts of goods which previously required a state to provide. The result is a phenomenon whereby many plutocrats today see no reason to contribute anything to their host societies, and indeed actively make war on the idea that citizenship imbues them with any economic or social responsibilities. (People as different as Stephen Schwartzman and Sheldon Adelson fit this bill, as do the Koch brothers.) In sum, plutocratic insurgency is another way of characterizing the most ideologically ambitious bleeding edge of what sometimes gets terms "Neoliberalism" or "Thatcherism," or "Reaganism." "There's no such thing as society," Thatcher famously declared, thus issuing the *cri de coeur* of insurgent plutocrats everywhere.

Beyond the United States, the critical event for the rise of the global plutocratic insurgency was the ideological collapse of state socialism, which everywhere on earth shifted the Overton Window dramatically to the right. Not only was the threat of left-wing grabs largely neutralized by socialism's implosion, but counterrevolutionaries on the right were emboldened by this collapse to attempt to roll back even the moderate, liberal forms of the welfare state. Arguably the most successful plutocratic insurgency in history was staged by the so-called oligarchs who arose from the ruins of the Soviet collapse. These were (mainly Jewish[2]) men who had started their business careers in the dark-gray corners of the Soviet "second economy," learning how to profit by sharp and ruthless dealing that took state strictures as opportunities rather than limits. Aided by useful idiots like Jeffrey Sachs, they grabbed the vast majority of the state-owned assets that Yeltin was selling off in a drunken fire sale designed to ensure that Communism could never again return to Russia. Eventually, in the Aughts, the former KGBers led by Vladimir Putin would stage a counter-insurgency and defenestrate most of the first generation oligarchs. What the rise of Putin signalled was the end of the Russia's plutocratic insurgency, and the reassertion of the state's interests as prior to those of the wealthy.

It might seem like the story laid out here is a liberal, perhaps even a Marxist one. While it's true that liberals have <u>long fretted</u> about the "secession" of the rich, increasingly conservatives are also <u>getting alarmed</u>. Ultimately, however, I don't think this is really a liberal or conservative matter. It's a question of national and social coherence as such: do people living together in a contiguous territory feel themselves somehow to be "in the same boat," willing to share responsibilities and risks collectively? Those engaged in the plutocratic insurgency answer that question with a defiant "No!" The plutocratic insurgency from above thus mirrors the deviant globalization insurgency from below, and taken together they embody <u>the contemporary crisis of the nation-state</u>.

Notes

1. <u>http://smallprecautions.blogspot.com/2012/09/plutocratic-insurgency.html</u>.
2. I should clarify the significance of the dramatic overrepresentation of Jews among the first-generation Russian oligarchs, including Boris Berezovsky, Vladimir Gusinsky, Alexander Smolensky, Mikhail Khodorkovsky, Mikhail Friedman, Vitaly Malkin, and others. First, Jewishness was not incidental to these men becoming oligarchs in the first place. While many late Soviet Communist Party members were enriching themselves with bribes, official anti-semitism made it almost impossible for Jews to get ahead within the formal Communist hierarchy. The most effective (and perhaps only) way for Soviet Jews to get ahead commercially, therefore, was by participating in the organization of the "second" (black market) economy. Unsurprisingly, therefore, ambitious Jews were overrepresented among those involved in the second economy, particularly in and around Moscow. This made them well-positioned to take advantage as the state economy collapsed. The biographies of most of the aforementioned oligarchs conform broadly to this pattern. Second, the Jewishness of the oligarchs also helps explain the course of their eventual removal from the apex of the post-Soviet economy. The fact that these oligarchs were Jewish helps account not only for why their appropriation of former state assets was widely perceived by the (anti-semitic) Russian public and elite establishment as illegitimate, but also for why there was little domestic Russian outcry when Putin threw them out of the country or into jail.

Reading 2

Plutocratic Insurgency

Robert J. Bunker

First Published 6 September 2012 in Small Wars Journal [1]

Preface: I've been developing the concept of what would be termed a plutocratic insurgency since 2011. The concept ties into earlier work done by John Robb (*Onward to a Hollow State*, 2008), Nils Gilman (*Deviant Globalization*, 2010), and others. This new concept will be highly controversial—it involves global elites and lacks the traditional trappings of an insurgency (i.e. an armed struggle). It is a counterpart to the criminal insurgency concept initially developed by John Sullivan. However, instead of being based on illicit economies and bottom up in nature, it is derived from sovereign free economies and top down in nature. The following elegantly crafted blog entry [by Nils Gilman] is one of the first public discussions about plutocratic insurgency. You will be reading more about this concept in this venue and others in the future.

Plutocratic Insurgency

Notes

1. http://smallwarsjournal.com/blog/plutocratic-insurgency.

Reading 3

Op-Ed: Not Your Grandfather's Insurgency— Criminal, Spiritual, and Plutocratic

Robert J. Bunker

First Published 20 February 2014 at Strategic Studies Institute, US Army War College [1] Reprinted with permission of the Strategic Studies Institute and U.S. Army War College Press, U.S. Army War College.

The U.S. Army is facing both ongoing and projected austere economic times with deep troop and budget cuts. As a result, a concomitant rise in soul searching over the Army's "strategic Landpower" contribution to national defense is increasingly evident. This is a natural and expected occurrence for a Service that has been in the spotlight for over a decade in ground campaigns—albeit very much anti-insurgent focused—in Iraq and Afghanistan that, respectively, has and is coming to an end. This is taking place at the same time as two other major events. The first event is the continuing U.S. congressional disagreements associated with the federal budget, debt levels, sequestration, and sporadic governmental closures. The second event is that of the United States ramping up its engagement and containment posture in its relations with China, with the other Services now in the forefront. China will hopefully be a cooperative, rather than intransigent, power in this bilateral relationship, but it is an authoritarian great power rising nonetheless.

Still other globalization outcomes are in play and are of great strategic importance to both U.S. national security and the Army's relationship to it. These outcomes, derived from the rise of globalized capitalism, the migration of humanity to cyberspace, and related 21st-century advances and changes in the post-Cold War world are challenging not only our perceptions of the separation of crime and war, but of insurgency itself. Quite possibly, while it now finds itself in a reflective mood, the corporate Army will be more receptive to some of the insights provided herein, concerning the new forms of insurgencies. But first, before delving into how new insurgency forms are "new," we must ask the question what insurgencies were like in your grandfather's day.

Your Grandfather's Insurgency

Old school insurgency or "people's war" was typically dominated by Leninist, Trotskian, Maoist, and related revolutionary thought. Such insurgencies are ideological in nature and may also draw upon nationalistic underpinnings, as was utilized in Vietnam. Specific characteristics of this type of insurgency are: it is premeditated, driven by the political, established by a parallel (shadow) government, utilizes violence—typically targeted and instrumental in nature, with the desired end state being political control over a nation-state.

Depending on the relative sophistication of the insurgents, a phased approach to insurgency—initially based on sequential and later on simultaneous phases—is utilized. The conditions influencing an insurgency, i.e. the popular grievances, may also be artificially accelerated. Seminal works in your grandfather's insurgency literature include: *Guerrilla Warfare* (1937); *People's War, People's Army* (1962); and the *Minimanual of the Urban Guerrilla* (1969). These revolutionary-based insurgencies include those that took place in China, Cuba, Vietnam, Angola, and El Salvador.

Criminal, Spiritual, and Plutocratic Insurgency

Twenty-first century insurgencies are turning out to be very different than 20th century ones. An initial projection concerning the development of such insurgencies was penned by Dr. Steven Metz in his 1993 Strategic Studies Institute monograph, _The Future of Insurgency_. In that prophetic work, he posited that:

> Two forms of insurgency are likely to dominate the post-cold war world. Spiritual insurgency is the descendant of the cold war-era revolutionary insurgency. It will be driven by the problems of modernization, the search for meaning, and the pursuit of justice. The other form will be commercial insurgency. This will be driven less by the desire for justice than wealth. Its psychological foundation is a warped translation of Western popular culture which equates wealth, personal meaning, and power.

Over the course of the last 2 decades, reality has increasingly mirrored theory with two forms of commercial insurgency—criminal and plutocratic—now evident. Additionally, elements of spiritual insurgency are also now identifiable in today's world and appear to validate that projection. These new forms of insurgency can be summarized as follows:

- _Criminal Insurgency:_ This variant of commercial insurgency was first articulated in 2008 and pertained to the ongoing narco-conflict in Mexico.[2] It focuses on criminal enterprises—the gangs, cartels, and associated mercenary groups—competing with the state. The intent of this criminality, which transcends the symbiotic nature of older forms of organized crime, is to free itself from state control to maximize profits from illicit economic activities. Unlike traditional insurgency, this form of insurgency may not be premeditated and was not initially driven by political motivations. Eventual freedom from sovereign rule by such criminal groups, however, results in their *de facto* political control of the cities, towns, and regions under their influence. The Mexican states of Michoacán and Tamaulipas represent present examples of this reality.

- *Spiritual Insurgency:* This construct and its real world manifestations are less developed than the commercial insurgency variants but are increasingly evident. Elements of this insurgency form can be readily seen with the La Familia Michoacana cartel in Mexico and even more so in its successor, Los Caballeros Templarios (The Knights Templars). Santa Muerte sacrificial practices of Los Zetas cartel members must also be considered, along with the cult-like behaviors of the members of the Lord's Resistance Army in Central Africa. The narcocultura movement in Mexico and beyond—which promotes a criminal code, fast living, and rough justice with a gun—gives spiritual meaning, and a plethora of narcosaints to worship, to those that adhere to its values.

- *Plutocratic Insurgency:* This other variant of commercial insurgency, first identified in 2011 by the author, exists at the opposite end of the spectrum from a criminal and illicit economic based insurgency.[3] In this instance, the "winners of globalization," represented by multinational corporations and global elites, are seeking to remove themselves from the regulatory, taxation, and, ultimately, political authority of states. This is done by promoting an extra-sovereign economy: using foreign tax havens, playing states off against each other to maximize profit, being a nonresident citizen so as not to pay taxes, and employing a bevy of lawyers and lobbyists within states to gain special privileges and economic considerations. This is very much representative of a Gilded Age (1870-1900) redux, but at a globalized level. No sovereign authority presently exists to contend with such an insurgent form; one that is an unintended consequence of globalized capitalism and is resulting in growing economic inequalities in Western states, yet has been relatively violence free. Some might argue, however, that law enforcement and judicial elements of co-opted states can be "legally utilized" by the plutocratic insurgents to suppress anti-plutocratic protests and demonstrations.

The "So What" Factor

The question must then be asked as to what these new insurgency forms mean for both the United States and for the Army that defends our nation. In the case of criminal and spiritual insurgency, contending with such conflicts definitely falls within the U.S. Army mission yet, at the same time, these are missions better left to policing and federal law enforcement agencies. The confounding factor is that when Army forces are deployed overseas in support of federal governments, often local (and sometimes regional and even national) police and law enforcement agencies have been corrupted and co-opted by the criminal organizations themselves.

One logical outcome of identifying such new insurgency forms is that it causes us to stop and pause to reflect upon our Army's recent counterinsurgency (COIN) experiences in Iraq and Afghanistan. These were definitely not your grandfather's revolutionary insurgencies, yet at the same time they did not fully have the characteristics of the criminal insurgencies taking place in Mexico and in some of regions of Central America. Quite possibly, they can be considered a transitional blend of people's war (tribal rather than Marxist based), criminality, and radical Islamic spirituality.

The emergence of plutocratic insurgency is in some ways more troubling and problematic than that of the two other insurgency forms. It represents globalized capitalism at odds with state moderated capitalism. Such an extra-sovereign challenge to states is representative of a shifting international order. Since this is the capitalist system essentially turning on itself, the U.S. Army currently has no part to play in such relationships. Still that Army is facing austere economic times, as is the nation that it defends, partially due to the rise of extra-sovereign corporations and global elites seeking to escape state authority.

In conclusion, while many eyes are now on China and its ambitions, we must also be cognizant of how the nature of insurgency is changing. Metz's theory has now become our reality. This new reality—reflective of an emergent post-modern world—will require a new and second interpretation of "strategic Landpower" directed at nonstate entities (e.g., transnational criminal organizations) in addition to traditional interpretations addressing states. At the same time, we must move beyond the blinders of both realist (state focused) and liberal (free markets are infallible) school tenets in our perspectives on international relations and accede that: a) nonstate entities now have the power to challenge states; and, b) globalized capitalism is increasingly in variance with Western state moderated capitalism which seeks to mitigate large inequalities in our social class structures.

Notes

The views expressed in this op-ed are those of the author and do not necessarily reflect the official policy or position of the Department of the Army, the Department of Defense, or the U.S. Government. This opinion piece is cleared for public release; distribution is unlimited.

1. https://ssi.armywarcollege.edu/index.cfm/articles/Not-Your-Grandfathers-Insurgency-Criminal-Spiritual-and-Plutocratic/2014/02/20.
2. The criminal insurgency construct was first articulated by John Sullivan. See John P. Sullivan and Robert J. Bunker, "Rethinking insurgency: criminality, spirituality, and societal warfare in the Americas," Robert J. Bunker, ed., *Criminal Insurgencies in Mexico and the Americas: The Gangs and Cartels Wage War*, London, UK: Routledge, 2013, pp. 29-50.
3. See Robert Bunker, "Plutocratic Insurgency," *Small Wars Journal*, September 6, 2012, available from smallwarsjournal.com/blog/plutocratic-insurgency. A link to discussion notes with Nils Gilman—one of the editors of *Deviant Globalization* (Continuum, 2011)—concerning this construct accompanies the citation.

Reading 4

The Twin Insurgency—
Facing Plutocrats and Criminals

Nils Gilman

Published 5 September 2014 in Robert J. Bunker and Pamela
Ligouri Bunker, Eds., *Global Criminal and Sovereign Free
Economies and the Demise of the Western Democracies: Dark
Renaissance.* London: Routledge, 2015: xx-xxxvi.
Reprinted with permission of the publisher.

Everywhere the ceremony of innocence is drowned.

William Butler Yeats, 1919

States within the global political economy today face a twin insurgency,
one from below, another from above. On the one hand, there are a
series of interconnected *criminal insurgencies,* in which the global
disenfranchised resist, coopt, and route around states as they seek ways
to empower and enrich themselves in the shadows of the global economy.
Drug cartels, human traffickers, computer hackers, counterfeiters, arms
dealers and others exploit the loopholes, exceptions, and failures of
governance institutions to build global commercial empires that, in turn,
provide them the resources to corrupt, coopt, or challenge incumbent

political actors. On the other hand, there exists a *plutocratic insurgency,* in which globalized elites seek to disengage from traditional national obligations and responsibilities. From libertarian activists, to tax haven lawyers, to currency speculators, to mineral-extraction magnates, the new global super-rich and their hired help are waging a broad-based campaign that aims either to limit the reach and capacity of government tax-collectors and regulators or to manipulate these functions as a tool in their own cut-throat business competition. Unlike classic twentieth century insurgents, who sought control over the state apparatus in order to implement social reforms, criminal and plutocratic insurgents do not seek to take over the state. Nor do they wish to destroy the state, since they rely, like parasites, on the state to provide the legacy goods of social welfare: health, education, infrastructure, and so on. Rather, their aim is simpler: to carve out de facto zones of autonomy for themselves by crippling the state's ability to constrain their freedom of (economic) action.

The failures of social modernism

Understanding how we arrived at these twin insurgencies requires a brief return to the anterior period. During the social modernist era (1945-1971), virtually all states—whether capitalist or communist, industrialized or developmental, great power or postcolonial—aimed to legitimate themselves by serving the interests of a middle class whose size they sought to expand (Woodiwiss, 1993; Gilman, 2003). Both capitalist and communist accumulation strategies were based on the nurturing of industrial laborers, who were expected to work for a living, and who, in turn, were told that the state not only would steadily improve their standard of living, but also would cushion them from outrageous misfortune via various forms of social security (Westad, 2006). These states were "welfare states" in the sense that they sought to provide for the *general welfare,* rather than to protect or lift up the poor or defend the prerogatives of the rich. In the non-communist world, the wealthy were taxed not out of class hostility but in order to finance *public goods* for society as a whole (Lambert, 1993). Health care, pensions, schools, and so on were represented less as individual "entitlements" than as collectively enjoyed public goods. While a diversity of social contracts existed during this period (Evans et al., 1985; Esping-Andersen, 1990), in virtually every country elites felt a duty to play a "muscular and essential role in steering the economy and underwriting the well-being of the middle class" (Mizruchi, 2013), and inequality of income steadily decreased. For Western elites in particular, the fact that the Cold War order made thinkable radical alternatives to capitalism no doubt helped concentrate a certain commitment to larger moral, social, and political purposes.[1]

By the 1970s, however, it was becoming undeniable that social modernist states across each of the "three worlds of development" were failing to deliver on their promises (Pletsch, 1981; Slater, 2008). In the West, the stagflation of the 1970s undermined the technical foundations of the Bretton Woods financial order, as well as the technocratic consensus in favor of Keynesian demand management and the political consensus in favor of sharing productivity gains between labor and capital. In the East, centrally planned economies were revealing themselves as not only politically repressive but also economically inefficient and environmentally catastrophic. In the Global South, while the commodity boom of the 1970s led to a golden age for primary producers, Import Substitution Industrialization failed to deliver sustained growth and transition to high per capita incomes,[2] and the commodity price crash of the early 1980s precipitated a debt crisis which put to rest any dreams of global redistribution (Reinhart, 2008). From the late 1970s through the early twenty-first century, a period of reaction to state-centric models of development set in (Harvey, 2007; Caryl, 2013; Sargent, forthcoming). Levels of economic inequality began to grow again, eventually reaching heights not seen since the 1920s, and prompting some financial analysts to describe the new economy as a "plutonomy" (Kapur *et al.*, 2005). At the same time, states stopped trying to create a more egalitarian society or to provide for the general welfare; instead they increasingly sought legitimacy by claiming to maximize the opportunities of individuals (Bobbitt, 2002).

From this perspective, the creation of plutocrats counted not as a defeat, but as a success for the new model of governance.

When Communism collapsed in 1989, what died was not just the particular collectivist economic system and authoritarian politics of the Soviet Union and its satellites. Cremated along with the corpse of Communism was the civic-minded conception of development as the central responsibility of the state and allied elites—a conception shared by communists and liberals alike during the Cold War. It wasn't just that the state "retreated" (Strange, 1996) from the "commanding heights" (Yergin, 1998) of the economy, but also that the very ambitions of the state found itself in eclipse. The best face that the World Bank could put on the new order was to say that, henceforth, the role of the state would be to "steer" rather than to "row" (World Bank, 1997). By the turn of the millennium, even the left had come to doubt whether states could be relied on to effectively and disinterestedly promote the public interest (Scott, 1998).

The nature of the new order was made most explicit in two texts published the year that the Berlin Wall fell, Francis Fukuyama's "The End of History?" (1989) and John Williamson's "The Washington Consensus" (1990). Fukuyama proposed that big-H History (in the Hegelian sense of ideological contestation over the proper relationship between state and civil society) had come to an end with a universal agreement that liberal, democratic capitalism was not just the best but in fact the only reasonable form of socio-political-economic organization. Williamson's text was more pragmatic than metaphysical, filling in the details of this "post-historical" policy consensus with specific imperatives around fiscal discipline, the redirection of public spending away from subsidies, the rollback of progressive tax codes, the floating of currencies, the liberalization of trade and cross-border investment, the privatization of state enterprises and deregulation of private ones, and above all the sacrosanctification of private property rights. Taken together, these texts involved not just a dethroning of the state, but a wholesale challenge to the idea that technocratic leadership was the primary way to ensure collective social well-being. Pioneered as domestic policy in Margaret Thatcher's Great Britain and Ronald Reagan's United States, the programs associated with the Washington Consensus—above all, the privatization of national industrial assets (especially of state owned firms and utilities) and deregulation (especially of financial firms)—soon became a model that London and Washington sought to export to the Global South and the post-Communist world under the rubric of "structural adjustment" and "shock therapy" (Fourcade-Gourinchas & Babb, 2002; Rajan & Zingales, 2003). As Dani Rodrik concluded: "'Stabilize, privatize, and liberalize' became the mantra of a generation of technocrats who cut their teeth in the developing world and of the political leaders they counseled" (Rodrik, 2006).

This transformation of the role of the state in the wake of the Cold War has led to a very different sort of landscape of political contestation. With the social modernist state in ideological crisis, the middle classes whose interests it was designed to promote find themselves in an increasingly precarious position. From above, they are threatened by a global financial elite in league with ultra-wealthy compradors, who seek to cut the social services that are paid for by taxes that these elites depict as a form of illegitimate expropriation. From below, they find themselves exposed to various forms of criminals, who have reacted to the collapse of hope for inclusion in the middle class by taking their futures into their own hands. Let us consider each of these phenomena in turn.

Plutocratic Insurgency: The revolt of mainstream globalization's winners

This ideological retreat of the social modernist state represents the central event that has enabled plutocratic insurgency. During the 1990s, a new class of globetrotting economic elites emerged, enriched by the opportunities created by globalizing industrial firms, deregulated financial services, and new technology platforms. This new class is an order of magnitude richer in absolute terms than previous generations of the ultra-wealthy.[3] The rise of the new plutocrats reflects an historic shift in the structure of capital accumulation (Irvin, 2007).

The accumulation regime that predominated during the heyday of social modernism was predicated on creating a new class of workers who could afford the goods that they were producing (Harvey, 2001). The great fortunes of the late nineteenth and early twentieth century were built on the backs of masses of worker-consumers in primarily inward-looking national contexts. By contrast, today's plutocrats make their fortunes selling their goods and services globally—in real terms, therefore, their ongoing success is less connected to the fortunes of their fellow national citizens than was that of previous generations. Moreover, the two signature types of massive wealth accumulation in the early 21st century have been high technology and financial services—both industries that do not rely on masses of laborers, and whose productivity is therefore detached from the health of any particular national middle class. The result has been a dramatic rise in inequality within countries, even as wealth inequality transnationally has narrowed.

The rise in a new class of plutocrats has been marked by the emergence of new ideological self-conceptions (Freeland, 2013). Many of these contemporary plutocrats see themselves as "the deserving winners of a tough worldwide competition" (Freeland, 2011) and regard efforts to make them to pay for public goods as little more than organized theft. Whereas the threat of Communism during the Cold War acted as a check on the maximalist ambitions of the ultra-rich, the political and ideological collapse of the Soviet Union removed that constraint, enabling an ideological shift in how a significant segment of the new wealthy conceive their relationship with their societies. While some among the wealthy continue to see themselves as owing a debt of obligation to the societies in which they have enriched themselves, there exists a significant subset—particularly among financial elites (Huffschmid, 2008)—who do not see their personal achievements as tied to the success of the national societies in which they reside (Taylor & Harrison, 2008). Instead of seeing themselves as the ultimate winners of the systems in which they work (Domhoff, 2009), they characterize themselves as rebels, outsiders who have made it on their own despite the restraints presented by incumbents, loafers, and parasites in government and society (Frank, 2007). The popularity of the pseudo-philosophical novels of Ayn Rand—whose ideas George Monbiot (2012) refers to as "the Marxism of the new right"—represents the most visible manifestation of this ideology that poses the rich as "makers" as opposed to the mass of shiftless "takers" (Burns, 2009; Weiss, 2012). From Washington to London, plutocrat-funded think tanks are devoted to creating a body of usable ideas and policy proposals geared at dismantling social modernism (James, 1993; Medvetz, 2012). This ideological shift heralds the arrival of plutocratic insurgency.[4]

The defining feature of plutocratic insurgency is the effort on the part of holders of this ideology to *defund or de-provision public goods*, in order to defang a state that they see as a threat to their prerogatives (Pack, 1987).[5] Practically speaking, plutocratic insurgency takes the form of efforts to *lower taxes*, which necessitates the cutting of spending on public goods; to *reduce regulations* that restrict corporate action or that protect workers; and to *defund or privatize public institutions*, such as schools, health care, infrastructure, and social space. The political strategy associated with plutocratic insurgency is to use austerity in the face of economic shocks to *rewrite social contracts on the basis of a much narrower set of mutual social obligations* (Klein, 2007), with the ultimate effect of de-collectivizing social risks (Beck, 2008). As a palliative for the loss of public goods and state-backed programs to improve public welfare, plutocratic insurgents typically promote the idea of philanthropy—directed toward ends defined not democratically but, naturally, by themselves (Barkan, 2013). "There's no such thing as society," Margaret Thatcher famously declared, issuing the *cri de cœur* of insurgent plutocrats everywhere—since, if there's no such thing as society, then the very category of social services collapses, along with any responsibility on the part of the rich to contribute to them. From this perspective, plutocratic insurgency signifies the re-importation back into the industrial core of the aforementioned policies of structural adjustment that were applied across the Global South during the 1980s and 1990s.

For plutocratic insurgents, this strategy is dictated at bottom by a raw cost-benefit analysis: the price the social modernist state asks them to pay in taxes and the regulatory burdens it imposes on them outweighs the benefit they believe they personally receive from living in such a state. Plutocratic insurgents believe they can afford (and therefore everyone should be required) to buy for themselves the sorts of goods that before required a state to provide. They live in gated communities, travel via personal jets and private bus fleets, and send their children to exclusive schools (Freeland, 2012). While each of these decisions may at first be motivated by lifestyle choices or a desire for social differentiation, the result is a progressive moral disinvestment and civic disengagement from the quality of these traditionally public services (Bickford, 2000; Sengupta, 2008; Blakely, 2012), especially as the habit of opting out of public services trickles down from the oligarchs to the upper middle classes (Caldeira, 2000). Leaving aside the matter of the undemocratic nature of such private services, or the adverse selection problems that arise from partial privatizations, what marks the arrival of plutocratic insurgency is when the rich begin to revolt against paying taxes for public services they never plan to use. The result is a reinforcing cycle, whereby plutocratic insurgents increasingly see no reason to contribute anything to their host societies, and indeed actively make war on the idea that citizenship imbues them with economic or social responsibilities.

Criminal Insurgency: The revolt of deviant globalization's winners

Many of same processes that are driving plutocratic insurgency also underpin the process of criminal insurgency: the globalization of economic flows, growing wealth inequality, and a collapse of state provisioning of public goods and services. From Latin America to Africa to the former Eastern bloc, the 1980s and 1990s structural adjustment and shock therapy programs led to the "hollowing out" of the state: the physical buildings and institutions of "adjusted" states remained in place, but their ambitions and capacities shriveled (Milward & Provan, 2000). The states in these countries dramatically decreased their spending on social services—ranging from subsidies for food and fuel to broader social services like public health and pensions. State-owned industries were either shut down or privatized, with wages and employment slashed. The state, in other words, further decreased its capacity to deliver a decent life to its citizens, leading to a collapse in the popular expectation that the state should serve as a guarantor of progress (Duffield, 1998; Ferguson 1999; Parenti, 2011). At the same time, however, the economies of these countries opened rapidly to cross-border financial and trade flows. This combination of the failure of the public-goods providing state and a dramatic increase in the openness of national economies created both the opportunity for enterprising individuals to make money in new ways and an imperative to do so, as a matter of survival. These effects were in fact the explicit intention of the structural adjustment and shock therapy programs: rolling back the dirigiste state and opening up the economy was meant to unleash a flood of pent-up entrepreneurial energy and, indeed, it did.

Alas, structural-adjustment- and shock-therapy-driven globalization of the formerly closed economies of the Eastern Bloc and the Global South turned out to have an unfortunate bug (Los, 2003; Glenny, 2008). While the mainstream globalization celebrated by the likes of Thomas Friedman (2005) grabbed the headlines, what most distinguished the post-Cold War global economy from the earlier era was the parallel development of a shadowy "deviant" globalization in industries like narcotics, immigration, wildlife harvesting, and antiquities. Though the weakness of the post-communist and post-developmental state represented a dire problem for mainstream businesses and for imploding middle classes in these countries, it offered certain comparative advantages for illicit commerce. Deviant entrepreneurs realized that arbitraging the moral and regulatory differences that existed in different jurisdictions worldwide presented fantastic business opportunities. While big multinational corporations were able to sew up the licit opportunities afforded by the integration of the global economy, they were unable to play in arenas of goods and services banned for moral reasons (Gilman *et al.*, 2011). The great unsung globalizers of the 1990s and 2000s, therefore, were the criminals who rapidly scaled up their local mom-and-pop criminal organizations to become globe-spanning deviant commercial empires (Saviano, 2006; Keefe, 2012).

These avatars of deviant globalization are also the leaders of the second of our twin insurgencies—the criminal sort. What distinguishes criminal insurgents from classic social revolutionaries is that rather than seeking to build or capture institutionalized state power, they seek merely to protect their rents in various (usually deviant) markets that they control. Organizations such as the First Command of the Capital in Brazil, the 'Ndrangheta in Italy, or the Zetas in Mexico have no interest in taking over the states in which they operate. Instead, like plutocratic insurgents, what criminal insurgents seek is to cripple the state, that is, to establish a zone of economic autonomy while continuing to rely on the state to supply vestigial social services.[6] These actors thrive in (and indeed prefer and try to foster) weak-state environments, and their activities reinforce the conditions of this weakness. As deviant globalization takes root in a particular locale, however, it soon begins to generate a positive feedback loop, in much the same way that many successful animal and plant species, as they invade a natural ecosystem, reshape their ecosystem in ways that improve their ability to exclude competitors (Sullivan & Bunker, 2002; Manwaring, 2005; Arias, 2006). The state weakness that at first was merely a permissive enabling condition for their business becomes something that the now empowered criminal insurgents seek to perpetuate and even exacerbate. They siphon off money, loyalty, and sometimes territory; they increase corruption; and they undermine the rule of law. They also force well-functioning states in the global system to spend an inordinate amount of time, energy, and attention trying to control what comes in and out of their borders.

In building their business empires, deviant globalizers inevitably come into conflict with host states in three distinct ways that render them de facto political actors. First, they control huge, growing swathes of the global economy, operating most prominently in places where the state is hollowed or hollowing out. Corruption fueled by drug money on both sides of the US-Mexico border exemplifies this point (Miller, 2009). Second, many deviant entrepreneurs control and deploy a significant quota of violence—an occupational hazard for people working in extra-legal industries, who cannot count on the state to adjudicate their contractual disputes. This use of violence brings deviant entrepreneurs into primal conflict with one of the state's central sources of legitimacy, namely its monopoly (in principle) over the socially sanctioned use of force, transforming them from merely deviant businessmen into criminal insurgents. Third, these criminal insurgents in some cases are begin to emerge as private providers of justice, health care, and infrastructure—that is, precisely the kind of goods that functional states are supposed to provide to their citizens. (However, since they are provided privately, to the deviant entrepreneurs' personal constituents, they are not 'public goods' in the sense of goods equally accessible to all citizens.) Criminal syndicates in Brazil (Langewiesche, 2007), the MEND in Nigeria (Junger, 2007), narco-traffickers like the Sinaloa Cartel in Mexico (Keefe, 2012)—all are criminal insurgents who not only have demonstrated that they can shut down areas of their host states' basic functional capacity, thereby upsetting global markets half a world away, but who are also providing social services to local constituencies (Robb, 2007).

Criminal insurgency is thus the form that deviant globalization takes as it scales and reaches political self-consciousness. On the one hand, the more deviant industries grow, the more damage they do to the political legitimacy of the states within which the criminal insurgents operate, thus undermining the capacity of the state to provide the infrastructure and services that the criminal insurgents want to free ride on. On the other hand, the people living in the semi-autonomous zones controlled by criminal insurgents increasingly recognize the insurgents rather than the hollowed out state as the real source of local power and authority (Finnegan, 2010). Of course, just because these deviant providers of alternative governance functions end up seeming "legitimate" in the eyes of local stakeholders, this type of governance is usually poorly institutionalized and untransparent about both ends and means. Nonetheless, as these groups take over functions that would have been expected of the state, their stakeholders increasingly lose interest in the hollowed-out formal state institutions (Davis, 2010).

Thus, even though criminal insurgents have no desire to kill their host state, they may end up precipitating a process whereby the state implodes catastrophically.

The Enclavization of Microsovereignties and the End of the Middle Class

During the 1990s, it became fashionable to declare that in the new post-cold war era, the state was destined to wither away. In fact, something more subtle was taking place: the double collapse of social modernist state's capacity and legitimacy was giving birth not to the post-historical utopia of universal consensus in favor of liberal democratic capitalism, but rather to a conjoined monster in the form of plutocratic secession and deviant globalization. Instead of projects of collective emancipation, what both plutocratic and criminal insurgents desire is for the social modernist state to remain intact *except insofar as it impinges on them personally*. Neither criminal nor plutocratic insurgents are revolutionaries in the classic modernist sense of political actors who seek to take over the state.[7] As the social modernist state failed to realize its promise, the very notion of a revolution that aspires to a project of national-scale collective social reform (Skocpol, 1979) has come to seem quaint. Neither category of insurgent is interested in taking control over the state to enact a process of national (or international) social reform. Nor do they seek a political revolution in the Arendtian or Burkean sense of a contest for direct operational and ideological control over the organs of the state (Arendt, 1963; Burke, 1983). Instead of being in revolt against a particular political regime, with the goal of building better government, they aim instead to cripple their hosts states in order to gain de facto zones of private autonomy that can enable individual, tribal, or interest-group enrichment.[8] They are thus parasitic in a very specific sense: they wish to free ride on the institutional legacy of social modernism so as to avoid costs to their businesses.

Seen from a spatial perspective, what both insurgencies represent is the replacement of the liberal ideal of uniform authority and rights within national spaces by *a kaleidoscopic array of de facto and de jure microsovereignties*. Rather than a single national space in which power is exercised and rights are enjoyed in a consist and homogeneous way by all residents, the cartography of the dual insurgency represents diverse enclaves of political authority and of social service provisioning arrangements (Ong, 2000; Sidaway, 2007). As these unique arrangements emerge, national and local authorities proliferate a variety of increasingly one-off exceptions to the general rules, incrementally traducing the liberal notion of equality before the law. Just as the 1930s saw a multiplication of conditions poised between war and peace, so our present conjuncture witnesses the multiplication of various forms of authority between the full-blown modern state and outright anarchy, symbolized by the blurring lines between police, military, and private security contractors, in terms of both kinetic capabilities and legal authorities (Singer, 2001; Lambert, 2013; Shank & Beavers, 2013). The process itself is, of course, self-reinforcing: the proliferation of exceptional and unique microsovereignties only increases the scope for the insurgents to engage in jurisdictional arbitrage, and further demands by other insurgents for their own personalized sovereign exceptions. In the space of the dual insurgency, citizenship no longer signifies the liberal ideal of an identical package of rights for all, but instead means very different things depending on where individuals are in physical and social space (Krijnen & Fawaz, 2010).

Within plutocratic enclaves, the source of authority and loyalty is, at bottom, money. From a geographic perspective, plutocratic insurgents seek to create zones of private authority and legal autonomy where they can privately command goods once considered public, including not just security (Caldeira, 2000; Hope, 2000; Abrahamsen & Williams 2011) but also increasingly schooling, transportation, health care, shopping, legal enforcement, and so on (Dezelay & Garth, 1998; Rodenbeck, 2013). The paradigmatic case for plutocratic spatial segregation and secession are so-called gated communities, which rightly have become the subject of a minor academic subfield (Lister et al., 2003). These spaces are much more than simple residential enclaves, but increasingly offer full-service operations that contain virtually everything their denizens need, so that residents only need to leave in order to travel to other such enclaves (Connell, 1999; Webster, 2001; Sengupta, 2008; Breitung, 2012). Rights within such spaces, it goes with out saying, accrue to dollars rather than to citizenship. The vision of the future here is of a global archipelago of "privatopias" (McKenzie, 1996), linked by air and internet to other such spaces, protected by high ramparts from the roiling dystopian ocean of the hoi polloi (Graham & Marvin, 2001; Davis, 2005). Moreover, in addition to these zones of physical separation, plutocratic insurgents also seek out (or seek to create) virtual zones of legal exception, in the form of offshore tax havens (which allows them to avoid income taxes—Baldacchino, 2010; Shaxson, 2011) and special economic zones (which allows them to avoid tariffs as well as laws designed to protect labor or the environment—Bach, 2011). Plutocratic insurgents are adept at playing off one jurisdiction against another, threatening to take their capital elsewhere if the local authorities do not grant them the exceptions that they seek.

The enclaves of the criminal insurgents are more precarious, as one would expect. Unlike the visible separation that the plutocratic insurgents enjoy in the form of high walls and armed guards, the autonomous zones of the underclass are more temporary and, naturally, less secure for their masters. From the favelas of Sao Paolo (Langewiesche, 2007), the slums of Karachi (Kaker, 2014), the waterfront of Kingston (Kilcullen, 2013), and the suburbs of Beirut (Fawaz et al., 2012) or Naples (Saviano, 2006) to the remotest corners of Afghanistan (Hetherington, 2011), Honduras (Schwartz, 2014) or Sudan (Omeje, 2010), such autonomous spaces take the form of feral "no-go zones" (no-go, that is, to the rich) in which some notionally social modernist state may claim authority, but in which true power is wielded by warlords, gangsters, or other kinds of organized criminals, who take de facto control over local security and whatever meager social service provisioning may be on offer (Norton, 2003; Bunker & Sullivan, 2011; Marten, 2012). In these zones, sources of authority and loyalty and the application of raw power tends toward what might be called "neo-tribalism"—"neo" in the sense that primal loyalties adhere not just to those who share (perceived) bonds of ancient kinship, but rather in accordance to all manner of intense and ritualized personal connections among young male specialists in the use of violence (Ronfeldt, 2006; Robb, 2007). In short, while globalization is indeed undermining national political institutions and thus national identities and loyalties, what appears to be replacing the national is not a "global" political identity—as "cosmopolitical" dreamers have long aspired to (Cheah & Robbins, 1998)—but rather a return to localized identities rooted in clan, sect, ethnicity, corporation, and gang. Understanding the nature of social relations in such spaces of social fracture may best be approached by a literary rather than a strictly social scientific sensibility (DiMaggio, 2011).

The central difficulty that both plutocratic and criminal insurgents face is that it is unclear whether the political objective they seek can produce stable equilibria of governance. There are least two separate reasons to question the ability of these arrangements to produce stability. First, the fracturing of sovereign homogeneity increases transaction costs for people traversing them—it requires a constant expenditure of time and effort to determine exactly what zone of governance one is in and who, therefore, is due respect and obeisance. This is equally true whether one considers the spaces of the plutocratic or the criminal insurgency: in the former case, the price is paid to lawyers, in the second to gangsters. Second, the kaleidoscope proliferates opportunities for arbitrage and defection of customers and foot soldiers to other governance spaces (Hirschman, 1970). The ultimate losers in all of this, of course, are the middle classes—the sorts of people who try to "play by the rules" by going to school and getting traditional middle class jobs whose chief virtue is stability. These sorts of people—who lack the ruthlessness to act as criminal insurgents and the resources to act as plutocratic insurgents—can only watch with a certain passivity as the institutions which were built over the course of the twentieth century to ensure a high quality of life for a broad majority of citizens are progressively eroded. As the social bases of solidaristic collective action crumble, individuals within the middle classes increasingly face the choice between accepting a progressive loss of social security and de facto social degradation, or attempting to join one of the two insurgencies.[9]

Notes

This essay—written as the foreword for *Global Criminal and Sovereign Free Economies and the Demise of the Western Democracies*—was also published in *The American Interest*, https://www.the-american-interest.com/2014/06/15/the-twin-insurgency/.

1. The ideal of the modernist welfare state may have been mainly honored in the breach but the point is that it was in fact honored despite contestation of the liberal-welfarist model by various actors, whether by leftists who sought a more explicit policy of class leveling, or by rightists who sought to uphold or enforce various forms of racial, national, or class-based exclusions. The liberal welfare state remained firmly ensconced as the hegemonic model during this period—that is, as the baseline against which other political discourses and proposed political-economic models had to define themselves. With that said, the relations between labor and management in the West (and particularly in the United States) were conflictual even during the postwar heyday of social modernism. Plutocratic pushback against both organized labor and the regulatory and tax reach of the liberal state was present from the beginning of the New Deal and became a formal political strategy by mid-1940s (Phillips-Fein, 2006; Phillips-Fein, 2009; Burgin, 2012). As Nelson Lichtenstein has observed, "There was no 'labor-management accord,' although labor's strength did generate a kind of armed truce in key oligopolistic sectors of the economy" (Lichtenstein, 2000: 261). Despite this pre-history of the plutocratic insurgency, however, it is clear that the end of the Cold War represented a watershed. One cannot help but contrast Tony Judt's (2005) descriptions of Europe's public-minded postwar statesmen to the shameless way that ex-Presidents (GHW Bush, Clinton) and Chancellors (Schroeder) and Prime Ministers (Blair) are happy to receive $100m+ payouts from hedge funds and foreign governments upon leaving office.
2. Key texts in the normative shift away from ISI were Baer, 1972 and Balassa, 1978.
3. Just a few statistics give a sense of the scale. When *Forbes* magazine first started tracking the ultra rich in 1982, there were 12 billionaires in the United States; by 2012, there were 425 (Kroll, 2012). In 1982, there were fewer than 200,000 millionaires in the United States; by 2012, there were over 3.7m (CapGemini, 2013). In 2013, there were also 98,700 "ultra-high net worth individuals" (with assets > $50m), of which 45% were American (Credit Suisse, 2013). To speak of the habits, ideological or otherwise, of the very rich is thus largely to speak of Americans.
4. The locus of the plutocratic insurgency today lies in West—in particular, the world headquarters for the global plutocratic insurgency is London, the world's largest

"offshore" financial center that is home to (or at any rate has the homes of) more plutocrats than any other city (Vellacott, 2012; Shaxson, 2013). Elsewhere, the evidence is less clear: Russia experienced a huge plutocratic insurgency in the 1990s, but the arrival of Putin and the defenestration of the first-generation oligarchs represented the reassertion of the prerogatives of the state—that is, a successful *plutocratic counterinsurgency*. In China, the rise of the super-rich has happened mainly through state-sponsored (though not state-owned) enterprises, which means that plutocrats there remain dependent on the state and the Communist Party and, as such, relatively insecure politically. There, and elsewhere in East Asia, rent-seeking rather than insurgent remains the norm among plutocrats.

5. Conceptually, plutocratic insurgencies differ from kleptocracies—the latter involve the using the institutions of state to loot the population, whereas the former wish to neutralize those institutions in order to facilitate private sector looting. In practice, these may overlap or co-mingle.

6. Liberal enthusiasts of globalization (most prominently: Barnett, 2005 and Friedman, 2005) assert poverty, insecurity, and state fragility are the result of "disconnectedness" from the world economy. This is false: even paradigmatically "failed" states—Congo, Somalia, Afghanistan—are deeply connected to the global economy. While it is true that they remain weakly connected to the *formal* and *legal* parts of the global economy, such places are *deviantly* connected—via the illicit trade in minerals, via piracy, or via the global drug trade, and so on. The crucial issue, in other words, is not connectedness or disconnectedness, but rather *what kind* of connectedness.

7. Rebels who seek to take over or direct the state toward projects of social reform do continue to exist of course—from Marx-inspired movements like the Zapatistas in Mexico or the Naxalites in India to Allah-inspired movements like Al-Shabaab in Somalia or the Moro insurgency in the Philippines. These sorts of movements, as well as the so-called "color revolutions" that have befallen various post-Soviet states represent a different phenomenon than either described in this essay.

8. The ideological collapse of the labor-centric, social welfare-providing nationalist state helps to explain why the post-2007 crisis has failed to produce organized opposition movements geared at reining in the secessionist impulses of plutocrats or at addressing the abjections that drive deviant globalization (Fraser, 2013).

9. The popularity of the American television series "Breaking Bad" stems in no small part from its dramatization of this precise moral dilemma.

References

Abrahamsen, R., & Williams, M. (2011) *Security beyond the State: Private Security in International Politics.* Cambridge: Cambridge University Press.

Arendt, H. (1963) *On Revolution.* New York: Penguin.

Arias, E. (2006) 'The Dynamics of Criminal Governance: Networks and Social Order in Rio de Janeiro'. *Journal of Latin American Studies.* Vol. 38. No. 2.: 293-325.

Bach, J. (2011) 'Modernity and the Urban Imagination in Economic Zones'. *Theory, Culture & Society.* Vol. 28. No. 5.: 98-122.

Baer, W. (1972) 'Import Substitution and Industrialization in Latin America: Experiences and Interpretations'. *Latin American Research Review.* Vol. 7. No. 1.: 301-328.

Balassa, B. (1978) 'Exports and Economic Growth: Further Evidence'. *Journal of Development Economics.* Vol. 5. No. 2.: 181-189.

Baldacchino, G. (2010) *Island Enclaves: Offshoring Strategies, Creative Governance, and Subnational Island* Jurisdictions. Montreal: McGill-Queen's Press.

Barkan, J. (2013) 'Plutocrats at Work: How Big Philanthropy Undermines Democracy'. *Dissent.* Fall, http://www.dissentmagazine.org/article/plutocrats-at-work-how-big-philanthropy-undermines-democracy.

Barnett, T. (2005) *The Pentagon's New Map: War and Peace in the Twenty-First Century.* New York: Putnam.

Beck, U. (2008) *World at Risk.* New York: Polity, 2008.

Bickford, S. (2000) 'Constructing Inequality: City Spaces and the Architecture of Citizenship'. *Political Theory.* Vol. 28. No. 3.: 355-376.

Blakely, E. (2012) 'In Gated Communities, a Dangerous Mind-Set'. *Washington Post.* 6 April, http://www.washingtonpost.com/opinions/in-gated-communities-such-as-where-trayvon-martin-died-a-dangerous-mind-set/2012/04/06/gIQAwWG8zS_story.html.

Bobbitt, P. (2002) *The Shield of Achilles: War, Peace, and the Course of History*. New York: Knopf.

Breitung, W. (2012) 'Enclave Urbanism in China: Attitudes towards Gated Communities in Guangzhou'. *Urban Geography*. Vol. 33. No. 2.: 278-294.

Bunker, R., & Sullivan, J. (2011) 'Integrating Feral Cities and Third Phase Cartels/Third Generation Gangs Research: The Rise of Criminal (Narco) City Networks and BlackFor'. *Small Wars & Insurgencies*. Vol. 22. No. 5.: 764-786.

Burgin, A. (2012) *The Great Persuasion: Reinventing Free Markets since the* Depression. Cambridge: Harvard University Press.

Burke, E. (1983 [1790]) *Reflections on the Revolution in France*. New York: Penguin.

Burns, J. (2009) *Goddess of the Market: Ayn Rand and the American* Right. New York: Oxford University Press.

Caldeira, T. (2000) *City of Walls: Crime, Segregation, and Citizenship in São Paulo*. Berkeley: University of California Press.

CapGemini (2013) 'World Wealth Report 2013', http://www.capgemini. com/resource-file access/resource/pdf/wwr_2013_0.pdf.

Caryl, C. (2013) *Strange Rebels: 1979 and the Birth of the 21ˢᵗ Century*. New York: Basic Books.

Cheah, P., & Robbins, P., eds. (1998) *Cosmopolitics: Thinking and Feeling beyond the Nation*. Minneapolis: University of Minnesota Press.

Connell, J. (1999) 'Beyond Manila: Walls, Malls, and Private Spaces'. *Environment and Planning A*. Vol. 31. No. 3.: 417-439.

Credit Suisse (2013) 'Global Wealth Report 2013', https:// publications.credit-suisse.com/tasks/render/file/?fileID= BCDB1364-A105-0560-1332EC9100FF5C83.

Davis, D. (2010) 'Irregular Armed Forces, Shifting Patterns of Commitment, and Fragmented Sovereignty in the Developing World'. *Theory and Society*. Vol. 39. No. 3-4.: 397-413.

Davis, M. (2005) *Evil Paradises: Dreamworlds of Neoliberalism*. New York: The New Press.

Dezelay, Y., & Garth, B. (1998) *Dealing in Virtue: International Commercial Arbitration and the Construction of a Transnational Legal Order.* Chicago: University of Chicago Press.

DiMaggio, K. (2011) 'Seceding from the Narrative: How the Criminal Underworlds in William Burroughs' Naked Lunch Map out a Non-Linear Narrative through the Creation of 'Temporary Autonomous Zones''. *International Journal of the Book.* Vol. 8. No. 1.: 11-18.

Domhoff, G. (2009) *Who Rules America? The Triumph of the Corporate Rich,* 7th ed. New York: McGraw-Hill.

Duffield, M. (1998) 'Post-modern Conflict: Warlords, Post-adjustment States and Private Protection'. *Civil Wars.* Vol. 1. No. 1: 65-102.

Esping-Andersen, G. (1990) *The Three Worlds of Welfare Capitalism.* Cambridge: Polity Press.

Evans, P., Rueschemeyer, D., & Skocpol, T., eds. (1985) *Bringing the State Back In.* Cambridge: Cambridge University Press.

Fawaz, M., Harb, M., & Gharbieh, A. (2012) 'Living Beirut's Security Zones: An Investigation of the Modalities and Practice of Urban Security'. *City & Society.* Vol. 24. No. 2.: 173-195.

Ferguson, J. (1999) *Expectations of Modernity: Myths and Meanings of Urban Life on the Zambian Copperbelt.* Berkeley: University of California.

Finnegan, W. (2010) 'Silver or Lead'. *The New Yorker.* 31 May, http://www.newyorker.com/reporting/2010/05/31/100531fa_fact_finnegan.

Fourcade-Gourinchas, M., & Babb, S. (2002) 'The Rebirth of the Liberal Creed: Paths to Neoliberalism in Four Countries'. *American Journal of Sociology.* Vol. 108. No. 3.: 533-579.

Fraser, N. (2013) 'A Triple Movement?'. *New Left Review.* Vol. 81. May-June, http://newleftreview.org/II/81/nancy-fraser-a-triple-movement.

Frank, R. (2007) *Richistan: A Journey Through the 21st Century Wealth Boom and the Lives of the New Rich.* New York: Piatkus.

Freeland, C. (2011) 'The Rise of the New Global Elite'. *The Atlantic.* Vol. 307. No. 1: 44-55.

Freeland, C. (2012) *Plutocrats: The Rise of the New Global Super-Rich and the Fall of Everyone Else.* New York: Penguin.

Freeland, C. (2013) 'An Elite Deserving of the Name'. *Democracy: A Journal of Ideas.* Iss. 29. Summer, http://www.democracyjournal. org/29/an-elite-deserving-of-the-name.php?page=all.

Friedman, T. (2005) *The World is Flat: A Brief History of the Twenty-First Century.* New York: Macmillan.

Fukuyama, F. (1989) 'The End of History?'. *The National Interest.* Vol. 16. No. 3.: 3-18.

Gilman, N. (2003) *Mandarins of the Future: Modernization Theory in Cold War America.* Baltimore: Johns Hopkins University Press.

Gilman, N., Goldhammer, J., & Weber, S., eds. (2011) *Deviant Globalization: Black Market Economy in the 21st Century.* New York: Continuum.

Glenny, M. (2008) *McMafia: A Journey Through the Global Criminal Underworld.* New York: Knopf.

Graham, S., & Marvin, S. (2001) *Splintering Urbanism: Networked Infrastructures, Technological Mobilities and the Urban Condition.* New York: Routledge.

Harvey, D. (2001) *Spaces of Capital: Toward a Critical Geography.* New York: Routledge.

Harvey, D. (2007) *A Brief History of* Neoliberalism. New York: Oxford University Press.

Hetherington, T. (2011) 'Into the Korengal'. *World Policy Journal.* Vol. 28. No. 1: 60-70.

Hirschman, A. (1970) *Exit, Voice, and* Loyalty. Cambridge: Harvard University Press.

Hope, T. (2000) 'Inequality and the Clubbing of Private'. Hope, T. & Sparks, R., eds., *Crime, Risk, and Insecurity: Law and Order in Everyday Life and Political Discourse.* New York: Routledge: 83-106.

Huffschmid, J. (2008) 'Finance as a driver of privatization'. *Transfer: European Review of Labour and Research.* Vol. 14. No. 2.: 209-236.

Irvin, G. (2007) 'Growing Inequality in the Neo-liberal Heartland'. *Post-Autistic Economics Review.* Vol. 43.: 1-23.

James, S. (1993) 'The Idea Brokers: The Impact of Think Tanks on British Government'. *Public Administration.* Vol. 71. No. 4.: 491-506.

Judt, T. (2005) *Postwar: A History of Europe Since* 1945. New York: Penguin.

Junger, S. (2007) 'Blood Oil'. *Vanity Fair.* February, http://www.vanityfair.com/politics/features/2007/02/junger200702.

Kaker, S. (2014) 'Enclaves, insecurity and violence in Karachi'. *South Asian History and Culture.* Vol. 5. No. 1.: 1-15.

Kapur, A., Macleod, N., & Singh, N. (2005) 'Plutonomy: Buying Luxury, Explaining Global Imbalances'. Citigroup Research. 16 October, http://cryptome.org/0005/rich-pander.pdf (Mirrored).

Keefe, P. (2012) 'How a Drug Cartel Makes its Billions'. *New York Times.* 15 June, http://www.nytimes.com/2012/06/17/magazine/how-a-mexican-drug-cartel-makes-its-billions.html?_r=0.

Kilcullen, D. (2013) *Out of the Mountains: The Coming Age of the Urban Guerrilla.* New York: Oxford University Press.

Klein, N. (2007) *The Shock Doctrine: The Rise of Disaster Capitalism.* New York: Knopf.

Krijnen, M., & Fawaz, M. (2010) 'Exception as the Rule: High-end Developments in Neoliberal Beirut'. *Built Environment.* Vol. 36. No. 2.: 245-259.

Kroll, L. (2012) 'Forbes World's Billionaires 2012'. *Forbes.* 3 July, http://www.forbes.com/sites/luisakroll/2012/03/07/forbes-worlds-billionaires-2012/.

Lambert, L. (2013) *Weaponized Architecture: The Impossibility of Innocence.* Barcelona: DPR-Barcelona.

Lambert, P. (1993) *The Distribution and Redistribution of Income.* Manchester: Manchester University Press.

Langewiesche, W. (2007) 'City of Fear'. *Vanity Fair.* 1 April, http://www.vanityfair.com/politics/features/2007/04/langewiesche200704.

Lichtenstein, N. (2000) 'Class Politics and the State during World War Two'. *International Labor and Working-Class History*. No. 58: 261-274.

Lister, D., Atkinson, R., & Flint, J. (2003) *Gated Communities: A Systematic Review of the Research Evidence*. Bristol: ESRC Centre for Neighbourhood Research.

Los, M. (2003) 'Crime in Transition: The Post-Communist State, Markets, and Crime'. *Crime, Law & Social Change*. Vol. 40. No. 2-3.: 145-169.

Manwaring, M. (2005) *Street Gangs: The New Urban Insurgency*. Carlisle: Strategic Studies Institute, US Army War College. 1 March, http://www.strategicstudiesinstitute.army.mil/pubs/display.cfm?pubID=597.

Marten, K. (2012) *Warlords: Strong-Armed Brokers in Weak* States. Ithaca: Cornell University Press.

McKenzie, E. (1996) *Privatopia: Homeowner Associations and the Rise of Residential Private Government*. New Haven: Yale University Press.

Medvetz, T. (2012) *Think Tanks in America*. Chicago: University of Chicago Press.

Miller, J. (2009) 'The Mexicanization of American Law Enforcement'. *City Journal*. Vol. 19. No. 4. Autumn, http://www.city-journal.org/2009/19_4_corruption.html.

Milward, H., & Provan, K. (2000) 'Governing the Hollow State'. *Journal of Public Administration Research and Theory*. Vol. 10. No. 2.: 359-380.

Mizruchi, M. (2013) *The Fracturing of the American Corporate Elite*. Cambridge: Harvard University Press.

Monbiot, G. (2012) 'A Manifesto for Psychopaths'. *The Guardian*. 6 March, http://www.monbiot.com/2012/03/05/a-manifesto-for-psychopaths/ (Mirrored).

Norton, R. (2003) 'Feral Cities: The New Strategic Environment'. *Naval War College Review*. Vol. 56. No. 4.: 97-106.

Omeje, K. (2010) 'Markets or Oligopolies of Violence? The Case of Sudan'. *African Security*. Vol. 3. No. 3.: 168-189.

Ong, A. (2000) 'Graduated Sovereignty in South-East Asia'. *Theory, Culture & Society.* Vol. 17. No. 4.: 55-75.

Pack, J. (1987) 'Privatization of Public-Sector Services in Theory and Practice'. *Journal of Policy Analysis and Management.* Vol. 6. No. 4.: 523-540.

Parenti, C. (2011) *Tropic of Chaos: Climate Change and the Geography of Violence.* New York: Nation Books.

Phillips-Fein, K. (2006) 'American Counterrevolutionary: Lemuel Ricketts Boulware and General Electric, 1950–1960'. Lichtenstein, N., ed., *American Capitalism: Social Thought and Political Economy in the Twentieth* Century. Philadelphia: University of Pennsylvania Press: 249-270.

Phillips-Fein, K. (2009) 'Business Conservatives and the Mont Pèlerin Society'. Mirowski, P., & Plehwe, D., eds., *The Road from Mont Pèlerin: The Making of the Neoliberal Thought Collective.* Cambridge: Harvard University Press: 280-301.

Pletsch, C. (1981) 'The Three Worlds, or the Division of Social Scientific Labor, circa 1950-1975'. *Comparative Studies in Society and History.* Vol. 23. No. 4.: 565-590.

Rajan, R., & Zingales, L. (2003) 'The Great Reversals: The Politics of Financial Development in the Twentieth Century'. *Journal of Financial Economics.* Vol. 69. No. 1.: 5-50.

Reinhart, C. & Reinhart, V. (2008) *Capital Flow Bonanzas: An Encompassing View of the Past and Present.* No. w14321. National Bureau of Economic Research. September, http://www.nber.org/papers/w14321.

Robb, J. (2007) *Brave New* War. New York: Wiley.

Rodenbeck, E. (2013) 'Mapping Silicon Valley's Gentrification Problem Through Corporate Shuttle Routes'. *Wired.* 9 June, http://www.wired.com/opinion/2013/09/mapping-silicon-valleys-corporate-shuttle-problem/.

Rodrik, D. (2006) 'Goodbye Washington Consensus, Hello Washington Confusion? A Review of the World Bank's Economic Growth in the 1990s: Learning from a Decade of Reform'. *Journal of Economic Literature.* Vol. 44. No. 4.: 973-987.

Ronfeldt, D. (2006) *Tribes: The Once and Forever Form*. WR-433-RPC. Santa Monica: RAND Corporation. December, http://www.rand.org/content/dam/rand/pubs/working_papers/2007/RAND_WR433.pdf.

Sargent, D. (forthcoming) *A Superpower Transformed: History, Strategy, and American Foreign Policy in the 1970s*. New York: Oxford University Press.

Saviano, R. (2006) *Gomorrah: A Personal Journey into the Violent International Empire of Naples' Organized Crime* System. Milan: Mondadori.

Scott, J. (1998) *Seeing Like a State: How Some Schemes to Improve the Human Condition Have Failed*. New Haven: Yale University Press.

Schwartz, M. (2014) 'A Mission Gone Wrong: Why Are We Still Fighting the Drug War?'. *New Yorker*. 6 January, http://www.newyorker.com/reporting/2014/01/06/140106fa_fact_schwartz.

Sengupta, S. (2008) 'Inside Gate, India's Good Life; Outside, the Servants' Slums'. *New York Times*. 9 June, http://www.nytimes.com/2008/06/09/world/asia/09gated.html.

Shank, M., & Beavers, E. (2013) 'America's Police Are Looking More and More Like the Military'. *The Guardian*. 7 October, http://www.theguardian.com/commentisfree/2013/oct/07/militarization-local-police-america.

Shaxson, N. (2011) *Treasure Islands: Tax Havens and the Men Who Stole the World*. London: Bodley Head.

Shaxson, N. (2013) 'A Tale of Two Londons'. *Vanity Fair*. 1 April, http://www.vanityfair.com/society/2013/04/mysterious-residents-one-hyde-park-london.

Sidaway, J. (2007) 'Enclave Space: A New Metageography of Development?'. *Area*. Vol. 39. No. 3.: 331-339.

Singer, P. (2001) *Corporate Warriors: The Rise of the Privatized Military Industry*. Ithaca: Cornell University Press.

Skocpol, T. (1979) *States and Social Revolution: A Comparative Analysis of France, Russia and China*. Cambridge: Cambridge University Press.

Slater, D. (2008) *Geopolitics and the Post-Colonial: Rethinking North-South Relations*. Malden: Blackwell.

Strange, S. (1996) *The Retreat of the State: The Diffusion of Power in the World Economy*. Cambridge: Cambridge University Press.

Sullivan, J., & Bunker, R. (2002) 'Drug Cartels, Street Gangs, and Warlords'. *Small Wars & Insurgencies*. Vol. 13. No. 2.: 40-53.

Taylor, J., & Harrison, D. (2008) *The New Elite: Inside the Minds of the Truly Wealthy*. New York: Amacom.

Vellacott, C. (2012) 'London Impoverished by Rise of the Plutocrats'. *Reuters*. 20 March, http://uk.reuters.com/article/2012/03/20/uk-london-incomedisparity-idUKLNE82J02420120320.

Williamson, J. (1990) 'What Washington Means by Policy Reform'. Williamson, J., ed., *Latin American Adjustment: How Much Has Changed*. Washington: Institute for International Economics: 7-40.

Webster, C. (2001) 'Gated cities of tomorrow'. *The Town Planning Review*. Vol. 72. No. 2.:149-170.

Weiss, G. (2012) *Ayn Rand Nation: The Hidden Struggle for America's Soul*. New York: St. Martin's Press.

Westad, O. (2006) *The Global Cold War: Third World Interventions and the Making of Our Times*. Cambridge: Cambridge University Press.

Woodiwiss, A. (1993) *Postmodernity USA: The Crisis of Social Modernism in Postwar America*. Thousand Oaks: Sage Publications.

World Bank Staff (1997) *World Development Report 1997: The State in a Changing World*. New York: Oxford University Press.

Yergin, D. (1998) *The Commanding Heights: The Battle between Government and the Marketplace That is Remaking the Modern World*. New York: The Free Press.

Reading 5

Public Looting for Private Gain: Predatory Capitalism, MNCs and Global Elites, and Plutocratic Insurgency

Robert J. Bunker

First published 5 September 2014 in Robert J. Bunker and Pamela Ligouri Bunker, Eds., *Global Criminal and Sovereign Free Economies and the Demise of the Western Democracies: Dark Renaissance.* London: Routledge, 2015: 134-162. Reprinted with permission of the publisher.

We love capitalism. But can capitalism be made to love us?

The end of the Cold War represented the climactic finish to a forty-year-old global struggle between competing ideologies derived from adversarial forms of political and economic organization. This struggle, albeit with minimized direct confrontations due to the rise of nuclear arms, reflected the twilight of the wars between industrialized states as a vestige of the modern Westphalian era. At its conclusion, we witnessed the economic implosion of the USSR and its subsequent partition and the rejection of a centrally planned economy by China that gave rise to its extensive market economy reforms. These events proved to unequivocally exorcise the 19th century legacy of Marx, Engels, and their adherents by discrediting a school of political and economic thought at whose basis was that of a class struggle between the owners of production (the bourgeoisie; *the propertied class—the Capitalists*) and the oppressed workers (the proletariat; *the propertyless class*) (Marx & Engels, 1886).

Still, recent concerns over class conflict—even warfare—have been espoused by capitalist scholars whose work is far removed from the tenets of historical materialism. In hindsight, it would be accurate to state that the victory of capitalism over Marxism in many ways resulted in the seeds of its own demise—at least in the sense of the continuing existence of a moderated capitalism subordinate to the needs of the Western states and their peoples.[1] The advent of globalization has in many respects gone sideways—a condition that has been commented on by a number of authors (Hertz, 2001; Stiglitz, 2003; Gilman et al., 2011; Rodrik, 2012). Back in the early 1990s, however, few individuals—be they scholar, policymaker, or common citizen—would have bet on these dark horses of globalization to even finish, much less sweep the competition, in what was then viewed as the start of a bright new era.[2] Still, this 'trifecta of dark globalization' derived from the rise of predatory capitalism, the increasing wealth accumulated by multinational corporations and global elites; the proverbial 1% controlling them, and the resulting emergence of a 'plutocratic insurgency' endangering the Western states and their peoples is winning out. Each of these components of this trifecta, symptomatic of the rise of a new and aberrant form of post-modern political economy, will be addressed in turn in this chapter and the public looting—that is the extraction of wealth from the middle classes and public institutions of the US and UK—which has ensued will be addressed. Further, a comparison of plutocratic insurgency to the earlier recognized construct of criminal insurgency will be highlighted as will some thoughts on the intersection between the extra sovereign and illicit economies upon which they are linked.

Predatory Capitalism

Capitalism can be defined as "an economic and political system in which a country's trade and industry are controlled by private owners for profit, rather than by the state" (*Oxford Dictionaries*, 2013a). Implicit in such a system is the duality of the free-market—"an economic system in which prices are determined by unrestricted competition between privately owned businesses" (*Oxford Dictionaries*, 2013b) and some sort of moderating state influence which ensures that its citizens—the majority of whom are labor (workers) in the middle and lower classes—are not exploited by the owners of capital (e.g. national elites). This 'political compromise' has been the traditional Western neo-liberal approach to capitalism following the excesses of the gilded age (1870-1900) and the gradual enshrinement of reformist labor laws and tax codes in the United States (Pizzigati, 2012) and in Western Europe (Maier, 1975). It resulted in the creation of a symbiotic partnership between big business and states with the later the dominant partner in this relationship.

This political compromise began to breakdown by the 1980s and, with the advent of globalization, the process by which states function as a moderating force was increasingly besieged by the owners of capital who by then had become multinational and extra-sovereign in size and scope—representative of a new class of global elites (Rothkopf, 2008; Collins, 2012; Freeland, 2012) and indicative of what is being called a second gilded age by numerous writers (Fraser, 2008; Schulz, 2011; Delong, 2012). A new form of capitalism befitting such elites—one with 'predatory' attributes—has since emerged. Predatory capitalism—that is, capitalism that is exploitive and oppressive of others and given to bribery, corruption, and coercion by its practitioners to achieve their profit seeking ends—is finding its way back into today's world or at the very least, as many scholars would argue that it never left the Global South, is now finding its way into the Western democracies; a brutish reality that is becoming increasingly recognized (Warner, 2007; Reich, 2012; Smith, 2013; Stiglitz, 2013). Such capitalism is reminiscent of European colonialism—who can forget the 19th century

British plundering of India via excessive levels of taxation (Naoriji, 1881) and the experience of Africa carved up like a holiday roast at the Berlin Conference of 1884-1885 (Rodney, 1972). Yet, in this scenario, it is turned inwards with cities like Detroit, with its $18 billion bankruptcy and 21,000 imperiled public pensioners, and other rust belt disasters becoming the poster children of this new reality (Reeves, 2013). These are poster children, by the way, further preyed upon by the on going looting of public pension funds via alliances between politicians, who gained sizeable campaign donations, and New York based hedge fund managers who profit from the back door deals (Taibbi, 2013). Juxtapose this middle American reality with 'tomorrow economy' cities, such as San Francisco with their $900,000 median home sales, where the 1% and their retainers congregate and techies utilize private buses to commute to social media campuses in the Silicon Valley (Egan, 2013).

Part of this process is attributed to increasing globalization with the flight of investment capital away from the traditional centers of concentration and its flow into emerging markets where labor is cheap and profit margins are high. In fact, according to Richard Wolff:

> After 200 years of concentrating its centers in western Europe, north America, and Japan, capitalism is moving most of its centers elsewhere and especially to China, India, Brazil and so on…
>
> …Among the social effects of capitalism's withdrawal from many old capitalist centers in the US are rapidly widening wealth and income inequalities there. These in turn provoke rising tensions within and between the two major political parties and a growing disaffection of the population with political leadership in general…
>
> …The consequence of political dysfunction (on top of the crises that punctuate capitalism's withdrawal) is to reinforce that withdrawal. The October shutdown and the ongoing stalemate over the national debt ceiling and federal budgets are events that force corporations,

wealthy individuals, and central banks to rethink the proportions of their portfolios held in US-based assets. Comparable rethinking affects the proportions allocated to Western Europe and Japan (2013).

The above quote captures many of the concerns raised in this work. The changing nature of capitalism—one that allows CEOs to loot their companies with excessive bonuses while denying basic benefits to common workers and allowing corporations to pretend to be nationalistic companies until it is time to pay their taxes—is resulting in an implosion of both the Western middle class and the liberal state supporting it (Barnett, 2011; Faux, 2012; Rothkopf, 2012).

Descriptions of capitalism that have escaped the moderating influence of modern democratic (liberal) states is representative of both pre and post 20th century realities. Caricatures of Ebenezer Scrooge in his counting-house and the more ravenous Robber Baron's of the 19th Century can easily be juxtaposed with Gordon—'Greed is Good'—Gekko and his cohort of modern day Wall Street cronies at Goldman Sachs and related firms. Literally, the hard won social contract between the common citizen and the liberal state has been torn up and cast aside. Unfettered capitalism does not result in a utopian world—rather 'self-regulating markets' are not regulated at all but result in concentrations of wealth in the hands of the few (Polanyi, 1944).

As a result, the 21st century market focuses on private gain and enrichment in an increasingly zero-sum and mercantilist-like struggle. Public good is of little consequence in a globalized economic system where anything goes—be it toxic waste dumping off the coast of Somalia, doctored baby formula produced in China, or small arms illicitly being smuggled into contested states—with *caveat emptor* being the new watch word of the day. It should be noted, however, that this privatized, and many times pseudo-dynastic, onslaught is not representative of some monolithic or centralized conspiracy. Quite the opposite—rather it is an evolutionary and structural response by massive corporations and holding conglomerates, and the elites who own them, to an evolving and hypercompetitive globalized economy.

Identifiable elements of this response—in essence predatory capitalistic activities—are as follows:

- *Stress profit and equity gain at all costs.* The *raison d'être* of predatory capitalism is the accumulation of wealth by all means possible—especially preying on the misfortunes of others because this helps to maximize profits. Disaster capitalism (Klein, 2007) is ideal, utilizing complexity, anonymity, secrecy, and conspiracy is prudent *(The Economist*, 2013b), and the use of 'unconscionable' practices, such as what foreign companies are doing in Africa's mining sector (Annan, 2013), represent acceptable operating procedures. As of March 2013, Moody's estimated that US linked multinationals had $1.45 trillion in cash reserves with 68% of it held overseas to avoid taxation (Semuels, 2013).

- *Follow the principals of hyper-rationalism.* The overreliance on the use of cost-benefit calculations makes this form of capitalism amoral and soulless. If a few % points of profit can be squeezed out by altering a design, changing suppliers, or moving a factory, the principals of hyper-rationalism will be followed. Further, the creation of substandard goods or engineered defects, known points of failure, which result in expensive parts replacements or shorten the lifecycle of a product also follows this logic (*The Engineer*, 2008). Other examples include renouncing US citizenship in order to gain preferable tax treatment prior to a corporate IPO launch (Wolverson & Walt, 2012) and the creation of ever quicker (in the low milliseconds) networks which allow high-frequency traders to pull boatloads of pennies out of the market via each transaction with zero market exposure at the end of the day (Adler, 2012).

- *Show no loyalty to workers, suppliers, customers, or even nations.* Another tenet of predatory capitalism is to have no affinity or sense of responsibility to anyone but yourself, family, and close allies (cronies). This zero-sum world view and lack of emotional attachment allows for high capital mobility—to quickly take advantage of profit making opportunities in a globalized economy. It results in a 24/7 'its just business' philosophy that replaces the social contract with a business contract that includes fine print prejudicial to anyone who signs it. A favored game of those engaging in this form of capitalism is playing laborer (employee and contract), city, region-state, and sovereign against their peers in a multilevel and global bidding war focused on lowering operating costs and gaining concessions (*The Economist*, 2013a; Inman, 2007; Reich, 2013).

- *Increasingly operate within a sovereign free economy.* This form of economy—also know as 'off the books'—represents an attempt by multinational corporations and global elites to gain freedom from the oversight, regulation, and taxation of sovereign states, especially Western ones. Essentially, a parallel supra-national economy is being constructed by global elites to facilitate predatory capitalist endeavors. Techniques include the use of the 'active financing exception' which "is the main tool GE uses to avoid nearly all U.S. corporate income tax" (Carney, 2013) and the use of offshore tax havens with potentially $32 trillion in offshore accounts in 2010 (Hsu, 2012). The efforts of Apple computer to profit from such chicanery have been well publicized (Neate, 2012; McCoy, 2013a; McCoy, 2013b).

- *Utilize corruption, co-option, and coercive force as required.* Another component of this form of capitalism is using subtle and targeted 'carrot and stick' tactics to manipulate the political environment and market in which global elites are operating. These tactics include corrupting and co-opting Congressional members in the US who gain from 'abnormal' stock profits while in office, benefit from big money campaign donations, and after leaving office look forward to being invited to become members of high salaried corporate boards (Richardson, 2011; Schweizer & Boyer, 2011; Palmer & Schneer, 2013). Such 'crony capitalism' found in the United States (Stockman, 2013) of course also extends to Europe and across the globe where plutocratic collaborators hold public office. At the other extreme, we see the use of legions of lawyers—legal 'hitmen'—who can stall and manipulate a judicial system where actual innocence of a crime is less important than having the economic resources to purchase a court ruling of such innocence. For this reason, ¿Plata O Abogado? (Silver or Lawyer) might become the new catchwords of predatory capitalism. Outside of Western societies, though, nothing matches the coercive capability of hiring a private military corporation (PMC) to do your bidding Project Censored, 1999).

- *Have a willingness to profit from the informal, and even the illicit, economy.* Global firms such as Proctor & Gamble, Colgate-Palmolive, and Unilever have for some time now learned how to reach past the formal economy into 'System D' transactions. These are all cash micro-level transactions and even include the bartering of goods and services via street vendor distribution in the developing world (Kostigen, 2012; Neuwirth, 2012). Multinationals disposing of commercial vessels to be broken up on the shores of Gujarat, India and bulk recycling of precious metals from old computers and electronics systems in Agbogbloshie, Ghana by masses of underpaid workers represent other aspects of semi-informal transactions, which by the way, create high levels of unregulated pollution (UNESCO, 2000; PBS, 2009). On the illicit side, major banks and brokerages have readily involved themselves with 'Black Market Peso Exchanges' in the Americas and currency debt swaps as in the case of Goldman Sachs in 2002 conspiring with national officials to hide actual debt levels in Greece (Martinuzzi, 2010; Martinuzzi & Petrakis, 2010). These linkages appear to be just the tip of the iceberg.

The last bullet takes us to an interesting component of the rise of the predatory capitalism; that is it's relationship to the illicit economy. The pioneering work of Ed Vulliamy, author of *Amexica* (2010), discusses this phenomenon from both the micro and macro perspectives. On a city level in northern Mexico, we see that:

...Juarez has imploded into a state of criminal anarchy—the cartels, acting like any corporation, have outsourced violence to gangs affiliated or unaffiliated with them, who compete for tenders with corrupt police officers. The army plays it own mercurial role...Juarez is also a model for the capitalist economy. Recruits for the drug war come from the vast sprawling *maquiladora*—bonded assembly plants where, for rock-bottom wages, workers make the goods that fill America's supermarket shelves or become America's automobiles, imported duty-free. Now, the corporations can do it cheaper in Asia, casually shedding their Mexican workers, and Juarez has become a teeming recruitment pool for the cartels and killers. It is a city that follows religiously the philosophy of a free market (Vulliamy, 2011b).

We are getting a blurring effect between predatory (mostly formal) capitalism, and the participating extra sovereign entities, and illicit capitalism, and the participating subnational entities. These capitalist forms are where the profit margins lie—state moderated capitalism, on the other hand, saddled with both bureaucratic rules and ethical guidelines, is not only noncompetitive with these emergent forms of capitalism but vulnerable to their co-optive power. For instance, at the global level, stemming from the Wachovia bank and Sinaloa cartel money laundering scandal (in the hundreds of billions of dollars)—it was determined that this may have only been one of numerous illegal transactions:

At the height of the 2008 banking crisis, Antonio Maria Costa, then head of the United Nations office on drugs and crime, said he had evidence to suggest the proceeds from drugs and crime were "the only liquid investment capital" available to banks on the brink of collapse. "Inter-bank loans were funded by money that originated from the drugs trade," he said. "There

were signs that some banks were rescued that way"
(Vulliamy, 2011a).

According to this same author:

> Antonio Maria Costa, who was executive director
> of the UN's office on drugs and crime from May 2002
> to August 2010, charts the history of the contamination
> of the global banking industry by drug and criminal
> money since his first initiatives to try to curb it from
> the European commission during the 1990s. "The
> connection between organised crime and financial
> institutions started in the late 1970s, early 1980s," he
> says, "when the mafia became globalised."
>
> Until then, criminal money had circulated largely
> in cash, with the authorities making the occasional,
> spectacular "sting" or haul. During Costa's time as
> director for economics and finance at the EC in Brussels,
> from 1987, inroads were made against penetration of
> banks by criminal laundering, and "criminal money
> started moving back to cash, out of the financial
> institutions and banks.["] Then two things happened:
> the financial crisis in Russia, after the emergence of the
> Russian mafia, and the crises of 2003 and 2007-08.
>
> "With these crises," says Costa, "the banking sector
> was short of liquidity, the banks exposed themselves
> to the criminal syndicates, who had cash in hand"
> (Vulliamy, 2011a).

While the relationship between predatory capitalism and the
darker illicit economy is of great interest other matters are also of
significance. The concern now is to focus on the extra sovereign entities,
and elites behind them, who are participating in the demise of the
Western Democracies. The next, necessary short overview, strives to
understand whom they and the powerful individuals associated with

those corporations are now that their predatory motives have become clear.

Multinational Corporations & Global Elites

Multinational corporations—which can also now be considered extra sovereign entities—have grown in size over the last half a century to become economic behemoths. Corporations such as Exxon Mobil have greater revenues than most states and have become laws onto themselves (Coll, 2012). In fact, such corporations have sterling AAA credit ratings that are higher than many sovereign states, and as a result, have become a preferred investment options over sovereign bonds in many instances (Pertuno, 2011; Foroohar, 2012). Walmart, for example, is:

> ...the world's largest private organization, has a bigger population than several United Nations member countries. Its revenue base is larger than many of the world's economies. And its borders extend far beyond the US (Heskett, 2013).

Various lists exist which show the power rankings of these corporations against that of states (revenues vs. GDP). For instance, in one list Proctor & Gamble is wealthier than Libya, Bank of America is wealthier than Vietnam, and ConocoPhillips is wealthier than Pakistan. Walmart would now rank as the world's 25th most powerful country and Exxon Mobil as its 30th if we went by these revenue indices. In fact, of the top one-hundred economic entities, half are states and the other half are now corporations (Hertz, 2003; Trivett, 2011). Another list put out by *Forbes* determines the world's largest corporations by determining their ranking via a composite score of their sales, profits, assets and market value (Decarlo, 2013).

Increasingly, we only half-jokingly ask if a massive corporation like a JPMorgan Chase or a Royal Dutch Shell were to get into a full blown conflict with a sovereign like Angola or even Greece, where the smart money bets would go. A number of books and studies have been coming out in this regard recognizing the increasing power and size of these non-sovereign entities and the threat that they now represent to sovereign states. Earlier works include David Korten's *When Corporations Rule the World* (2001), John Cavanagh's *Alternatives to Economic Globalization* (2004), and Joel Bakan's *The Corporation* (2005).

Additionally, research into the rise of these corporations by a team of researchers in Zurich has focused on the relationships between 43,000 individual business entities. The findings of this network analysis suggest that a core of 1,300 companies with interlocking ownerships control most of the global economy via their possession of the majority of shares of multinational blue chips and manufacturing firms. At the core of these companies was a 'super-entity' of 147 even more closely linked corporations composed mostly of financial institutions such as JPMorgan Chase, Goldman Sachs, and Barclays Bank (Coghlan & MacKenzie, 2011; Vitali et al., 2011).

In tandem with the rise of these super corporations is the increasing wealth of their masters. Terms for these ultra-rich individuals varies; superclass, global power elite, new global super-rich, plutocrats, new robber barons, the 1%, the .1%, the .01% with the list ongoing. Awareness of the rise of this privileged economic class has grown increasingly over the last decade. Numerous reports, news stories, and commentaries have highlighted their excesses and the growing concentration of wealth that they hold—such as the title of this article from *The Guardian*:

> The new robber barons: how taxpayers subsidise CEOs' multimillion salaries: A new report finds many top executives are taking home more than their corporations pay in taxes—at our expense (Chatterjee, 2012).

Even the internal financial documents pertaining to these groups recognize this new reality. In what has become an infamous Citigroup 'Equity Strategy' industry note from 2005, the following wording is used:

The World is dividing into two blocs—the Plutonomy and the rest. The U.S., UK, and Canada are the key Plutonomies—economies powered by the wealthy...

...We will posit that: 1) the world is dividing into two blocs—the plutonomies, where economic growth is powered by and largely consumed by the wealthy few, and the rest...

...2) We project that the plutonomies (the U.S., U.K., and Canada) will likely see even more income inequality, disproportionately feeding off a further rise in the profit share in their economies, capitalist-friendly governments, more technology-driven productivity, and globalization.

...The usual analysis of the "average" U.S. consumer is flawed from the start. To continue with the U.S., the top 1% of households also account for 33% of net worth, greater than the bottom 90% of households put together. It gets better (or worse, depending on your political stripe)—the top 1% of households account for 40% of *financial* net worth, more than the bottom 95% of households put together... (Kapur et al., 2005).

Each scholar and research group addressing this issue provides its own metric of who these new plutocrats are and the estimated amount of wealth and power that they control. David Rothkopf analyses a micro focused population of six thousand individuals as representative of this superclass. He focuses on the international influence, rather than simply wealth or achievements, of this group that has moved beyond borders and has become part of an exclusive global community. At the time of his analysis, 95,000 Ultra-High-Net-Worth Individuals (UHNWIs) with assets in excess of $30 million controlled $13 trillion. About a thousand or so billionaires also existed—though the superclass was by no means highly correlated with the former grouping (2008). Chrystia Freeland, on the other hand, focuses on the 0.1% of globe's individuals as representative of the new super-rich. She provides overviews of these new working rich, alpha geeks, and citizens of the world and how 'the billionaire's circle' transformed the global banking business (2012). Jeff Faux is more limited in his analysis with a focus on America's elite creating a servant economy in that nation (2012) while Sam Pizzigati also focuses on America's rich (2012). Another more recent study characterizes the global plutocratic grouping, based on UHNWIs whose cohort has since grown in size, as follows:

> There were nearly 200,000 people worth $30 million or more globally in 2013, with a combined wealth of $27.8 trillion. Wealth-X predicts that figure will exceed $40 trillion by 2020 (Zeveloff, 2014).

These global elites, in what can be considered a Gilded Age redux, would make Mark Twain feel quite at home. In 1871, Twain penned the satirical "Revised Catechism" in the *New York Tribune* as a response to the excesses of Tammany Hall under 'Boss' Tweed:

> Q. What is the chief end of man?
> A. To get rich.
> Q. In what way?
> A. Dishonestly if we can; honestly if we must.
> Q. Who is God, the only one and true?
> A. Money is God—gold and greenbacks and stocks—father, son, and the ghost of the same—three persons in one: these are the true and only God, mighty and supreme; and William Tweed is his prophet.

Twain would readily recognize this new plutocratic offensive except for the fact that the conspirators have become far more sophisticated, now operate on a globalized level, and have achieved supra-national status outside of the confines of state moderated capitalism. This new offensive has been gradually developing since the 1970s and 1980s and represents what David Rothkopf terms, via the subtitle of *Power, Inc.*, as "The Epic Rivalry Between Big Business and Government—and the Reckoning That Lies Ahead" (2012). Basically, the thesis is that private power is now concentrated in a few thousand global corporations held by wealthy elites and their families. These plutocrats—via their corporations and trusts—now wield more power than a majority of modern states. One of the more recent factors that are leading to the creation of this powerful class of global 'super-citizens' is how the legal status of corporations have changed in America. This can be viewed in the recent *Citizens United v. FEC* 558 U.S. 310 (2010) decision. Corporations are now considered to be artificial—albeit immortal—people given the same rights as US citizens. Politically, this has helped to undermine the democratic process by opening up free speech and campaign donations to corruptive influences by corporations seeking to gain special economic and legal concessions (Rothkopf, 2012). Some years ago—back in 1997—Jessica Mathew's identified the 'power shift' that was taking place between such corporations and nations. Her perceptions were that:

> National governments are not simply losing autonomy in a globalizing economy. They are sharing powers—including political, social, and security roles at the core of sovereignty—with businesses, with international organizations, and with a multitude of citizens groups, known as nongovernmental organizations (NGOs). The steady concentration of power in the hands of states that began in 1648 with the Peace of Westphalia is over, at least for a while (Mathews, 1997).

This power shift also extends to elite American, and to a slightly lesser extent British, educational institutions—which means unbiased research and analysis concerning what is taking place within the international political-economy may at some point also become co-opted. Look at FY2013 endowments for the most prestigious and elite colleges in the United States; Harvard has a $32.7 billion endowment,

Yale has a $20.8 billion endowment, and Stanford has a $18.7 billion endowment (*Harvard Magazine*, 2013; *Yale News*, 2013; *Stanford News*, 2013). Cambridge comes in at a paltry £4.9 billion and Oxford at £3.7 billion for a prior FY (Dent, 2014). Student tuition is now basically meaningless for these and other hugely endowed universities, though they still readily seek it, while they continue to pull down sizeable donations from their elite alumni and corporate gift programs with Stanford adding $1 billion by such means to its FY2013 endowment (Lewin, 2013). Harvard, in fact, has been characterized as a massive hedge fund that now engages in teaching on the side. Emphasis is now fully placed on fund management and those financial elites that oversee it:

> Harvard's Division of Arts and Sciences—the central core of academic activity—contains approximately 450 full professors, whose annual salaries tend to average the highest at any university in America. Each year, these hundreds of great scholars and teachers receive aggregate total pay of around $85 million. But in fiscal 2004, just the five top managers of the Harvard endowment fund shared total compensation of $78 million, an amount which was also roughly 100 times the salary of Harvard's own president. These figures clearly demonstrate the relative importance accorded to the financial and academic sides of Harvard's activities (Unz, 2012).

Further, if the affluent family of a lackluster student seeks to be admitted they can make a donation to the university known as the 'Harvard Price' now estimated to be $10 million (Golden, 2007; Unz, 2012). While at first glance a steep price, it represents quite a deal for the heir apparent of a global fortune. Attending prestigious colleges is extremely critical because they facilitate a closed loop cycle of educating plutocratic elites—and their retainers, as members of an administrative meritocracy— whose associations with each other continue on for a lifetime and are beginning to extend to their children and grandchildren as the new social classes of the 1% and beyond begin to solidify. These serve to cement early functional relationships as does the yearly World Economic Forum (WEF) meeting in Davos, Switzerland and the Aspen Institute gathering in Colorado for the networking of older plutocrats who descend via hundreds of private jets to these locales to cut their backroom deals and then once again scatter across the globe (Rothkopf, 2008; Freeland, 2012).

These globetrotters behave much like swarms of predators looking for fresh business opportunities in order to squeeze out additional profits for their portfolios. It can be said that the new world that they helping to create is one of *Evil Paradises* (Davis & Monk, 2008) and dark and deviant realms (Heine & Thakur, 2011; Gilman et al., 2011) free of state moderated capitalism and built upon skewed perceptions of social and political organization. We have begun to see the erection of the plutocratic playgrounds of the future, already now upon us, in which anything or anyone can be bought or sold—or at least rented or timeshared—built upon masses of Filipino maids, Indian laborers, and other miserably paid developing world workers. Throw in a stratum of European or American expats for their technical skills and expertise, who can't find such lucrative contracts back home and desperately need to provide for their families, and you have the makings of an emerging world gone very bad indeed.

For the elites who are building these playgrounds no *noblesse oblige* exists—rather, as an Apple executive recently quoted said, "We sell iPhones in over a hundred countries…We don't have an obligation to solve America's problems. Our only obligation is making the best product possible" (Duhigg & Bradsher, 2012). The rest of his thinking surely went something like this, "We just want you to purchase our products, make us fat and rich, and then you and your petty states are to just leave us alone and allow us to live in our own enclaves and cities." As US corporations and their jobs have moved beyond the national interest so others in the Western democracies follow—though London and New York still make for some of their favorite abodes (Foroohar, 2012; *The Telegraph*, 2013; Zeveloff, 2014).

Plutocratic Insurgency

Building upon our explorations and analysis of predatory capitalism and the global elites and their corporations who promote it, we come to the emergence of what is known as plutocratic insurgency. That insurgency form is a derivative of the 'commercial insurgency' construct first articulated by Steven Metz in 1993. The *raison d'être* of commercial insurgency draws upon psychological factors affecting discontented individuals:

> *Commercial Insurgency and the Search for Wealth.* In the pursuit of personal meaning in the developing world, there is an alternative to violent nativism or other forms of spiritual insurgency. When the discontented define personal meaning by material possessions rather than psychic fulfillment, they create the environment for commercial insurgency. This was made possible when Western materialism penetrated nearly every corner of the Third World via electronic communications and widespread travel. Commercial insurgency is a quasi-political distortion of materialism (Metz, 1993).

Another, and better known, derivate of this insurgency construct is that of the 'criminal insurgency' form first developed by John Sullivan in 2008. That form is illicit economy based and was developed to better describe the conflict being waged by the gangs and cartels in Mexico and Central America (Sullivan, 2008). Plutocratic insurgency, on the other hand, is somewhat counter-intuitive vis-a-vis the initial commercial archetype. It is not meant to be descriptive of 'personal meaning in the developing world' but rather is directed towards the developed world and the hyper-materialistic individuals within it who already hold great wealth and power. The term was first coined in 2011 by the author in an attempt to characterize rising inequalities in the United States and Western Europe with the advent of the 1% and is viewed as a natural compliment to the earlier identified criminal insurgency form (Bunker, 2012). The construct was further developed for this book project via what was initially a private exchange in 2012 with Nils Gilman who was asked to periodize and further comment on it vis-à-vis his *Deviant Globalization* research (Gilman et al., 2011).

Just as criminal insurgency is derived from interaction between the illicit economy and increasingly politicized—either intentional or *de facto*—violent non-state actors (eg. gangs, organized crime, and cartels), plutocratic insurgency emerges from interaction between the sovereign free economy, with its predatory capitalist behaviors, and the multinationals (and the global elites controlling them). To better understand the plutocratic insurgency construct and place in context the threat that it represents to the Western states, it is compared to the criminal insurgency construct in Table 1. This table compares and contrasts these two constructs in the categories of actors involved, relationship to formal IPE, orientation to public goods, economic effect on the state, military (crime) effect on the state, citizen threat perceptions when facing such an insurgency, TTPs (tactics, techniques, & procedures) involved, and the types of capitalism represented.

A brief summary of what a plutocratic insurgency looks like goes like this. Multinational corporations and a segment of the global elites (the .1% & .01%) are distancing themselves from the rest of humanity by the amount of wealth and power that they hold. This elite includes foreign royalty—autocrats—controlling Sovereign Wealth Funds such as the Saudi ruling families. These vast corporations and important individuals are considered the 'winners' of globalization and hold high legitimacy. They are global insiders and powerbrokers. Because of their immense wealth and status these individuals retreat to exclusive and privatized spaces protected by private security (mercenary) forces and high walls. These elites also see a different internet than the rest of us (Fertik, 2013). They have no need for public goods—they can directly purchase anything that they need—and in fact eschew collective societal risk strategies in favor of individual and family based ones. States suffer which come in contact with these individuals and their business interests due to a denial of tax revenues—a bevy of lawyers and lobbyists ensure that they pay as little taxes as feasible via accounting tricks, special privileges, and other concessions gained. Middle class families suffer via loss of formal economy jobs due to outsourcing and corporate economies of scale making their small business endeavors non-competitive. At best, such families end up servicing the elites in a servant economy relationship (Faux, 2012). The plutocrats engage in rampant cronyism with white collar crime becoming institutionalized—family and friends simply come first. Individuals showing high competency become their retainers. This meritocracy, composed of skilled knowledge workers and armed guards, protect these global elites and help to ensure that they enjoy impunity from the laws of sovereign states.

The political effect on the state is pronounced. Public goods are both privatized and defunded and, in essence, just become another commodity to be bought and sold. This extends to the criminal justice and courts system whose scales are weighted in favor of those with the most wealth. Democratic governance is further undermined by elite campaigns to rewrite social contacts or, at a minimum, have them narrowly interpreted. This results in a crisis of legitimacy for the state as democratic consensus within the political process is lost and polarization of viewpoints becomes entrenched. At some point, the election process can become almost meaningless. Ultimately, the state slowly becomes reconfigured to plutocratic values. The average citizen on the street does not understand the larger context of what is taking place but feels the effects. They become fearful, and rightly so, of seeing their middle class lifestyle imperiled, have personal debt concerns as they try to maintain that lifestyle, and recognize a lack of future social mobility for their children. This adds to societal stress levels and tensions. Police state-like behaviors can also manifest themselves when the bureaucracies of a state get mixed signals from polarized governance. Without a policy consensus, those bureaucracies turn in on themselves and, as a result, create greater and greater levels of efficiency with regard to domestic policing and homeland security. These measures may ultimately promote draconian policies with zero-tolerance for non-compliance.

The tactics, techniques, and procedures (TTPs) of plutocratic insurgency are one of *¿Plata O Abogado?* (Silver or Lawyer). Lawyers and lobbyists are used in generous measure and elected officials are selectively co-opted by means of campaign and party donations in order to gain special privileges. Lucrative corporate board deals come later as rewards for collaboration with plutocratic interests. Offshore financial schemes and the use of tax havens and other tax avoidance measures help promote the extra sovereign economy which goes hand-in-hand with the extra sovereign (resident non-citizen) non-domicile status the 1% (and more exclusive groupings) seek to achieve in the political communities within which they live. Ultimately, plutocratic insurgency is representative of a supra-national globalized form of predatory capitalism that is attempting to move beyond the confines of mere sovereign states.

Table 1. Plutocratic Insurgency and Criminal Insurgency Constructs

	Plutocratic Insurgency	*Criminal Insurgency*
Actors	Multinational Corporations (MNCs) & a segment of the Global Elites (1% to .01%); Includes Foreign Royalty controlling Sovereign Wealth Funds (SWFs)	Criminals, Gangs, Organized Crime (Domestic and Transnational), and other Violent Non-State Actors (VNSAs)
Relationship to the International Political Economy (Formal)	Insiders ('Winners'); High Wealth and Legitimacy	Outsiders ('Losers'); Mostly Low Wealth (Kingpin and group exceptions) and Illegitimacy
Orientation to Public Goods	Public Spaces Replaced by Gated/Private Communities; Police Replaced by Private Security/Mercenaries; Collective Societal Risk Replaced by Individual /Family Risk Strategy	Public Spaces Replaced by 'No Go Zones'; Police Replaced by Armed Gangs and Private Armies; Collective Societal Risk Replaced by Tribal Risk Strategy
Economic Effect on the State	Denial of Tax Revenues; Increasingly Knowledge and Service Oriented Economy Polarization	Denial of Tax Revenues— Extortion (Street Taxation) of Businesses/Individuals; Theft of Governmental Assets/Property

Military (Crime) Effect on the State	Rampant Cronyism; White Collar Crime Becomes Institutionalized; Elites Enjoy Impunity	Impunity of Criminal Activities (Assaults, Killings, etc); Danger of Corruption of Police/Courts
Political Effect on the State	Defunding or Privatizing of Public Goods (& Institutions); Social Contracts Rewritten/ Narrowly Interpreted; Loss of Democratic Consensus/ Polarization; State Reconfiguration to Plutocratic Values	*De Facto* Loss of Governmental Control in Areas; Public Goods Co-opted by Criminals; Environmental Modification/ Resocialization of Citizens (Narco Cultura); State Reconfiguration to Criminal Values
Citizen Threat Perceptions	Middle Class Lifestyle Imperiled; Personal Debt Concerns; No Social Mobility for Children; Government is Draconian (Police State-like)	Safety & Security of Individuals Imperiled; Children are Suffering (PTSD); Government is Ineffective &/or Corrupt
Tactics, Techniques, & Procedures (TTPs)	*¿Plata O Abogado?* (Silver or Lawyer); Use of Lawyers, Lobbyists, & Elected Officials (Co-opted); Campaign/ Party Donations for Special Privileges; Offshore Finance; Promote Extra-Sovereign (Off the Books) Economy	*¿Plata O Plomo?* (Silver or Lead); Use of Terrorism; Suppression/ Control of Journalists/Media; Smuggling Activities; Money Laundering/Co-option of Formal Businesses
Type of Capitalism	Predatory (Formal based); Supra-National Globalized	Criminalized (Illicit based); Sub-National Globalized

Sources: Steven Metz, *The Future of Insurgency*. Carlisle: Strategic Studies Institute, US Army War College, 10 December 1993 (for the original 'commercial insurgency' construct); John P. Sullivan and Robert J. Bunker, 'Rethinking insurgency: Criminality, spirituality and societal warfare in the Americas'. Special Issue: Criminal Insurgencies in Mexico and the Americas: The Gangs and Cartels Wage War. *Small Wars & Insurgencies*, Vol. 22. No. 5 (2011): 742-762; Nils Gilman (and Robert J. Bunker), 'Plutocratic Insurgency'. *Small Precautions*, 5 September 2012, http:// smallprecautions.blogspot.com/2012/09/plutocratic-insurgency.html; preface and postscript information from this book project and additional discussions between John P. Sullivan, Nils Gilman, and the author.

The plutocratic and criminal insurgency forms tie back into broader strategic concerns discussed in the overview to this book, specifically, that we are seeing a 'Dark Renaissance' taking place as an outcome of globalized capitalism and information technologies which is incrementally leading to a process of Westphalian state deconstruction. Quite possibly, the intersection of these two insurgency forms can best be summed up as follows by a *Forbes* reporter looking back at tweets about Mexico in 2012—"…#Mexico is 'a contradictory situation – economy is doing relatively well, but security = problem.'" (Flannery, 2013). This tweet only tells us part of the story, however. While it is agreed that the criminal insurgencies are now well advanced in that state with over 10% of Mexico—or 2,437 cities—now under gang and cartel control (Reyes, 2013), the formal economy itself is not doing well. Criminal control over cities in Mexico means that local populations and businesses in their areas of control pay extortion and street taxes before governmental taxes and fees. Also, the aging and underperforming State oil monopoly—PEMEX—which represents a major share of federal revenues has now seen over 1,300 incidents of pipeline thefts (via breaches) by criminal organizations in 2011 alone, resulting in over 3.35 million barrels of fuel stolen (Reuters, 2012). Rather the illicit—as seen above with the addition of tens of billions of dollars of narcotics revenues—and sovereign free economies, via multinational production (*eg.* the maquiladoras) and sales in Mexico and segments of the tourism industry, are the ones prospering. Thus money from the illicit economy, and to a far more limited extent the sovereign free one, are helping to prop Mexico up and make the overall economy appear to be doing well.

Fortunately, such criminal insurgencies as seen in Mexico—which also are taking place in other parts of Latin America—have not, as of yet, gained a significant foothold in the Western Democracies. Still, with an estimated 1.4 million gang members (street, prison, and outlay motorcycle) now existing within the US, we should at least be cognizant of such potentials as these numbers grow (NGIC, 2011). Additionally, Western Europe is also plagued by its own gang member radicalization concerns in Britain (Peachy, 2013), the 751 *Zones Urbaines Sensibles* (Sensitive Urban Zones) in France alone (Pipes, 2013 [2006]), and 3,600 organized crime groups now operating throughout the larger continent (Europol, 2013). Still, for the West, the plutocratic insurgency underway may now represent more of a threat; albeit a subtler (and cognitive dissonance based) one given the celebrated Horatio Alger mythos—now spread by Hollywood imagery—of idolizing the rich from humble origins who are able to enjoy the monetary successes of their hard work.

Public Looting for Private Gain

The outcomes of this 'trifecta of dark globalization'—predatory capitalism, the rise in dominance of multinational corporations and the elites (1%) behind them, and the emergence of what can be termed plutocratic insurgency—are undermining both Western states and the middle classes found within them. The economic erosion is readily evident when Western governmental and household (family) debt levels are viewed. US governmental debt recently crossed over the $17 trillion threshold and now represents 73% of US GDP (National Debt Clocks, 2013; Schroeder, 2013). Far less known is that US state and local governmental debts levels also climbing:

> Across America, elected officials, taxpayer groups, and other researchers have launched a forensic accounting of state and municipal debt, and their fact-finding mission is rewriting the country's balance sheet. Just a few years ago, most experts estimated that state and local governments owed about $2.5 trillion, mostly in the form of municipal bonds and other debt securities. But late last year, the States Project, a joint venture of Harvard's Institute of Politics and the University of Pennsylvania's Fels Institute of Government, projected that if you also count promises made to retired government workers and money borrowed without taxpayer approval, the figure might be higher than $7 trillion (Malanga, 2013).

Further, it was determined that within the US "States often manipulate their accounting rules to show a balanced budget, when in actuality a deficit exists" and that "Federal fiscal stimulus to states has ended. As a result, states have faced budget gaps totaling $55 billion in FY 2013" (Harvard Institute of Politics, 2012). European governmental debt levels are also significant. For example, the United Kingdom's basic debt level is £1 billion or 70% of its GDP. The national debts (& GDP %) of Spain, France, and Italy are €.615 trillion (77%), €1.83 trillion (95%), and €1.99 trillion (141%), respectively (National Debt Clocks, 2013).

Such excessive national debt levels raises concerns of credit down grades—such as the August 2011 Standard and Poor's US downgrade from AAA (outstanding) to AA+ (excellent) and the more recent February 2013 Moody's UK downgrade from AAA (highest quality) to Aa1 (high quality/very low risk) (O'Toole, 2013; Standard & Poors, 2011). Fitch, in April 2013, also downgraded the UK from AAA to AA+ rating and, in October 2013, put the US on its downgrade watchlist (McGarth, 2013; Patnaude, 2013). These downgrades can ultimately increase the costs of borrowing for a state if its prime investment grade ratings are lost. Excessive national debt levels also signal the potential dysfunction of national economies due to the strains placed upon them by large interest servicing payments, a reduction in internal influence, and ultimately raise the specter of sovereign bankruptcy (Buchhelt *et al.*, 2013; Neu, Mao & Cook, 2013). End of FY 2013 US national debt payments were $227.75 billion (6.23 % of all federal outlays) which has been manageable only because of the Federal Reserve's aggressive policy of ensuing that the "U.S. government is paying historically low rates on its debt" which is presently at 2.43% and is not sustainable (Desilver, 2013).

We should also turn our attention to household and family debt in the United States and the United Kingdom. For the US, aggregated family net worth suffered a 40% drop between 2007 and 2010—from $126,400 to $77,300—which is the equivalent of 18 years of family savings and investments (Riley, 2012). These figures are misleading, though, because wealth is polarized within American society with the elites holding stocks and bonds while the rest of America, those with any form of savings (20% of Americans have $0 or negative net worth), generally have it tied to the equity of their homes—an asset that suffered a greater drop in values than financial investments during that period

(Mishel et al., 2012). Factored into the aggregate net worth figures is the fact that one year later—in 2011—median household debt had increased to $70,000 (Gottschalck, Vornovytsky, & Smith, 2013) which suggests that family debt levels in the 2010-2011 period were slightly under 50% of assets. A sizeable chunk of this debt comes from student debt that has doubled since 2007 and crossed the $1.2 trillion threshold (Denhart, 2013; Flores, 2013).

Based on the median US family income of $51,000 in December 2011 (Davidson, 2012), this would place family debt levels to income at 137% that, while not a national debt to GDP equivalent, provides insights into the economic health of families. Such family to income debt levels would of course be skewed with easily over 50% of American society—including 45 million individuals on food stamps (the Supplemental Nutrition Assistance Program; SNAP) (Ellis, 2011)—having much higher rates and the upper 1% having little to no family debt to income levels. The lower class situation is likely even graver given that, in June 2013, the food stamp situation further deteriorated with a "record 23,116,928 American households" enrolled—more than the entire number of estimated households that exist in the entire Northeastern United States (Jeffrey, 2013). This can be contrasted to the 'sucking money pit' the greater DC metro region has become. It contains half of the top 20 median income counties in the US flush with governmental contractors—many of which support homeland security and intelligence agencies—tied to big business interests (Ferguson, 2012).

In the United Kingdom, family wealth and debt level variances are also very pronounced. A full 10% of British households are said to now hold assets of £1 million, derived primarily from the value of sky high London properties, a surge in stock prices, and the future valuation of occupational pensions. Though the future valuation of public pensions—in one example set at £1.3 million for a career police inspector—is speculative as it assumes municipal solvency in the face of underfunded public retirement programs (Clark, 2013). For example, the police pension fund in Britain was underfunded by £481 million in 2007-2008 more than twice that of 2006-2007 (Doward, 2009).

These concerns are warranted given that by 2008 the UK had the become biggest debtor of the developed world, even more so than debt laden Japan, and in 2011 was at 492% of GDP when all "aggregate indebtedness of the UK is considered" (Peston, 2013). Thus less than 10% of the British households can be considered truly wealthy while at the other extreme:

> The bottom 50% of households in Britain have just £4,400 of cash, property and pensions…according to an Office for National Statistics report which lays bare the vast disparities in wealth across the UK (Collinson, 2012).

As a result, British society is very much mimicking the have and have not character of American society with a shrinking middle class and ongoing governmental debt spending to sustain social welfare programs (*eg.* public goods) for increasing numbers of households that exist within the lower classes. At the same time, as discussed earlier in this chapter, the net worth of global elites has been accelerating, with the global elite (1%) now controlling 46% of the world's wealth (Kharpal, 2013). In the US, the 1% took home about 22% of the income earned by Americans (Lowrey, 2013) while in Britain "The share of the top 1% of income earners increased from 7.1% in 1970 to 14.3% in 2005" (Ramesh, 2011) with additional yearly gains expected.

Conclusion

Drawing upon a Western capitalist—and post-Marxist—interpretation of these developments, we must accept that we are witnessing a 'civil war' amongst ourselves (e.g. the capitalists). We have a supra-bourgeoisie composed of transnational elites—that new global class super-rich according to Freeland (2013)—in a class struggle with the petty-bourgeoisie—middle class shop owners, small business people, and moderately skilled professional workers. An example of this conflict can be readily seen each time a Walmart, Costco, or similar big box store is sited in a small city or urban neighborhood within the United States or Western Europe. Local shops and businesses in city downtowns and strip malls are unable to compete and as a result go under. Additionally, the part-time replacement jobs generated by these mega-stores do not meet 'living wage' standards—at least in the sense of adult workers providing for dependent children. This can be juxtaposed with the fact that high-end 'ritzy' malls catering to the elite are flourishing in the US—not so, of course, for the lower end 'middle class' malls which are struggling to generate profits in the face of growing vacancies (Matthews, 2012).

Another example of this conflict is that of major insurance companies and networks becoming the middlemen of health care. Medical doctors are seeing their incomes falling, with independent general practitioners becoming a legacy of the past—while quality of service is going down (increased waiting times, scripted care, and use of nurse practitioners) and medical insurance premiums are going up. Once again, both incomes and expenses for the petty-bourgeoisie are negatively impacted. In both examples, and numerous others not provided, savvy corporations and multinationals—drawing upon their bevy of lobbyists, lawyers, and accountants—are able to maximize shareholder profits for the economic elites.

Resulting from such a changing global economy, with its predatory underpinnings, and coupled with a massive recession, many American workers have been hit hard. However, America has had the resources to extend federal unemployment benefits and provide welfare and aid payments, during and after the great recession of December 2007 to June 2009 (US BLS, 2012). Ongoing US federal budget deficits and the recent governmental shutdown, however, are putting a strain on the governmental system and causing intense bipartisan schisms. Presently, 1.3 million long-term jobless Americans are set to lose their benefits at the end of 2013 if a congressional compromise can't be reached (Green, 2013).

The focus on the importance of now having a secure job to be considered part of the middle-class can be seen in a 2012 PEW Research report. In the 2012 report, 86% of the adults surveyed considered a secure job the most important attribute while, in a 1991 survey, 70% of adults surveyed said that home ownership was more important (Drake, 2013). This shift portrays the partial devolution of the US petty-bourgeoisie away from capital accumulation (home ownership) into more of a proletariat (renter) mindset. This comes at the same time that a Cornell and Stanford University study found that "Fewer people are living in middle-class neighborhoods in America as people increasingly dwell in areas segregated by income extremes" (Li, 2013). The study found that in 1970 about 65% of American families lived in middle-class neighborhoods—a level in 2009 that dropped to 42%. Extreme types of neighborhoods, with either well-off and poor residents, increased during these periods from 15% to 33% of American families (Li, 2013). By 2007, this already resulted in a shift in which more Americans below the poverty line could be found in the suburbs rather than in US inner cities (Tyre & Philips, 2007). Further exacerbating this trend is the fact that the institution of marriage is receding for the less affluent in the United States. These concerns were expressed by Bradford Wilcox who lead a university research team looking at this subject:

> [He]…is concerned that marriage is "withering" among middle and lower social groups, with potentially disastrous effects on American society and the economy.
> "I think we are moving towards a classically Latin model, where the powerful and the privileged have strong, stable families and access to decent income and assets. And everyone who is not in that upper third is worse and worse off" (Wheeler, 2012).

The United Kingdom is also becoming a nation of renters, with housing stock being purchased by the global elites and their wealth funds (Warner, 2012), and is suffering its own erosion of the institution of marriage in its working classes, making marriage more of an elite and surviving middle class phenomena (*The Guardian*, 2010; Marsden,

2013). Across Western Europe—writ large—the issue of retrograde social mobility is also now a very real concern. While the lower population Baltic states (Norway, Sweden, Finland and Denmark) have done better than the United Kingdom and other larger states such as Spain, France, and Italy, the overall trending in what is known as the 'Great Gatsby Curve' is not promosing.[3] This graph portrays the relationship between generational social mobility (y) and income inequality (x) with high levels in both ratings indicative of states in which the poor are likely to remain poor and the income gap between the elites and the poor is sizeable. The score is derived from a 1985 Gini coefficient (Greeley, 2013). Bottom rankings are evident in the United Kingdom (0.5 & 0.3) and France (0.41 & 0.27). A score of (0.18 & 0.21) for Finland is reflective of a low ranking (Krueger, 2012; Bloomberg, 2013). Per the *White House Blog*:

> The curve shows that children from poor families are less likely to improve their economic status as adults in countries where income inequality was higher – meaning wealth was concentrated in fewer hands – around the time those children were growing up (Vandivier, 2013).

Needless to say, the United States has faired even worse with its Gatsby score than the European states with a score of (0.47 & 0.34) and a further sizeable increase into 2010 (Bloomberg, 2013). Children born into low-income households, in essence, remain have nots throughout their lives and have little chance of joining the dwindling ranks of the middle class. It is of little wonder then that mass Occupy and related anti-1% protests (*eg.* #Occupy, *We are the 99%*) should sweep the United States and areas of Europe where the middle class was imperiled, and in many other regions of the globe from September 2011 through February 2012 (Castells, 2012; Wolff & Barsamian, 2012).[4] Protests broke out in hundreds of cities including the major Western centers of Rome, Madrid, London, New York, and Los Angeles. Such protests are reminiscent of the 16th century Peasant's War in Germany when the free peasants were forced into serfdom via increased taxation; however, in this modern incarnation, bloodshed was kept to a minimum even though the outcome was very much the same with victory going to the elites. In the case of the European Union, the winners were appointed (not democratically elected) technocrats and allied multinational business interests and in the US were global elite investors hidden behind the trappings of liberal democracy.

Still, we are only in the mid-phases of this plutocratic onslaught and conditions have the potential—via either the enactment of police state-like policies (via over centralization) and/or state failure (via fragmentation)—to get far more severe. These potentials can be seen in Juarez, Mexico where the extra sovereign and illicit meet at a dystopian—feral and criminal city—level (Bunker & Sullivan, 2012). The bloodshed with nearly 10,000 deaths (Dudley, 2013) over the last half dozen years has not been moderated. The reason is that Mexico has both lost control over parts of the country to criminal forces and it does not have the resources—based on how its state institutions are designed— to 'buy off the populace' via a social safety net (as in the US and the UK) because the resources simply do not exist. As a result, destitute and unemployed individuals have no choice but to hit the streets and work for the gangs and cartels that dominate the illicit economy. Formerly autocratic states, such as a transitioning Mexico, are thus being hit even harder by both the plutocratic (supra-national) and criminal (sub-national) insurgencies coming together in a vice grip compressing state institutions. Nils Gilman and Michael Costigan would call this process 'the arbitrage of the nation-state' (2012). From an Epochal Warfare theory perspective, this is the ultimate expression of the process by which the era of dominance of Westphalian states is coming to a close. For the US and Western Europe, a level of state stability and civility within the populace still exist. The question we must now ask is for how long. Quite possibly, the answer will be until the public and formerly middle class family monies run out.

Notes

1. See the Nils Gilman preface to this work concerning the nurturing of industrial workers—both capitalist and communist based—during the high social modernist era (1945-1971).
2. Instead, the post-Cold War honeymoon period was just beginning with only one superpower still standing after a decades long ideological slug fest. Francis Fukuyama's 'The End of History' (1989, 1992) heralded the triumph of neo-liberalism and democracy and became the watchwords of this era.
3. It should be noted that Germany is mid-range on the Gatsby curve and with its population of 82 million is lessening the effects in Europe. Still, from 1985 to 2008, it had a significant increase on the curve along with notable increase in the Baltic states highlighted. See the 'Gini coefficients of income inequality, mid-1980s and late 2000s' (OECD, 2011: 24).
4. In a sense, these protests resembled developing world food riots as a reaction to mandated International Monetary Fund (IMF) during the late 1970s and 1980s. In this instance, it was not the very poor rebelling against the inequalities of predatory capitalism but the Western middle and lower classes. See Davis (2007: 161).

References

Addler, J. (2012) 'Raging Bulls'. *Wired*. September: 116-125.

Annan, K. (2013) 'Foreword'. *Equity in Extractives*. Africa Progress Panel, http://www.africaprogresspanel.org/wp-content/uploads/2013/08/2013_APR_Equity_in_Extractives_25062013_ENG_HR.pdf.

Barnett, T. (2011) *America's False Recovery: The Coming Sovereign Debt Crisis and Rise of Democratic Plutocracy*. Jacksonville: Merit & Justice Press.

Baskan, J. (2005) *The Corporation: The Pathological Pursuit of Profit and Power*. New York: Simon & Schuster.

Bloomberg Visual Data (2013) 'The Great Gatsby Curve: Declining Mobility'. 8 November, http://www.bloomberg.com/infographics/2013-10-08/the-great-gatsby-curve-explained.html.

Buchhelt, L., et al. (2013) 'Revisiting sovereign bankruptcy'. *Vox.* 12 November, http://www.voxeu.org/article/revisiting-sovereign-bankruptcy.

Bunker, R. (2012) 'Plutocratic Insurgency'. *Small Wars Journal.* 6 September, http://smallwarsjournal.com/blog/plutocratic-insurgency.

Bunker, R., & Sullivan, S. (2012) 'Integrating feral cities and 3rd phase cartels/3rd generation gangs research: the rise of criminal (narco) city networks and BlackFor'. Bunker, R., ed., *Criminal Insurgencies in Mexico and the Americas: The Gangs and Cartels Wage War.* Routledge: London, 765-787.

Carney, T. (2013) 'How corporate tax credits got in the 'cliff' deal'. Washington Examiner. 2 January, http://washingtonexaminer.com/tim-carney-how-corporate-tax-credits-got-in-the-cliff-deal/article/2517397.

Cavanagh, J. (2004) *Alternatives to Economic Globalization: A Better World Is Possible.* San Francisco: Berrett-Koehler Publishers.

Castells, M. (2012) *Networks of Outrage and Hope: Social Movements in the Internet Age.* Cambridge: Polity Press.

Chatterjee, P. (2012) 'The new robber barons: how taxpayers subsidise CEOs' multimillion salaries'. *The Guardian.* 19 August, http://www.theguardian.com/commentisfree/2012/aug/19/new-robber-barons-how-taxpayers-subsidise-ceos.

Clark, T. (2013) 'One British household in 10 has £1m assets'. *The Guardian.* 21 May, http://www.theguardian.com/money/2013/may/21/british-household-1m-assets.

Coglan, A. & MacKenzie, D. (2011) 'Revealed—the capitalist network that runs the world'. *New Scientist.* 24 October, http://www.newscientist.com/article/mg21228354.500-revealed--the-capitalist-network-that-runs-the-world.html.

Coll, S. (2012) *Private Empire: ExxonMobil and American Power.* New York: Penguin Press.

Collins, C. (2012) *99 to 1: How Wealth Inequality Is Wrecking the World and What We Can Do about It.* San Francisco: Berrett-Koehler Publishers.

Collinson, P. (2012) 'Richest 10% of UK households own 40% of wealth, ONS says'. *The Guardian*. 3 December, http://www.theguardian.com/money/2012/dec/03/richest-10-uk-households-40-per-cent-wealth-ons.

Davidson, P. (2012) 'U.S. median household income up 4% at end of 2011.' *USA Today*. 9 February, http://usatoday30.usatoday.com/money/economy/story/2012-02-09/income-rising/53033322/1.

Davis, M. (2007) *Planet of Slums*. London: Verso.

Davis, M., & Monk, D. (2008) *Evil Paradises: Dreamworlds of Neoliberalism*. New York: The New Press.

Decarlo, S. (2013) 'The World's Biggest Companies'. *Forbes*. 17 April, http://www.forbes.com/sites/scottdecarlo/2013/04/17/the-worlds-biggest-companies-2/.

DeLong, J. (2012) 'Inequality: Living in the Second Gilded Age'. For the *San Francisco Chronicle*. 28 October, http://delong.typepad.com/sdj/2012/10/inequality-living-in-the-second-gilded-age.html.

Denhart, C. (2013) 'How The $1.2 Trillion College Debt Crisis Is Crippling Students, Parents And The Economy'. *Forbes*. 7 August, http://www.forbes.com/sites/specialfeatures/2013/08/07/how-the-college-debt-is-crippling-students-parents-and-the-economy/.

Dent, K. (2014) 'Cambridge's endowment funds make it Britain's richest university'. *The Cambridge Student*. 16 January, http://www.tcs.cam.ac.uk/news/0030480-cambridges-endowment-funds-make-it-britains-richest-university.html.

Desilver, D. (2013) '5 facts about the national debt: What you should know'. Pew Research Center. 9 October, http://www.pewresearch.org/fact-tank/2013/10/09/5-facts-about-the-national-debt-what-you-should-know/.

Doward, J. (2009) 'Taxpayers in £481m police pension top-up'. *The Guardian*. 21 November, http://www.theguardian.com/politics/2009/nov/22/police-pension-funding-shortfall.

Drake, B. (2013) *Having a secure job replaces homeownership as the key to being middle-class*. August 9, http://www.pewresearch.org/fact-tank/2013/08/09/having-a-secure-job-replaces-homeownership-as-the-key-to-being-middle-class/.

Dudley, S. (2013) 'How Juarez's Police, Politicians Picked Winners of Gang War'. *InsightCrime*. 13 February, http://www.insightcrime.org/juarez-war-stability-and-the-future/juarez-police-politicians-picked-winners-gang-war.

Duhigg, C., & Bradsher, K. (2012) 'How the U.S. Lost Out on iPhone Work'. *The New York Times*. 21 January, http://www.nytimes.com/2012/01/22/business/apple-america-and-a-squeezed-middle-class.html?pagewanted=all.

The Economist (2013a) 'Sweet land of subsidy'. 27 April: 27-28.

The Economist (2013b) 'Subject: Asset protection and regime change'. 11 May: 16.

Egan, T. (2013) 'Dystopia by the Bay'. *New York Times*. 5 December, http://www.nytimes.com/2013/12/06/opinion/dystopia-by-the-bay.html?_r=0.

Ellis, B. (2011) 'Food stamp use rises to record 45.8 million'. *CNN*. 4 August, http://money.cnn.com/2011/08/04/pf/food_stamps_record_high/.

The Engineer (2008) 'Defective body armour'. 10 October, http://www.theengineer.co.uk/news/defective-body-armour/308333.article.

Europol (2013) *EU Serious and Organised Crime Threat Assessment (SOCTA 2013)*. 19 March, https://www.europol.europa.eu/content/eu-serious-and-organised-crime-threat-assessment-socta.

Faux, J. (2012) *The Servant Economy: Where America's Elite is Sending the Middle Class*. Hoboken: John Wiley & Sons, Inc.

Ferguson, A. (2012). 'Bubble on the Potomac'. *Time*. 28 May: 46-52.

Fertik, M. (2013) 'The Rich See a Different Internet Than the Poor'. *Scientific American*. 18 February, http://www.scientificamerican.com/article.cfm?id=rich-see-different-internet-than-the-poor.

Flannery, N. (2013) 'Looking Back at 2012: A Year of #Mexico #Drugwar Tweets'. *Forbes*. 4 January, http://www.forbes.com/sites/nathanielparishflannery/2013/01/04/looking-back-at-2012-a-year-of-mexico-drugwar-tweets/.

Flores, A. (2013) 'Student debt nearly doubles since 2007'. *Los Angeles Times*. 20 June: B4.

Foroohar, R. (2012) 'Stocks for Safety?' *Time*. 9 January, http://content.time.com/time/magazine/article/0,9171,2103281,00.html.

Foroohar, R. (2012) 'Companies Are the New Countries'. *Time*. 13 February: 21.

Fraser, S. (2008) 'Tomgram: Steve Fraser, The Two Gilded Ages'. 22 April, http://www.tomdispatch.com/post/174922.

Freeland, C. (2012) *Plutocrats: The Rise of the New Global Super-Rich and the Fall of Everyone Else*. New York: Penguin Books.

Fukuyama, F. (1989) 'The End of History'. *The National Interest*. Summer, Vol. 16. No. 3.: 3-18.

Fukuyama, F. (1992) *The End of History and the Last Man*. New York: Free Press.

Gilman, S., Goldhammer, J., & Weber, S. (2011) *Deviant Globalization: Black Market Economy in the 21st Century*. New York: Continuum.

Gilman, N. (2012) 'Plutocratic Insurgency'. *Small Precautions*. 5 September, http://smallprecautions.blogspot.com/2012/09/plutocratic-insurgency.html.

Gilman, N., & Costigan, M. (2012) 'The Arbitage of the Nation-State'. *Breakthrough Journal*. February, http://thebreakthrough.org/index.php/journal/debates/against-cosmopolitanism-a-breakthrough-debate//the-arbitrage-of-the-nation-state/.

Golden, D. (2007) *The Price of Admission: How America's Ruling Class Buys Its Way into Elite Colleges—and Who Gets Left Outside the Gates*. New York: Random House.

Gottschalck, A., Vornovytsky, M., & Smith, A. (2013) 'Household Wealth and Debt in the U.S.: 2000 to 2011'. United States Census Bureau, http://blogs.census.gov/2013/03/21/household-wealth-and-debt-in-the-u-s-2000-to-2011/.

Greeley, B. (2013) 'The Gatsby Curve: How Inequality Became a Household Word'. *Bloomberg Businessweek*. 12 December, http://www.businessweek.com/articles/2013-12-05/obama-talks-inequality-and-mobility-going-full-gatsby.

Green, J. (2013) 'Congress: 1.3 Million Americans Are About to Have a Terrible Christmas'. *Bloomberg Businessweek*. 9 December, http://www.businessweek.com/articles/2013-12-09/1-dot-3-million-americans-are-about-to-have-a-terrible-christmas.

The Guardian (2010) 'Marriage rates in the UK'. 11 February, http://www.theguardian.com/news/datablog/2010/feb/11/marriage-rates-uk-data.

Harvard Magazine (2013) 'Endowment Value Rises to $32.7 Billion'. 24 September, http://harvardmagazine.com/2013/09/harvard-endowment-up-2-billion-to-32-7-billion.

Harvard University Institute of Politics (2012) 'Harvard's Institute of Politics, UPENN's Fels Institute of Government and AEF Produce U.S. State Annual Reports'. 27 November, http://www.iop.harvard.edu/november-27-2012-harvard's-institute-politics-upenn's-fels-institute-government-and-aef-produce-us.

Heine, J., & Thakur, R., eds. (2011) *The Dark Side of Globalization*. New York: United Nations University.

Hertz, N. (2001) *The Silent Takeover: Global Capitalism and the Death of Democracy*. New York: The Free Press.

Heskett, J. (2013) 'Is Walmart Defying Economic Gravity?'. *Forbes*. 5 December, http://www.forbes.com/sites/hbsworkingknowledge/2013/12/05/is-walmart-defying-economic-gravity/.

Hsu, T. (2012) 'Wealthy May Hide as Much $32 Trillion Offshore, Report Says'. *Los Angeles Times*. 23 July, http://articles.latimes.com/2012/jul/23/business/la-fi-mo-tax-havens-20120723.

Inman, P. (2007) 'Amicus moves to create multinational 'super-union'.' *The Guardian*. 1 January, http://www.theguardian.com/business/2007/jan/02/politics.tradeunions.

Jeffrey, T. (2013) '23,116,928 to 20,618,000: Households on Food Stamps Now Outnumber All Households in Northeast U.S.' *CNS News*. 17 September, http://cnsnews.com/news/article/terence-p-jeffrey/23116928-20618000-households-food-stamps-now-outnumber-all-households.

Kapur, A., Macleod, N., & Singh, N. (2005) 'Equity Strategy: Plutonomy: Buying Luxury, Explaining Global Imbalance. Citigroup Equity Note. 16 October: 1-32.

Klein, N. (2007) *The Shock Doctrine: The Rise of Disaster Capitalism*. New York: Metropolitan Books.

Kharpal, A. (2013) 'Global wealth hit $241 trillion, but distribution skewed'. *CNBC News*. 11 October, http://www.cnbc.com/id/101105809.

Korten, D. (2001) *When Corporations Rule the World*. San Francisco: Berrett-Koehler Publishers.

Kostigen, T. (2012) 'Informal economy: Huge and growing'. *MSN Money*. 16 January, http://money.msn.com/investing/informal-economy-massive-and-growing-marketwatch.aspx.

Krueger, A. (2012) 'The Rise and Consequences of Inequality in the United States: charts'. Charts prepared for a speech by A. Krueger, Chairman of the Council of Economic Advisers, on January 12 at the Center for American Progress, http://www.slideshare.net/whitehouse/the-rise-and-consequences-of-inequality-in-the-united-states-charts.

Lewin, T. (2013) 'Report Says Stanford Is First University to Raise $1 Billion in a Single Year'. *The New York Times*. 20 February, http://www.nytimes.com/2013/02/21/education/stanfords-fund-raising-topped-1-billion-in-2012.html?_r=0.

Li, S. (2013) 'Middle-class neighborhoods losing residents'. *Los Angeles Times*. 18 October: B2.

Lowrey, A. (2013) 'Top 1 percent take record share of U.S. income'. *The Seattle Times*. 10 September, http://seattletimes.com/html/nationworld/2021795994_incomegapxml.html.

Maier, C. (1975) *Recasting Bourgeois Europe*. Princeton: Princeton University Press.

Malanga, S. (2013) 'The Indebted States of America.' *City Journal*. Summer, Vol. 23. No. 3., http://www.city-journal.org/2013/23_3_state-debt.html.

Marsden, S. (2013) 'Job insecurity leaves marriage the preserve of middle-class couples – study'. *The Telegraph*. 13 August, http://

www.telegraph.co.uk/news/politics/10238664/Job-insecurity-leaves-marriage-the-preserve-of-middle-class-couples-study.html.

Martinuzzi, E. (2010) 'Goldman Sachs, Greece Didn't Disclose Swap Contract (Update1)'. Bloomberg. 17 February, http://www.bloomberg.com/apps/news?pid=newsarchive&sid=akqC4y5U7MnU.

Martinuzzi, E., & Petrakis, M. (2010) 'EU Seeks Greek Swaps Disclosure After Ministry Probe (Update2)'. *Bloomberg*. 15 February, http://www.bloomberg.com/apps/news?pid=newsarchive&sid=a5MJFT2dMyIU.

Marx, K., & Engels, F. (1886) *Manifesto of the Communists*. London: International Publishing Co. See also http://www.bl.uk/learning/images/21cc/waves/large1745.html.

Mathews, J. (1997) 'Power Shift: The Rise of Global Civil Society'. *Foreign Affairs*. January-February, http://www.foreignaffairs.com/articles/52644/jessica-t-mathews/power-shift.

Matthews, C. (2012). 'Ritz Retail: Why shopping developers are catering to the well-off'. *Time*. 17 September: 18.

McCoy, K. (2013a) 'Did Apple do Irish jig around taxes?'. *USA Today*. 21 May: 3B

McCoy, K. (2013b) 'Apple's tax ingenuity a tough sell'. *USA Today*. 22 May: 1B-2B.

McGarth, M. (2013) 'Fitch Puts U.S. On Credit Downgrade Watch'. *Forbes*. 15 October, http://www.forbes.com/sites/maggiemcgrath/2013/10/15/fitch-puts-u-s-on-credit-downgrade-watch/.

Metz, S. (1993) *The Future of Insurgency*. Carlisle: Strategic Studies Institute, US Army War College. 10 December, http://www.strategicstudiesinstitute.army.mil/pubs/display.cfm?pubID=344.

Mishel, L., et al. (2012) *The State of Working America*. 12th Ed. Ithaca: Cornell University Press. EPI digital edition overview, http://stateofworkingamerica.org/files/book/Chapter1-Overview.pdf.

Naoriji, D. (1881) *No. 3. Memorandium on a Few Statements in the Report of the Indian Famine Commission, 1880.* Posted 28 July 2013, http://sabhlokcity.com/2013/07/british-rule-in-india-was-plunder-of-an-unceasing-foreign-invasion-naorojis-1880-statement/#sthash.G0amJuiG.dpuf.

National Debt Clocks (2013) 16 December, http://www.nationaldebtclocks.org.

National Gang Intelligence Center (2011) *National Gang Threat Assessment—Emerging Trends.* Washington, DC., http://www.fbi.gov/stats-services/publications/2011-national-gang-threat-assessment/2011-national-gang-threat-assessment-emerging-trends.

Neate, R. (2012) 'Apple paid less than 2% tax on overseas profits last year'. *The Guardian.* 4 November, http://www.theguardian.com/technology/2012/nov/04/apple-paid-low-overseas-tax.

Neu, C., Mao, Z., & Cook, I. (2013) *Fiscal Performance and U.S. International Influence.* Santa Monica: RAND, http://www.rand.org/pubs/research_reports/RR353.html.

Neuwirth, R. (2012) *Stealth of Nations: The Global Rise of the Informal Economy.* New York: Anchor Books.

The Organisation for Economic Co-operation and Development (OECD) (2011) 'An Overview of Growing Income Inequalities in OECD Countries: Main Findings'. Paris, http://www.oecd.org/els/soc/49499779.pdf.

O'Toole, J. (2013) 'Moody's downgrades United Kingdom from AAA'. *CNN Money.* 22 February, http://money.cnn.com/2013/02/22/news/economy/moodys-uk-downgrade/.

Oxford Dictionaries (2013a) Definition of 'capitalism'. Oxford: Oxford University Press, http://www.oxforddictionaries.com/definition/english/capitalism.

Oxford Dictionaries (2013b) Definition of 'free market'. Oxford: Oxford University Press, http://www.oxforddictionaries.com/definition/english/free-market?q=free+market.

Palmer, M., & Schneer, B. (2013) 'Capitol Gains: Retired Members of Congress and Corporate Board Directorships'. Prepared for the Annual Meeting of the Southern Political Science Association, New Orleans, Louisiana, January 9-11, 2014, http://maxwellpalmer.com/files/capitol_gains.pdf.

Patnaude, A. (2013) 'Fitch Downgrades U.K. Rating'. *The Wall Street Journal*. 19 April, http://online.wsj.com/news/articles/SB1000 14241278873244937045784327761463111892.

Public Broadcasting System (PBS) (2009) 'Ghana: Digital Dumping Ground'. 23 June, http://www.pbs.org/frontlineworld/stories/ ghana804/video/video_index.html.

Peachy, P. (2014) 'Lee Rigby murder: UK's street gangs 'are the next breeding ground for new brand of extremist''. *The Independent*. 7 January, http://www.independent.co.uk/news/uk/crime/lee-rigby-murder-uks-street-gangs--are-the-next-breeding-ground-for-new-brand-of-extremist-9016698.html.

Pertuno, T. (2011) 'Corporate power grows as government wanes'. *Los Angeles Times*. 19 November: B1, B4.

Peston, R. (2011) 'UK's debts 'biggest in the world''. *BBC News*. 21 November, http://www.bbc.co.uk/news/business-15820601.

Pipes, D. (2013 [2006]) 'The 751 No-Go Zones of France'. *Daniel Pipes Middle East Forum*. 22 November [14 November], http://www. danielpipes.org/blog/2006/11/the-751-no-go-zones-of-france.

Pizzigati, S. (2012) *The Rich Don't Always Win: The Forgotten Triumph Over Plutocracy that Created the American Middle Class, 1900-1970*. New York: Seven Stories Press.

Polanyi, K. (1944) *The Great Transformation*. New York, Toronto, Farrar & Rinehart, Inc.

Project Censored (1999) 'Mercenary Armies in Service to Global Corporations', http://www.projectcensored.org/16-mercenary -armies-in-service-to-global-corporations/.

Ramesh, R. (2011) 'Income inequality growing faster in UK than any other rich country, says OECD'. *The Guardian*. 5 December, http://www.theguardian.com/society/2011/dec/05/ income-inequality-growing-faster-uk.

Reeves, J. (2013) '19 shocking facts about Detroit's bankruptcy'. *USA Today*. 3 December, http://www.usatoday.com/story/

money/personalfinance/2013/12/02/19-facts-about-detroit-bankruptcy/3823355/.

Reich, R. (2012) *Beyond Outrage: Expanded Edition: What has gone wrong with our economy and our democracy, and how to fix it.* New York: Vintage.

Reich, R. (2013) 'Global Capital and the Nation State'. 20 May, http://robertreich.org/post/50890974932.

Reuters. (2012) 'RPT-Theft on Mexico fuel pipelines jumps 55 pct–Pemex'. 23 April, http://uk.reuters.com/article/2012/04/23/mexico-oil-idUKL2E8FNC6320120423.

Reyes, I. (2013) 'El 10% del país en "estado fallido"'. *24 Horas*. 10 December, http://www.24-horas.mx/el-10-del-pais-en-estado-fallido/.

Richardson, V. (2011) 'House members in the know score 'abnormal' stock profits, study says'. *The Washington Times*. 25 May, http://www.washingtontimes.com/news/2011/may/25/house-members-stock-market-success-questioned/?page=all.

Riley, C. (2012) 'Family net worth plummets nearly 40%.' *CNN Money*. 12 June, http://money.cnn.com/2012/06/11/news/economy/fed-family-net-worth/.

Rodney, W. (1972) *How Europe Underdeveloped Africa*. London: Bogle L'Ouverture Press.

Rodrik, D. (2012) *The Globalization Paradox: Democracy and the Future of the World Economy*. New York: W. W. Norton & Company.

Rothkopf, D. (2008) *Superclass: The Global Power Elite and the World They Are Making*. New York: Farrar, Straus, and Giroux.

Rothkopf, D. (2012) *Power, Inc. The Epic Rivalry Between Big Business and Government—and the Reckoning That Lies Ahead*. New York: Farrar, Straus, and Giroux.

Schroeder, R. (2013) 'U.S. on 'unsustainable' budget course: CBO'. *MarketWatch: The Wall Street Journal*. 17 September, http://www.marketwatch.com/story/cbo-issues-fresh-long-term-debt-warning-2013-09-17?link=MW_pulse.

Schulz, T. (2011) 'The Second Gilded Age: Has America Become an Oligarchy?'. *Spiegel Online International*. 28 October, http://www.spiegel.de/international/

spiegel/the-second-gilded-age-has-america-become-an-oligarchy-a-793896.html.

Schweizer, P., & Boyer, P. (2011) 'The Wonk Who Slays Washington'. *Newsweek*. 21 November: 32-37.

Semuels, A. (2013) 'U.S. Firms' cash hoard: $1.45 trillion'. *Los Angeles Times*. 21 March: B5.

Smith, H. (2013) *Who Stole the American Dream?* New York: Random House.

Standard & Poors (2011) 'United States of America Long-Term Rating Lowered To 'AA+' Due To Political Risks, Rising Debt Burden; Outlook Negative'. 5 August, http://www.standardandpoors.com/ratings/articles/en/us/?assetID=1245316529563.

Stanford News (2013) 'Stanford Management Company releases 2013 results'. 25 September, http://news.stanford.edu/news/2013/september/stanford-management-company-092513.html.

Stiglitz, J. (2003) *Globalization and Its Discontents*. New York: W. W. Norton & Company.

Stiglitz, J. (2013) *The Price of Inequality: How Today's Divided Society Endangers Our Future*. New York: W. W. Norton & Company.

Stockman, D. (2013) *The Great Deformation: The Corruption of Capitalism in America*. New York: Public Affairs.

Sullivan, J. (2008) 'Transnational Gangs: The Impact of Third Generation Gangs in Central America'. *Air & Space Power Journal—Spanish Edition*. Second Trimester, http://www.airpower.maxwell.af.mil/apjinternational/apj-s/2008/2tri08/sullivaneng.htm.

Taibbi, M. (2013) 'Looting the Pension Funds'. *Rolling Stone*. 26 September, http://www.rollingstone.com/politics/news/looting-the-pension-funds-20130926.

The Telegraph (2013) 'Energy companies 'turning their noses up' at Parliament and consumers, says MP'. 29 October, http://www.telegraph.co.uk/earth/energy/10411192/Energy-companies-turning-their-noses-up-at-Parliament-and-consumers-says-MP.html.

Trivett, V. (2011) '25 US Mega Corporations: Where They Rank If They Were Countries'. *Business Insider.*27 June, http://www.businessinsider.com/25-corporations-bigger-tan-countries-2011-6?op=1.

Twain, M. (1871) 'The Revised Catechism'. *New York Tribune.* 27 September.

Tyre, P., & Philips, M. (2007) 'Poor Among Plenty'. *Newsweek.* 12 February: 54.

United Nations Educational, Scientific and Cultural Organization (UNESCO) (2000) 'Gujarat - Ship-Breaking and Coastal Pollution'. 29 May, http://www.unesco.org/csi/act/india/IndiaGujR.htm.

Unz, R. (2012) 'Paying Tuition to a Giant Hedge Fund'. *The American Conservative.* 4 December, http://www.theamericanconservative.com/articles/paying-tuition-to-a-giant-hedge-fund/.

US Bureau of Labor Statistics (2012) 'BLS Spotlight on Statistics: The Recession of 2007-2009'. February, http://www.bls.gov/spotlight/2012/recession/pdf/recession_bls_spotlight.pdf.

Vandivier, D. (2013) 'What is the Great Gatsby Curve?' *The White House Blog.* 11 June, http://www.whitehouse.gov/blog/2013/05/28/great-gatsby-curve.

Vitali, S., Glattfelder, J., & Battiston, S. (2011) 'The Network of Global Corporate Control'. *PLOS One.* 26 October, http://www.plosone.org/article/info%3Adoi%2F10.1371%2Fjournal.pone.0025995.

Vulliamy, E. (2010) *Amexica: War Along the Borderline.* New York: Picador.

Vulliamy, E. (2011a) 'How a big US bank laundered billions from Mexico's murderous drug gangs'. *The Observer.* 2 April, http://www.theguardian.com/world/2011/apr/03/us-bank-mexico-drug-gangs.

Vulliamy, E. (2011b) 'Ciudad Juarez is all our futures. This is the inevitable war of capitalism gone mad'. *The Guardian.* 20 June, http://www.theguardian.com/commentisfree/2011/jun/20/war-capitalism-mexico-drug-cartels.

Warner, C. (2007) *The Best System Money Can Buy: Corruption in the European Union*. Ithaca: Cornell University Press.

Warner, J. (2012) 'Britain is becoming a nation of renters as overseas investors gobble up the housing stock'. *The Telegraph*. 11 December, http://blogs.telegraph.co.uk/finance/jeremywarner/100021775/britain-is-becoming-a-nation-of-renters-and-overseas-investors-gobble-up-the-housing-stock/.

Wheeler, B. (2012) 'Why is the US marriage rate falling sharply?' *BBC News*. 9 January, http://www.bbc.co.uk/news/magazine-16274740.

Wolff, R. (2013) 'US Political Dysfunction and Capitalism's Withdrawal'. *e-International Relations*. 27 October, http://www.e-ir.info/2013/10/27/us-political-dysfunction-and-capitalisms-withdrawal/.

Wolff, R., & Barsamian, D. (2012) *Occupy the Economy: Challenging Capitalism*. San Francisco: City Lights Publishers.

Wolverson, R., & Walt, V. (2012) 'Take the Money and Run'. *Time*. 30 July: 13.

Yale News (2013) 'Endowment earns 12.5% return'. 24 September, http://news.yale.edu/2013/09/24/endowment-earns-125-return.

Zeveloff, J. (2014) 'Where The World's Super-Rich Spend Their Millions On Real Estate [MAP]'. *Business Insider*. 16 January, http://www.businessinsider.com/where-super-rich-spend-money-on-real-estate-map-2014-1.

Reading 6

The Plutocratic Insurgency

Rich Couch

First Published 23 July 2014 in Let's Talk Books and Politics Blog [1]
Reprinted with permission.

There seems to be general agreement that somewhere in the 1970s-1980s there was a fundamental change in attitude towards the role of government in society, and that this was accompanied by a new economic order. This was clearly the timeframe in which globalization began to have a major impact on societies and economies, but that, by itself, could not have caused a change in how a society viewed governance. What were the causes of these changes and where are we headed?

Nils Gilman addresses these issues in an article in *The American Interest*: The Twin Insurgency. Gilman begins with this intriguing lede:

> "The postmodern state is under siege from plutocrats and criminals who unknowingly compound each other's insidiousness."

Both insurgencies depend on a weakened but still functional government that can be utilized to further their economic and social interests. Both are active political players.

"From above comes the plutocratic insurgency, in which globalized elites seek to disengage from traditional national obligations and responsibilities. From libertarian activists to tax-haven lawyers to currency speculators to mineral-extraction magnates, the new global super-rich and their hired help are waging a broad-based campaign to limit the reach and capacity of government tax-collectors and regulators, or to manipulate these functions as a tool in their own cut-throat business competition."

"From below comes a series of interconnected criminal insurgencies in which the global disenfranchised resist, coopt, and route around states as they seek ways to empower and enrich themselves in the shadows of the global economy. Drug cartels, human traffickers, computer hackers, counterfeiters, arms dealers, and others exploit the loopholes, exceptions, and failures of governance institutions to build global commercial empires. These empires then deploy their resources to corrupt, coopt, or challenge incumbent political actors."

Of interest here is the plutocratic insurgency.

"….plutocratic insurgents do not seek to take over the state. Nor do they wish to destroy the state, since they rely parasitically on it to provide the legacy goods of social welfare: health, education, infrastructure, and so on. Rather, their aim is simpler: to carve out de facto zones of autonomy for themselves by crippling the state's ability to constrain their freedom of (economic) action."

The philosophical underpinnings of plutocrats must provide justification for their wealth and power. They have come to see themselves as deserving winners in a meritocratic economic order. If they are deserving of their status and think of themselves as "winners," then everyone else must be a "loser" and also be deserving of their lower status. In order to continue their "justified" winning ways they must convince or delude society into believing that what is good for the plutocrats is good for everyone.

> "The defining feature of the plutocratic insurgency is its goal: to defund or de-provision public goods in order to defang a state that its adherents see as a threat to their prerogatives. (Note that, conceptually, plutocratic insurgencies differ from kleptocracies; the latter use the institutions of state to loot the population, whereas the former wish to neutralize those institutions in order to facilitate private-sector looting. In practice, these may overlap or co-mingle.) Practically speaking, plutocratic insurgency takes the form of efforts to lower taxes, which necessitates cutting spending on public goods; reducing regulations that restrict corporate action or protect workers; and defunding or privatizing public institutions such as schools, health care, infrastructure, and social space."

The political strategy used by plutocrats is to demand austerity as the solution to all economic problems, of which budget deficits are among the worst. A typical ploy is to demand a balanced budget in all situations. Combining this with a demand that taxes can never be raised will inevitably lead to smaller and less effective government.

> "….the ultimate effect being to de-collectivize social risks. As a palliative for the loss of public goods and state-backed programs to improve public welfare, plutocratic insurgents typically promote philanthropy (directed toward ends defined not democratically but, naturally, by themselves alone)."

Plutocrats will be able to conclude that state-provided services are not cost effective for them and are more of a burden than a benefit.

> "....the hallmark of the arrival of plutocratic insurgency is when the rich begin to revolt against paying taxes for public services they never plan to use. As these public services deteriorate in quality, the result is a self-reinforcing cycle whereby plutocratic insurgents increasingly see no reason to contribute anything to their host societies and, indeed, actively contest the idea that citizenship comes with economic responsibilities."

How did our society, in the United States, arrive at a period in which we are taken advantage of by the wealthy and yet we seem to be applauding them for their efforts?

Gilman is a bit vague in describing what generated the societal transition that occurred and made the world more welcoming to the wealthy. He refers to the postwar period when Europe and the US expanded their governments to provide greater social and economic security to their populations as the "social modernist era." He concludes that, in some way, governments faltered in their promise to deliver economic security to their middle classes.

> "By the 1970s, however, it was becoming clear that the social modernist states were increasingly failing to deliver on their promises. In the West, inflation eroded the technical foundations of the Bretton Woods financial order, and economic stagnation undermined the technocratic consensus in favor of Keynesian demand management and the political consensus in favor of sharing productivity gains between labor and capital."

The fall of the Communist states was taken as confirmation that the aggressive form of capitalism practiced in the US and UK was the reason for Western victory. Free-market capitalism was elevated to the level of economic dogma and governments retreated from attempts to place controls on it.

Gilman provides a description of what happened, but observations are not explanations. It is interesting that he recognizes the rise of the "Washington Consensus" as global economic policy, but he does not directly tie it to his notion of a plutocratic insurgency even though it was clearly intended to propagate economic strategies favorable to plutocrats throughout the world.

> "The Washington Consensus, in particular, promoted not just a dethroning of the state, but a wholesale challenge to the idea that technocratic leadership constituted the primary way to ensure collective social well-being. Pioneered as domestic policy in Margaret Thatcher's Great Britain and Ronald Reagan's United States, but continued thereafter in administrations controlled by their respective political opposites, the programs associated with the Washington Consensus—above all, the privatization of national industrial assets (especially of state-owned firms and utilities) and deregulation (especially of financial firms)—soon became the model London and Washington sought to export to the Global South and the post-Communist world under the rubric of 'structural adjustment' and 'shock therapy'."

Some have ascribed the decline in popularity of the social modernist state to a forgetting of the conditions that made such a state a necessity. Others merely conclude that people have become more individualistic. Perhaps the best rendering of the attitudes and intellectual debates in the US is provided by Daniel T. Rodgers in his book *Age of Fracture*.

Rodgers provides this description of the transformation in attitudes that occurred in the US.

> "….in the last quarter of the [twentieth] century, through more and more domains of social thought and argument, the terms that had dominated post-World War II intellectual life began to fracture. One heard less about society, history, and power and more about individuals, contingency, and choice. The importance of economic institutions gave way to notions of flexible and instantly acting markets. History was said to accelerate into a multitude of almost instantaneously accessible possibilities. Identities became fluid and elective. Ideas of power thinned out and receded. In politics and institutional fact and in social imagination, the 1930s, 1940s, and 1950s had been the era of consolidation. In the last quarter of the century, the dominant tendency of the age was toward disaggregation."

He attributes the fall from dominance of the modernist state to the disruptions caused by economic changes and globalization that shattered expectations in terms of economic security. People began to see themselves more individuals with a need to take more responsibility for their own futures as old guarantees of economic well-being dissipated. New conceptions of reality had to be developed.

> "What crossed between these widely flung fronts of thought and argument was not a single, dominant idea—postmodern, new right, or neoliberal—but a contagion of metaphors. Intellectual models slipped across the normal divisions of intellectual life. Market ideas moved out of economics departments to become the new standard currency of the social sciences….Fluid, partial notions of identity, worked out in painful debates among African American and women's movement intellectuals slipped into universal usage. Protean, spill-over words like 'choice' were called upon to do more and more work in more and more circumstances. In the

process some words and phrases began to seem more natural than the rest—not similes or approximations but reality itself."

Rodgers wishes to believe that these developments were a natural development given the evolution of circumstances. He does allow that there might have been conscious efforts to control the intellectual debates. Rodgers does not use the phrase "plutocratic insurgency," but what he describes as occurring during this period could well have been described as such.

> "In this reading of late twentieth-century U.S. history, the key to the age was the conscious efforts of conservative intellectuals and their institutional sponsors to reshape not only the terms of political debate but the mechanics of intellectual production itself. By the late 1970s, Nixon's former secretary of the Treasury, the Wall Street investor William E. Simon, was urging that 'the only thing that can save the republican Party….is a counterintelligentsia,' created by funneling funds to writers, journalists, and social scientists whose ideas had been frozen out of general circulation by the 'dominant socialist-statist-collectivist orthodoxy' prevailing in the universities and the media."
>
> "Within a decade, Simon's project had dramatically reshaped the production and dissemination of ideas."

Rodgers warns against attributing too much influence to this effort, but in a subsequent *article* in *The American Prospect* he includes this statement:

> "….the modern Republican Party's embrace of an anti-statist agenda that would have dismayed its founders has been a feat of ideological struggle as conscious and successfully managed as any in American history."

This seems to attribute quite a bit of influence by this conscious and premeditated campaign to propagate conservative/plutocratic concepts. Rodgers also brings to our attention what is the critical accomplishment of the plutocratic insurgency: the takeover of the Republican Party.

Isaac William Martin has produced, in his book <u>*Rich People's Movements: Grassroots Campaigns to Untax the One Percent*</u>, an illuminating study that suggests a plutocratic insurgency has been active since the implementation of the federal income tax. The goals then were the same as the goals now: limit taxation and limit the government's role in the economy. These plutocratic efforts met with various degrees of success until finally culminating in the capture of the Republican Party.

During this period of transition in attitudes, there was another transition taking place: the migration of Southern Democrats to the Republican Party. This development is usually discussed as an instance of pandering to the racial attitudes of the Southern whites. However, the accommodation of Southerners in the Party had other, perhaps more significant ramifications. Consider what was desired by Southern politicians in order to maintain the "Southern way of life." They wished to have single party states dominated by wealthy political and economic elites. Politicians were dedicated to maintaining a low-wage society with as little interference as possible from the federal government in terms of regulation, worker safety, healthcare, and other benefits. The gradual progression from slaves to sharecroppers to Walmart associates was not accidental. The Southerners were the perfect allies for the resident Republican plutocrats.

Martin concludes:

> "Rich people's movements have been thoroughly institutionalized and thereby tamed. Many former activists are now well entrenched in the Republican Party and its allied think tanks, and their tactics are now correspondingly oriented toward inside lobbying. Some movement goals remain unrealized only because they are nigh unachievable."

It is not unreasonable to conclude that plutocratic insurgency is not a recent phenomenon, but rather one that has always been active. It is not a recent response to newfound wealth, but a fundamental response to wealth itself in which conservation and propagation are required. What is new is the degree of success of the insurgency.

Martin's final conclusion:

> "Rich people's movements have a permanent place in the American political bestiary. As long as one of our great political parties is allied with the radical rich, it is safe to predict that rich people's movements will continue to influence public policy in ways that preserve—and perhaps even increase—the extremes of inequality in America."

Conspiracy theories are popular because, occasionally, one actually exists.

Notes

1. http://letstalkbooksandpolitics.blogspot.com/2014/07/the-plutocratic-insurgency.html.

Reading 7

Donald Trump and the "Twin Insurgency": He's Half Plutocrat, Half Criminal and Entirely Ruthless

Paul Rosenberg

First Published 30 October 2016 in Salon Magazine [1]
Reprinted with permission.

Trump's campaign marks the collision of two campaigns against the democratic state—from tycoons and thugs.

As the Donald Trump campaign implodes into the black hole of his damaged psyche, it's important not to lose sight of the bigger picture, because it's not simply going to vanish along with Trump's chances of winning the presidency. Perhaps one of the most helpful ways of framing that big picture can be found in "The Twin Insurgency," a 2014 article by Nils Gilman in The American Interest, with the subhead "The postmodern state is under siege from plutocrats and criminals who unknowingly compound each other's insidiousness."

As Gilman argues, during the post-World War II "social modernist era," between 1945 and 1971, states around the world sought "to legitimate themselves by serving the interests of middle classes whose size they sought to expand." Gilman doesn't dwell on their relative successes—which were considerable in the industrialized West, at least—but concerns himself with what began happening as they fell short of their intended goals.

"Stagflation" in the West, central planning failure in the East and debt crisis in the global South were hallmarks of the different ways in which the model fell short. "By 1980, the reaction against the social modernist state had set in. Levels of economic inequality began to grow again, eventually reaching heights not seen since the 1920s," Gilman writes. "It wasn't just that the state 'retreated' from the 'commanding heights' of the economy, to use Daniel Yergin's terms, but also that the very ambition of the state receded. Many states stopped even pretending they wanted to create a more egalitarian society and instead sought to legitimate themselves by claiming they were maximizing individual opportunity."

Politically, leadership came from figures like Margaret Thatcher and Ronald Reagan. Gilman cites Thatcher's quote, "There's no such thing as society" as "the *cri de coeur* of insurgent plutocrats everywhere." The resulting retreat of the state left middle-class lives dramatically more precarious, especially vulnerable to threats on two fronts:

> From above, middle classes find themselves threatened by a global financial elite, in league with ultra-wealthy compradors, both of whom seek to cut social services and the taxes that pay for them—taxes that these elites depict as a form of illegitimate expropriation. From below, the middle classes find themselves exposed to a new resurgence of criminality, which has discovered in their plight a business opportunity.

That is the twin insurgency in a nutshell: predatory plutocratic elites above, criminal insurgencies below and an increasingly insecure immiserated middle class caught in between. And it helps us to understand Donald Trump's emergence with a clarity that's otherwise hard to muster.

On one hand, the erosion of the social modernist state that allows the twin insurgency to flourish is the very foundation of Trump's appeal. He is responding to legitimate, intensely felt grievances that have also fed ethno-nationalist movements elsewhere around the world, although it was Bernie Sanders, not Trump, who offered a concrete political program this year to restore at least some of what's been lost. "Trump is certainly feeding off the middle-class anxiety that the twin insurgency has produced," Gilman confirmed in an email to Salon.

On the other hand, Trump is the very embodiment of the twin insurgency, an insurgent plutocrat with suggestive links to criminality, who takes full advantage of areas free from the rule of law. He has long ruthlessly targeted other insurgents when it suited him—first as exploited business partners (even his bankers!) and now as designated villains in his grab for presidential power, which he understands in purely insurgent rather than constitutional terms.

Wayne Barrett, Trump's first biographer, is especially helpful here. In one Democracy Now! interview, Barrett described how, around 1990, Trump "was engaged in completely defrauding the banks, and the banks knew it. OK? And they were giving him the loans anyway." In part, Barrett said, this was because of Trump's ties with prosecutors, most notably Rudy Giuliani, whose future trajectory is well known. "So his relationships with prosecutors and the fact that the bankers— they were embarrassed by what they had done; they didn't want any investigation of this. So the combination of the two ... gave him a pass." Trump wasn't simply taking advantage of a corrupt system, he was *personally corrupting it.* He partnered with mobsters as well (more from Barrett on this below), though now he enjoys painting immigrants as gang members and criminals.

Gilman cited this willingness to attack other insurgents as one of Trump's greatest sources of strength:

> I think the paradox with him, in terms of my
> framework, is that he's the only candidate who has
> been willing to name and denounce both ends of the
> twin insurgency explicitly, whether that means railing

against the "criminals from Mexico" and in the "inner cities," on the one hand, and the bankers and "globalist parasites" exporting jobs, on the other. To be honest, it disturbs me that he is the only candidate willing to speak this truth, and I think part of his appeal is precisely that he does so. All of it is inflected through extremely ugly racist shit, of course, so it's not that his diagnosis is right, but at least he's naming the relevant elephants.

Trump has always been willing to cozy up to or attack other members of either insurgency by turns—the bankers who've saved his ass more than once, or the criminal enterprise-builders with whom he has partnered. There's nothing new in this, except what he's trying to get out of it.

Trump has sometimes acted like a pure plutocratic insurgent. The New York Times account of how he benefited from $885 million in tax breaks and subsidies offers a classic example of how plutocrats extract wealth from the postmodern state. But his dealings with mob figures since the 1970s, and his repeated backstabbing and double-crossing (a.k.a. "renegotiation") are unusual, to say the least. He also has business dealings around the globe, including countless hidden partnerships with other members of the global plutocracy. Thus, Trump is not your typical plutocrat. He represents a fascinating intersection of the two insurgencies in a number of different ways, and has exploited bureaucratic weaknesses both have helped create.

Consider Trump's exploitative business record, just for a start. Trump has made untold millions by defaulting on contracts with contractors and workers, taking advantage of erosions of the rule of law and of the social cohesion associated with it. This has been aided and abetted by the use and abuse of legal proceedings, such as burying less affluent adversaries in frivolous paperwork, and aggressively using nondisclosure agreements to shut people up as a condition of settling with them. He's been involved in 3,500 lawsuits, but apparently thinks that's a good thing, since he claims to have won more often than lost.

That's more a sign of how much legal muscle Trump has than anything else—a lesson he first learned from his mentor, Roy Cohn, once Sen. Joe McCarthy's top aide. Cohn was also chief counsel to the New York mob, providing Trump with a wealth of criminal connections from the earliest days of his business career. Barrett <u>discussed this in detail</u> with Democracy Now! host Amy Goodman early in July. New York mobsters were involved with Trump's projects in earlier years and were among his tenants. Even more crucially, the Philadelphia mob was involved, Barrett says, in an "intricate relationship that gave birth to Donald's casino empire in Atlantic City."

Trump's move from casinos into beauty pageants and eventually to hosting "The Apprentice" was facilitated by another example of his predatory nature, described in a <u>Boston Globe story</u> that dealt with just one of those 3,500 lawsuits:

> It began as a planned partnership between Trump and a Florida couple, George Houraney and Jill Harth, who operated American Dream Calendar Girls, staging elaborate events in which winning contestants were featured, provocatively posed, in wall calendars.
>
> Houraney and Harth were eager to tap into the cachet and glitz of Trump and his casinos. It ended in a bitter, drawn-out legal battle when the planned partnership crumbled after the first pageant.
>
> The couple alleged Trump broke his word, cheated them out of a $250,000 fee, and deprived them of up to $5 million in future business. More explosively, they said he continually made aggressive, unwanted sexual advances toward Harth, who was vice president of American Dream.

Regarded in isolation—or worse yet, in pieces: a business dispute here, a sexual harassment claim there—it's hard to appreciate the full significance of this story, although the Globe did underscore its significance for Trump's business trajectory, after first noting it revealed a darker side of Trump's playboy image at the time:

> The foray into the Calendar Girls pageant, however, also ushered in Trump's interest in the business of entertainment. He later bought the Miss Universe pageant and gained national renown for his reality show, "The Apprentice."
>
> "I don't believe there would have been an 'Apprentice' if there wasn't a pageant first," said Jim Gibson, a consultant and longtime pageant host who guided Trump into the pageant business and eventually to the Miss Universe event. "That got him in the higher hierarchies of the television business. And it did exactly what Donald wanted to do: It built his name."

None of the ventures named here were criminal, but Trump's sexual behavior around them may well have been. And then there's Trump's modeling agency, which <u>violated immigration laws</u>, supplied models for "The Apprentice" and had contracts and work arrangements that have been described as bordering on human trafficking.

Trump has apparently never come close to facing criminal charges for any of his alleged misdeeds, but in a way that's the point: The twin insurgency is very much about rolling back the rule of law, and Trump has had a field day exploiting the opportunities that result from that.

He's also had a vast number of foreign partnerships, which as <u>Newsweek's Kurt Eichenwald</u> has reported, create irresolvable conflicts of interest for a potential president, conflicts that epitomize where Trump's real interests lie as a member of the plutocratic insurgency. But there's a further danger of foreign criminal involvements as well, which could at least partially be exposed if his tax returns were made public.

Gilman's perspective illuminates the patterns of Trump's dealings in a different way than is commonly understood, but it also goes far beyond an indictment of Trump as an individual. It was above all the conventional conservatives, starting with Reagan and Thatcher, who opened the way for the twin insurgencies to flourish. And then it was neoliberals like Bill Clinton and Tony Blair who "pragmatically" "reinvented" their center-left political parties to go along with it.

As for Trump, Gilman concludes, "I don't think he's really a plutocratic insurgent himself. Maybe he used to be, though even in the past he was more of a crony capitalist than a plutocratic insurgent." That sounds like a barroom argument for another day. "Now he's evolving into something more like a would-be oligarch or warlord," Gilman says.

In his article, Gilman discussed warlords as typical wielders of power in the more precarious "enclaves of criminal insurgents," alongside more familiar kinds of gangsters or organized crime leaders. Which leads me to propose another way of thinking about Donald Trump: as a criminal conspirator. Lock him up!

Notes

1. https://www.salon.com/2016/10/30/donald-trump-and-the-twin-insurgency-hes-half-plutocrat-half-criminal-and-entirely-ruthless/.

Reading 8

Plutocratic Insurgency Note No. 1: Eight Individuals are Now as Wealthy as the Poorest Half of the World

Robert J. Bunker and Pamela Ligouri Bunker

First Published 9 February 2017 in Small Wars Journal [1]

Key Information: Deborah Hardoon, *An Economy for the 99%: It's time to build a human economy that benefits everyone, not just the privileged few.* OXFAM Briefing Paper. 16 January 2017: 48 pages, http://policy-practice.oxfam.org.uk/publications/an-economy-for-the-99-its-time-to-build-a-human-economy-that-benefits-everyone-620170:

New estimates show that just eight men own the same wealth as the poorest half of the world. As growth benefits the richest, the rest of society—especially the poorest—suffers. The very design of our economies and the principles of our economics have taken us to this extreme, unsustainable and unjust point. Our economy must stop excessively rewarding those at the top and start working for all people. Accountable and visionary governments, businesses that work in the interests of workers and producers, a valued environment, women's rights and a strong system of fair taxation, are central to this more human economy. The sources and methodology behind the headline facts in this paper are explained in the separate methodology note.

Key Information: Ben Hirschler, "World's eight richest as wealthy as half humanity, Oxfam tells Davos." *Reuters.* 16 January 2017, http://www.reuters.com/article/us-davos-meeting-inequality-idUSKBN150009:

> Just eight individuals, all men, own as much wealth as the poorest half of the world's population, Oxfam said on Monday in a report calling for action to curtail rewards for those at the top.
>
> As decision makers and many of the super-rich gather for this week's World Economic Forum (WEF) annual meeting in Davos, the charity's report suggests the wealth gap is wider than ever, with new data for China and India indicating that the poorest half of the world owns less than previously estimated.
>
> Oxfam, which described the gap as "obscene", said if the new data had been available before, it would have shown that in 2016 nine people owned the same as the 3.6 billion who make up the poorest half of humanity, rather than 62 estimated at the time.
>
> In 2010, by comparison, it took the combined assets of the 43 richest people to equal the wealth of the poorest 50 percent, according to the latest calculations.
>
> Inequality has moved up the agenda in recent years, with the head of the International Monetary Fund and the Pope among those warning of its corrosive effects, while resentment of elites has helped fuel an upsurge in populist politics...

Who: Eight richest individuals in the world; Bill Gates (Microsoft), Amancio Ortega (Inditex), Warren Buffett (Berkshire Hathaway), Carlos Slim (Grupo Carso), Jeff Bezos (Amazon), Mark Zuckerberg (Facebook), Larry Ellison (Oracle), and Michael Bloomberg (Bloomberg) who have a combined net worth of $426 billion dollars.

What: These eight individuals have a net worth equivalent to that of the economic bottom half of humanity—3.6 billion people. This phenomenon is a component of increasing global inequality and concentration of wealth (and power) in the hands of plutocratic individuals with extra-sovereign privileges. It is resulting in dystopian futures for large segments of humanity.

When: Present day; evolutionary process that has its origins in the 1980s with increasing privatization, loss of middle class incomes, and decline of the welfare state in the West linked to Reaganomics in the US and Thatchernomics in the UK; even earlier origins in other global regions with the failure of decolonization, development, and neo-liberalism vis-à-vis the rise of authoritarian regimes' and multinational corporations' (MNC) profiting seeking activities.

Where: Global phenomenon.

Why: This is a component of late stage (post-industrial/post-modern) capitalism in which sum-sum economic exchanges are increasingly being replaced by zero-sum economic exchanges which have resulted in the increasing polarization of global wealth in the hands of fewer and fewer individuals.

Analysis: The increasing trend towards the concentration of wealth in fewer and fewer individuals—from 43 in 2010 to 8 in 2016 who have equivalent wealth to the poorest half of the world—is indicative of the rise of global capitalism which is in variance with state moderated capitalism. It challenges Adam Smith's "Invisible Hand" metaphor, that pertains to the operations of a free market economy, by showing that some sort of sovereign economic regulation is indeed required in order to protect the public good. With few inhibitors, globalized capitalism becomes predatory in nature and efficiency seeking with the creation of vast holding companies and economic strangleholds. The resulting outcome is much like a later stage Monopoly game with wealth being concentrated in the hands of fewer and fewer players. What we are essentially witnessing is the rise of a 'global plutocratic class' with extra-sovereign prerogatives that has more in common amongst itself than with their fellow nationals or for that matter the rest of humanity. Unfortunately—unlike a Monopoly game that at some point will end and a new game will begin—no restart will take place within the global economy. The poorest half of the world presently has few, if any, opportunities to better their economic future or those of their children. This trend ultimately signifies the contemporary crisis of neo-liberalism and the rise of a deviant and mercantilist (zero-sum) form of capitalism that promotes authoritarianism and economic class polarization rather than traditional democratic and middle class institutional forms.

Key Words: Corruption, Crony Capitalism, Free Market Infallibility, Global Inequality, 1%, Plutocratic Insurgency, Profit Maximization

Further Reading

Robert Bunker, "Plutocratic Insurgency." *Small Wars Journal.* 6 September 2012, http://smallwarsjournal.com/blog/plutocratic-insurgency.

Nils Gilman, "Plutocratic Insurgency." *Small Precautions.* 5 September 2012, http://smallprecautions.blogspot.com/2012/09/plutocratic-insurgency.html.

Nils Gilman, "The Twin Insurgency." *The American Interest.* Vol. 9. No. 6., 15 June 2014, http://www.the-american-interest.com/2014/06/15/the-twin-insurgency/.

Robert J. Bunker and Pamela Ligouri Bunker, Editors. *Global Criminal and Sovereign Free Economies and the Demise of the Western Democracies: Dark Renaissance.* Routledge Advances in International Political Economy. New York: Routledge, 2016 (Reprint edition).

Notes

All opinions are strictly those of the authors and in no way reflect the viewpoints of any U.S. Governmental, academic, or corporate entity.

1. http://smallwarsjournal.com/jrnl/art/plutocratic-insurgency-note-no-1-eight-individuals-are-now-as-wealthy-as-the-poorest-half-o.

Reading 9

Plutocratic Insurgency Note No. 2: 69% of Americans Don't Even Have $1,000 in Savings

Pamela Ligouri Bunker and Robert J. Bunker

First Published 14 February 2017 in Small Wars Journal [1]

Key Information: Cameron Huddleston, "69% of Americans Have Less Than $1,000 in Savings." *GoBankingRates*. 19 September 2016, https://www.gobankingrates.com/personal-finance/data-americans-savings/:

Americans are falling short when it comes saving money—specifically, setting aside money in savings accounts—to create a financial cushion. In fact, they've gone from bad to worse, according to GOBankingRates.com's latest survey findings on savings amounts.

In 2015, we asked more than 5,000 adults how much they had saved in a savings account. The results were startling: 62 percent said they have less than $1,000 in savings.

Recently, GOBankingRates asked the question again, this time to more than 7,000 people to see if Americans' saving rates have improved in the last year or so. But the results are even more surprising—the percentage of Americans with less than $1,000 in savings has jumped to 69 percent…

Key Information: Sean Williams (Motley Fool), "Nearly 7 in 10 Americans have less than $1,000 in savings." *USA Today.* 9 October 2016, http://www.usatoday.com/story/money/personalfinance/2016/10/09/savings-study/91083712/:

> The U.S. is often referred to as the land of economic opportunity. Apparently, it's also the land of consumption and "spend everything you've got."
>
> We don't have to look far for confirmation that Americans are generally poor savers. Every month the St. Louis Federal Reserve releases data on personal household savings rates. In July 2016, the personal savings rate was just 5.7%. Comparatively, personal savings rates in the U.S. 50 years ago were double where they are today, and nearly all developed countries have a higher personal savings rate than the United States. In other words, Americans are saving less of their income than they should be—the recommendation is to save between 10% and 15% of your annual income—and they're being forced to do more with less in terms of investing…

Key Information (Archival): Elyssa Kirkham, "62% of Americans Have Under $1,000 in Savings, Survey Finds." *GoBankingRates.* 5 October 2015, https://www.gobankingrates.com/savings-account/62-percent-americans-under-1000-savings-survey-finds/:

> Having a savings fund is one of the keys to financial health. Yet trying to save is a struggle, especially because the biggest money challenge for Americans is sticking to a budget — a central skill to ensure enough money is left over each month to save.

"It's worrisome that such a large percentage of Americans have so little set aside in a savings account," said Cameron Huddleston, a personal finance expert and columnist for GOBankingRates. "It suggests that they likely don't have cash reserves to cover an emergency and will have to rely on credit, friends, and family, or even their retirement accounts to cover unexpected expenses."

Survey Finds Two-Thirds of Americans Don't Have Enough Money Saved

The overall results from the survey show that 62 percent of Americans have less than $1,000 in their savings accounts, and a third of those under-savers have no savings account at all. The portion of savers with balances over $1,000 is 29.1 percent.

The most frequently selected amount that people say they have in savings is also the lowest $0; 28 percent of people selected this answer. Even worse, the next-most-common answer is "I don't have a savings account," selected by one in five people (20.7 percent)…

Key Information (Archival): Maggie McGarth, "63% of American's Don't Have Enough Savings to Cover A $500 Emergency." *Forbes*. 6 January 2016, http://www.forbes.com/sites/maggiemcgrath/2016/01/06/63-of-americans-dont-have-enough-savings-to-cover-a-500-emergency/#655f9b996dde:

The car brakes go on the fritz. The refrigerator stops refrigerating. The dog gets his paws on a batch of chocolate chip cookies and earns himself a trip to the vet ER.

These are just three of any number of things that could go wrong during the course of the year. Recovering from any one will set you back about $500, which means these scenarios fall closer to the "undesirable inconvenience" category than they do the "massive calamity" one. And yet, nearly two-thirds of Americans do not have enough money in savings to cover the cost of a single one of these unplanned expenses.

According to a brand new survey from Bankrate. com, just 37% of Americans have enough savings to pay for a $500 or $1,000 emergency. The other 63% would have to resort to measures like cutting back spending in other areas (23%), charging to a credit card (15%) or borrowing funds from friends and family (15%) in order to meet the cost of the unexpected event.

Key Information (Archival): Tim Worstall, "It's Simply Not True That Most American's Don't Have $1,000 In Emergency Savings." *Fortune.* 14 January 2016, http://www.forbes.com/sites/timworstall/2016/01/14/its-simply-not-true-that-most-americans-dont-have-1000-in-emergency-savings/#3064d8d32db4:

I read Salon, yes, apologies, a dirty little secret. I do so because I love the intellectual challenge of working out why they've managed to grasp the wrong end of the stick on any economic issue. It's a bit like reading the opinion columns of The Guardian: you know they're wrong, the fun is in attempting to work out why and how on this specific point…

It's an interesting observation that most Americans have little in their checking and savings accounts. But to draw from that the opinion that the middle class doesn't exist is to be entirely wrong. The correct conclusion to draw is that these people are indeed middle class in a country with a well functioning financial system. Because of this they don't need savings because they have access to credit.

And if we're honest about it credit and savings are economically the same thing. They're both ways of gaining access to emergency funding. That one is not consuming now so as to be able to consume in an emergency, the other not consuming in the future to be able to consume in an emergency makes no difference economically…

And this of course has its public policy point. That most Americans don't have $500 or so of "savings" as conventionally defined simply doesn't matter. Because near all Americans have access to $500 of credit and thus are able to consume in such emergencies. And, as ever in the study of things economic, it is consumption which is the important point of it all. If people can consume in emergencies it doesn't matter whether that is through savings or credit.

Who: A representation of the U.S. internet population throughout all 50 states and Washington, DC. A margin of error of 1.70 percent exists for the 2015 survey consisting of 5,006 responses and a margin of error of 2.6 percent exists for the 2016 survey consisting of 7,052 responses.

What: Google Consumer Surveys conducted by *GoBankingRates. com* concerning how much money respondents had in their savings accounts.

When: The surveys were taken 11-13 September 2015 and 1-9 August 2016, respectively.

Where: The surveys were conducted by means of the internet with respondents who live within the United States.

Why: The website *GoBankingRates.com* conducted the surveys in support of its business strategy of having readers go to the site to a) get competitive interest rate information on financial services found nationwide and b) find out about informative personal finance content, news, and tools. The surveys represent both a public informational service and a newsworthy marketing tool that will steer more users to the website.

Analysis: The surveys identify a downward trend in personal savings rate for the American public. In 2015, of those surveyed, 62% have less than a $1,000.00 in savings while in 2016 this number rose to 69% of the respondents. No *GoBankingRates.com* personal savings rates data existed prior to the 2015 survey. At the other extreme of those surveyed in 2015, 14% had over $10,000 in savings—that rose to 15% in 2016 which may be suggestive of a gradual shift towards the class polarization between those at the top and bottom of American society. The 69% rate of respondents with less than $1,000.00 in savings is indicative of the growing underclass of working poor in the United States (see Further Reading). Some of the themes found in the later news articles commenting on the 2016 survey are troubling. First, they equate the fact that the mass of working poor Americans are simply living beyond their means and do not have responsible spending habits. While this may be partially accurate, those same Americans are being bombarded by corporate marketing ads to get them to purchase their products—much of which is initially funded by low to no interest rates on the credit extended. Additionally, for many middle class Americans, it is now basically impossible—given the demise of many public entitlement programs and services—for them to provide for the basic needs of their families without going deeper and deeper into debt. Second, access to credit does not equate to having money in one's bank account. This egregious theme is tied to the article written by Tim Worstall in *Fortune*. This can be seen with the pronouncement "That most Americans don't have $500 or so of "savings" as conventionally defined simply doesn't matter. Because near all Americans have access to $500 of credit and thus are able to consume in such emergencies." That he equates working and middle class access to credit—which represents taking on additional personal debt—as economically the same as having savings is beyond ludicrous. He essentially advocates a 'pay day advance' solution for Americans facing financial emergencies such as securing medical services for their children or obtaining heating oil for their rented housing in the dead of winter. While this trend towards the hollowing out of individual American savings is of concern, the fact those same Americans are being blamed for their dire economic situations should be as equally concerning. It is suggestive of a shift within the United States from state moderated capitalism that protected its citizens for decades to an emerging predatory capitalist form that is actively and efficiently extracting wealth from them to satisfy corporate and plutocratic earning sheets. In some ways this is reminiscent of the old company town model found in the United States—although, in this case, it is expanding writ large across the country.

Further Reading

Sasha Abramsky, *The American Way of Poverty: How the Other Half Still Lives*. New York: Nation Books, 2014.

Gary Rivlin, *Broke, USA: From Pawnshops to Poverty, Inc.—How the Working Poor Became Big Business*. New York: Harper Business, 2010.

Linda Tirado, *Hand to Mouth: Living in Bootstrap America*. New York: G.P. Putnam's Sons, 2014.

Notes

All opinions are strictly those of the authors and in no way reflect the viewpoints of any U.S. Governmental, academic, or corporate entity.

1. http://smallwarsjournal.com/jrnl/art/plutocratic-insurgency-note-no-2-69-of-americans-don't-even-have-1000-in-savings.

Reading 10

Plutocratic Insurgency Note No. 3: No Shoring: Job Obsolescence Via Artificial Intelligence (AI) and Robotics

Robert J. Bunker and Pamela Ligouri Bunker

First Published 22 February 2017 in Small Wars Journal

Key Information: Cade Metz, "The AI Threat is Not SKYNET. It's the End of the Middle Class." *Wired*. 10 February 2017, https://www.wired.com/2017/02/ai-threat-isnt-skynet-end-middle-class/:

...At a time when the Trump administration is promising to make America great again by restoring old-school manufacturing jobs, AI researchers aren't taking him too seriously. They know that these jobs are never coming back, thanks in no small part to their own research, which will eliminate so many other kinds of jobs in the years to come, as well. At Asilomar, they looked at the real US economy, the real reasons for the "hollowing out" of the middle class. The problem isn't immigration—far from it. The problem isn't offshoring or taxes or regulation. It's technology...

In the US, the number of manufacturing jobs peaked in 1979 and has steadily decreased ever since. At the same time, manufacturing has steadily increased, with the US now producing more goods than any other country but China. Machines aren't just taking the place of humans on the assembly line. They're doing a better job. And all this before the coming wave of AI upends so many other sectors of the economy. "I am less concerned with *Terminator* scenarios," MIT economist Andrew McAfee said on the first day at Asilomar. "If current trends continue, people are going to rise up well before the machines do."

McAfee pointed to newly collected data that shows a sharp decline in middle class job creation since the 1980s. Now, most new jobs are either at the very low end of the pay scale or the very high end. He also argued that these trends are reversible, that improved education and a greater emphasis on entrepreneurship and research can help feed new engines of growth, that economies have overcome the rise of new technologies before. But after his talk, in the hallways at Asilomar, so many of the researchers warned him that the coming revolution in AI would eliminate far more jobs far more quickly than he expected...

Key Information: Christopher Mims, "Technology's Long-Term Toll on the Middle Class." *The Wall Street Journal.* 23 January 2017: B-1, B-4, https://www.wsj.com/articles/technology-vs-the-middle-class-1485107698:

...When workers lose a middle-class manufacturing or clerical job and end up in the service sector, the effect on their wages, benefits and job security contributes to what economists call polarization. In a polarized labor market, a minority of highly skilled employees—the ones who can leverage technology to be more productive—effectively replace the labor of others and are paid accordingly. Everyone else sees their fortunes dwindle.

Polarization has hit the middle class hard, but the devaluation of human labor will continue up the income ladder, says Branko Milanovic, an economist who specializes in income inequality.

That's partly because, more than ever, we have the ability to eliminate higher-paying knowledge work. Ian Barkin, co-founder of Symphony Ventures, which helps some of the world's largest companies automate everything from call centers to human-resource departments, says this phenomenon is known as "no-shoring." The idea is that digitizing back-office tasks brings them back to the country in which a company operates, but without bringing back any jobs…

Key Information: Wolfgang Lehmacher, "Don't Blame China For Taking U.S. Jobs." *Fortune*. 8 November 2016, <ins>http://fortune. com/2016/11/08/china-automation-jobs/</ins>:

…The U.S. has lost 5 million factory jobs since 2000. And trade has indeed claimed production jobs - in particular when China joined the World Trade Organization in 2001. Nevertheless, there was no downturn in U.S. manufacturing output. As a matter of fact, U.S. production has been growing over the last decades. From 2006 to 2013, "manufacturing grew by 17.6%, or at roughly 2.2% per year," according to a report from Ball State University. The study reports as well that trade accounted for 13% of the lost U.S. factory jobs, but 88% of the jobs were taken by robots and other factors at home.

If not China, what then explains these jobs losses? It's simple: factories don't need as many workers as they used to, because robots increasingly do the work.

Investment in automation and software has doubled the output per U.S. manufacturing worker over the past two decades. Robots are replacing workers, regardless of trade at an accelerating pace. "The real robotics revolution is ready to begin" writes BCG and predicts that "the share of tasks that are performed by robots will rise from a global average of around 10% across all manufacturing industries today to around 25% by 2025."…

Key Information: "Robots will eliminate 6% of all US jobs by 2021, report says." *The Guardian*. 13 September 2016, https://www.theguardian.com/technology/2016/sep/13/artificial-intelligence-robots-threat-jobs-forrester-report:

By 2021, robots will have eliminated 6% of all jobs in the US, starting with customer service representatives and eventually truck and taxi drivers. That's just one cheery takeaway from a report released by market research company Forrester this week.

These robots, or intelligent agents, represent a set of AI-powered systems that can understand human behavior and make decisions on our behalf. Current technologies in this field include virtual assistants like Alexa, Cortana, Siri and Google Now as well as chatbots and automated robotic systems. For now, they are quite simple, but over the next five years they will become much better at making decisions on our behalf in more complex scenarios, which will enable mass adoption of breakthroughs like self-driving cars.

These robots can be helpful for companies looking to cut costs, but not so good if you're an employee working in a simple-to-automate field…

…"Six percent is huge. In an economy that's really not creating regular full-time jobs, the ability of people to easily find new employment is going to diminish. So we will have people wanting to work and struggling to find jobs because the same trends are beginning to occur in other historically richer job creation areas like banking, retail and healthcare," said Andy Stern, the former president of the Service Employees International Union.

"It's an early warning sign and I think it just portends a massive wind of change in the future."…

Who: Artificial intelligence (AI) and robots utilized by businesses and multinational corporations.

What: The ongoing elimination of American manufacturing, transportation, and customer service jobs as well as white collar and knowledge worker jobs as a component of globalization and the information revolution.

When: Contemporary era; since the 2010s increasing concerns expressed over artificial intelligence (AI) and robot use in the economy having reached a 'tipping point' where more human jobs were being lost than being gained by their ever growing utilization.

Where: Within the United States.

Why: The result of the replacement of human labor by machine labor (i.e. AI and robotics) in order to increase productivity and lower costs; the transition from human labor to advanced software and automation processes to achieve higher corporate profitability. A manifestation of post-industrial and cyber based economies in advanced 21st century societies.

Analysis: The migration of US manufacturing jobs overseas to China, Mexico, and other locales—commonly known as 'offshoring'—has been one of the flashpoints of globalization for US workers. Images of the Rust Belt towns in the mid-West and Eastern US—exemplified by Detroit and other hollowed out and depopulated city cores—as well as concerns over free trade agreements (NAFTA; North American Free

Trade Agreement and TTP; Trans-Pacific Partnership) and jokes about Indian call center employees trying to convince customers that they are based in the US are all components of the greater offshoring and globalization milieu. While much talk has focused on the critical need for the reshoring (aka; onshoring or repatriation) of US jobs in order to bolster the thinning US middle class—particularly in the present administration but a public policy issue also visibly cognizant in earlier ones—such efforts are not gaining momentum. The reason is that, rather than the reshoring of jobs, we have increasingly been witnessing the no shoring of jobs. The no shoring concept—articulated by Ian Barkin (in *The Wall Street Journal* article cited in this note)—is the process of talking off shored American jobs and bringing them back to the US for artificial intelligence programs and robotic lines to do. The net result is that the old job remains lost and not only have US workers lost this employment option but foreign off shore workers have now lost that job opportunity as well. This increasing trend is representative of the dystopian nightmare laid out in *Player Piano*—a 1952 science fiction novel written by Kurt Vonnegut. It results in a bifurcated society in which the haves—engineers, managers, and capitalists (corporate owners)—have productive lives while the lower classes—whose jobs have been automated—have little purpose for their existence. Such a scenario is representative of the crisis of post Modern capitalism in which state moderated capitalism, which is meant to protect middle class structures and provide public welfare benefits, is being subsumed by larger predatory and globalized multinational corporate activities. While the US is presently nowhere near a dystopian *Player Piano* future, the no shoring trend is of immense concern. Ultimately, it suggests that the new administration may have little to no power to institute any form of meaningful reshoring programs for US workers and the fragmentation of the middle class will continue unabated. If such fragmentation continues, it will undermine the American societal mythos derived from the Horatio Alger archetype of poor yet hard working, honest, and courageous boys (and girls) gaining upward mobility into the American middle class. While such a mythos may at first appear historically trite, socio-economic mobility has been a defining characteristic of American society for well over a century. The increased 'thinning' of the middle class—resulting from both the off shoring and no shoring of jobs—will mean that those born into the lower class will increasingly have fewer and fewer opportunities to leave it. Socio-economic mobility in American society is a defining component of the 'pursuit of happiness' and an unalienable right and, if that is taken away from the citizenry, the social contract between the state and the governed will be gravely imperiled.

Further Reading

Jagdish N. Bhagwati and Alan S. Blinder, *Offshoring of American Jobs: What Response from U.S. Economic Policy?* Benjamin M. Friedman, ed., Cambridge: MIT Press, 2009.

Martin Ford, *The Lights in the Tunnel: Automation, Accelerating Technology and the Economy of the Future.* Charleston: CreateSpace, 2009.

Martin Ford, *Rise of the Robots: Technology and the Threat of a Jobless Future.* New York: Basic Books, 2016 (Reprint).

Jerry Kaplan, *Humans Need Not Apply: A Guide to Wealth and Work in the Age of Artificial Intelligence.* New Haven: Yale University Press, 2016 (Reprint).

Notes

Disclaimer: All opinions are strictly those of the authors and in no way reflect the viewpoints of any U.S. Governmental, academic, or corporate entity.

1. http://smallwarsjournal.com/jrnl/art/plutocratic-insurgency-note-no-3-no-shoring-job-obsolescence-via-artificial-intelligence-ai.

Reading 11

Plutocratic Insurgency Note No. 4: Silencing the Middle Class— The Gradual Extinction of Tenure in American Universities

Pamela Ligouri Bunker and Robert J. Bunker

First Published 7 March 2017 in Small Wars Journal [1]

Key Information: Douglas Belkin, "Faculty's New Focus: Don't Offend." *The Wall Street Journal.* 28 February 2017: A3, https://www. wsj.com/articles/college-facultys-new-focus-dont-offend-1488200404 (Mirrored at http://www.todayevery.com/share/HkxiLuj-9e?hint=SB10 559519697244824476804582638013261645738?responsive=y/articles):

…Conservatives seized on this shift and used the term politically correct to connote what they saw as a creeping relativism and an attack on truth.

The meaning took on additional nuance in the past decade as college prices skyrocketed and parents began to expect more protection for their children on campus. Those expectations prompted schools to hire more university administrators to look after students' well-being, not to teach them, said Dr. Zimmerman.

That shifted the conversation about what is politically correct from the realm of the intellectual and cultural to the psychological and emotional…

…The unintended consequences come in the classroom where some faculty say they are now pulling their punches, particularly those without the job protections of tenure.

Renee Fraser, an adjunct who teaches western civilization at Moorpark Community College in California, said she is deeply concerned about receiving a bias complaint when she delivers a lecture this semester about nationalism.

"If you describe nationalism, you're describing Donald Trump, " she said, noting that students in her school are mostly conservative. "I'm embarrassed that I don't let the students have more freedom because I'm afraid for my job."

Andrea Quenette, who teaches communications at the University of Kansas, says she was on track for tenure until the fall of 2015 when students accused her of being racially insensitive…

Key Information: Douglas Belkin, "Universities, Facing Cuts, Target Tenure." *The Wall Street Journal.* 15 February 2017: A3, https://www.wsj.com/articles/colleges-faced-with-funding-cuts-target-tenure-trims-1487068202 (Mirrored at http://handbill.us/?p=82164):

…The institution of tenure—which provides job security and perks like regular sabbaticals—began in the U.S. early in the 20th century as a bulwark against interference from administrators, corporate interests and politicians who might not like professors' opinions or agree with their research.

Attacks on tenure have become commonplace in the wake of the recession as reductions in public support for colleges led to steep tuition increases that have driven up student debt and magnified scrutiny on the business practices of universities. Conservative lawmakers also have expressed mounting displeasure with university professors, saying they indoctrinate impressionable students with a liberal point of view...

...In 1975, 45% of faculty at public and private schools was tenured or tenure-track; the 2014 figure is 29%. The balance of the jobs are now filled by part-time adjunct professors who make, on average, less than half the salary of tenured professors, enjoying few of their benefits, and are excused from much of the administrative work. While the average salary of a full professor is $142,141, according to the American Association of University Professors, adjuncts are typically paid between $1,500 and $5,000 a course.

Schools across the country, mostly small, private colleges like Wartburg College in Iowa and the College of Saint Rose in New York, have been offering buyouts to cull their ranks of longtime faculty. Other schools have eliminated entire academic departments...

Key Information: National Center for Education Statistics, "Characteristics of Postsecondary Faculty." May 2016 Update, https://nces.ed.gov/programs/coe/indicator_csc.asp:

...From fall 1993 to fall 2013, the number of full-time faculty at degree-granting postsecondary institutions increased by 45 percent, while the number of part-time faculty increased by 104 percent. As a result of the faster increase in the number of part-time faculty, the percentage of all faculty who were part time increased from 40 to 49 percent during this period....

...In academic year 2013–14, approximately 49 percent of institutions had tenure systems. A tenure system guarantees that professors will not be terminated without just cause after a probationary period. The percentage of institutions with tenure systems ranged from 1 percent at private for-profit institutions to almost 100 percent at public doctoral institutions. Of full-time faculty at institutions with tenure systems, 48 percent had tenure in 2013–14, compared with 54 percent in 1999–2000. From 1999–2000 to 2013–14, the percentage of full-time faculty having tenure decreased by 5 percentage points at public institutions, by 4 percentage points at private nonprofit institutions, and by 58 percentage points at private for-profit institutions...

Key Information: Andrew Hibel and Gregory Scholtz, "Tenure in Academia, the Past, Present and Future." *HigherEdJobs*. 30 September 2013, https://www.higheredjobs.com/higheredcareers/interviews.cfm?ID=459:

...**Hibel:** *In a recent Bloomberg Business article, the author states, "Academic freedom is the esteemed argument made for tenure. This rationale dates back to the late 18th century, when professors at religious schools needed protection from trustees and donors who might demand termination of those faculty who taught outside the accepted doctrine." He goes on to say that "academic freedom is protected under the First Amendment and therefore tenure is not necessary, at least at public universities." Please explain the role and purpose of tenure in today's higher education system. Also, what are your thoughts on his comments?*

Scholtz: As I stated previously, the role and purpose of tenure in American higher education is to protect academic freedom in order to promote the discovery and dissemination of knowledge and thus serve the common good. Academic freedom, as understood by the AAUP, is a professor's freedom "to teach, both in and outside the classroom, to conduct research and to publish the results of those investigations, and to address any matter of institutional policy or action whether or not [one is] a member of an agency of institutional governance. Professors should also have the freedom to address the larger community with regard to any matter of social, political, economic, or other interest, without institutional discipline or restraint, save in response to fundamental violations of professional ethics or statements that suggest disciplinary incompetence" (From the executive summary of a 2009 AAUP report on the fallout from the Supreme Court's decision in *Garcetti v. Ceballos*).

According to academic freedom and Constitutional experts, the First and Fourteenth Amendments protect an individual faculty member at a public university from government interference that is external and based on content. They do not protect that faculty member from administrators and governing board members— or, indeed, from other members of the faculty—who would interfere in their teaching, their scholarship, or their speech about institutional matters and matters of public concern. For further elaboration, see Walter P. Metzger, "Profession and Constitution: Two Definitions of Academic Freedom in America" (Texas Law Review 1265 [1988]), David M. Rabban, "Academic Freedom," in *Encyclopedia of the American Constitution* 12 (1986); and Neil Hamilton, *Zealotry and Academic Freedom: A Legal and Historical Perspective* (1995), 187-194.

In other words, constitutional academic freedom in some ways falls far short of professional academic freedom, as commonly understood in American higher education. So the idea that tenure is not needed to protect academic freedom at public colleges and universities because Constitutional protections are adequate is incorrect. To understand the importance of tenure for protecting academic freedom at such institutions, all one need do is to talk to their faculty members who do not have tenure. And, as the Bloomberg author acknowledges, these Constitutional rights do not apply to faculty members in their professional capacities at private colleges and universities...

Key Information: Adriana Kezar and Daniel Maxey, "The Changing Academic Workforce." *Trusteeship Magazine.* May-June 2013, https://www.agb.org/trusteeship/2013/5/changing-academic-workforce:

...The large and growing reliance on non-tenure-track faculty throughout higher education has resulted in such faculty members now accounting for approximately 70 percent of the faculty providing instruction at nonprofit institutions nationwide. Yet, most campuses ignore the needs of this group, operating as though tenure-track faculty members are the norm. As non-tenure-track faculty have been hired in greater numbers, institutions have often not considered how their faculty policies and practices—and the working conditions encountered by adjuncts, particularly those working part time—may carry deeply troubling implications for student learning, equal-employment opportunities and nondiscrimination, and risk management...

...In 1969, tenured and tenure-track positions made up approximately 78.3 percent of the faculty, and non-tenure-track positions accounted for about 21.7 percent, according to The American Faculty, published in 2006 by Jack H. Schuster and Martin J. Finkelstein (Johns Hopkins University Press). By 2009, data from the National Center for Education Statistics' Integrated

Postsecondary Education Data System show these proportions had nearly flipped; tenured and tenure-track faculty had declined to 33.5 percent of the professoriate, and 66.5 percent of faculty were ineligible for tenure. Of the 66.5 percent, 18.8 percent were full-time, non-tenure-track, and 47.7 percent were part-time. While the numbers of non-tenure-track faculty have grown the most at community colleges, they make up a large portion of the faculty at all institutional types...

Who: Faculty in American colleges and universities who are increasingly becoming either full-time professors ineligible for tenure or adjunct and part-time professors with short term teaching contracts.

What: The elimination of tenure-track and tenured faculty in American higher education.

When: The shift towards hiring non-tenure track professors has progressed since the 1990s and continues today.

Where: Within the United States.

Why: Primarily implied to be a cost cutting measure at American non-profit universities. In the case of for-profit universities, which have proliferated in student numbers since the 1990s, adjunct and part-time professors form the basis of the business model to maximize corporate profits.

Analysis: While some disagreement exists concerning the rate of the shift of tenured and tenured-track faculty to contract and part-time (adjunct) faculty, the overall trend is not in dispute. The tenure system is slowly devolving and may at some point be in effect only in the most prestigious—read 'economically well-endowed'—private universities and a few select public hybrid institutions. The gradual demise of tenure on American college campuses mirrors the thinning of a middle class no longer required for 20th century based mass industrial production and conventional warfare utilizing large standing armies. With public support for colleges drying up and tuition bills rising, higher education has increasingly shifted from a public good to a commodity competing in the free market economy. Since tenured faculty are costly to maintain, they became a natural target of cost savings measures. Increasingly, powerful administrators—whose growing numbers have long been commented upon—have become complicit in this drive to limit the job security and salaries of PhD labor for the benefit of their university employers. While some perspectives portray tenured professors as extreme liberals out of touch with reality, or worse as non-productive deadwood contributing little to meaningful academic debate, in their justification to end university tenure, this is a simplistic and polarized view of the institution itself. The major benefit of the tenure system in higher education is to allow the middle class to have a voice—free of governmental, religious, administration, and plutocratic corporate interests—concerning the health and trajectory of American society. Without free and open debate, even criticism, of contemporary issues negatively impacting that class strata, its socio-economic and political interests are not advanced. The gradual silencing of the middle class in US public debate due to the increasing elimination of tenured faculty is a little recognized systemic phenomena. Still, numerous individual instances of contracted and tenure-track faculty fearing to offend students or even raise controversial subjects in the classroom—which could lead to a bias complaint and potentially dismissal—have been identified thus resulting in de facto self-censorship. The loss of the middle class voice at the intelligentsia level is another troubling component of plutocratic and sovereign-free economic practices hollowing out American society. Unfortunately, the process may be so well advanced, although generally unrecognized, that it is already a *fait accompli*. This fact along, with the knowledge that the American two party system has become increasingly divisive with the injection of emotive populism, suggests that not only are reasoned middle class debates disappearing but also any form of centrist political agreements themselves.

Further Reading

James L. Bess and Jay R. Dee, *Bridging the Divide between Faculty and Administration: A Guide to Understanding Conflict in the Academy*. New York: Routledge, 2014.

Jack H. Schuster and Martin J. Finkelstein, *The American Faculty: The Restructuring of Academic Work and Careers*. Baltimore: Johns Hopkins University Press, 2008.

Notes

All opinions are strictly those of the authors and in no way reflect the viewpoints of any U.S. Governmental, academic, or corporate entity.

1. http://smallwarsjournal.com/jrnl/art/plutocratic-insurgency-note-no-4.

Reading 12

The Rise of the "Plutocratic Insurgency"

George Thomas

*First Published 15 March 2017 at Quintus
Curtius: Fortress of the Mind* [1]
Reprinted with permission.

I've written before on the extreme social dangers that come about from <u>excessive concentrations of wealth in the hands of a few.</u> A very important series of articles by Robert and Pamela Bunker in *Small Wars Journal* has taken this idea one step further: they have identified the current vast income disparities as a form of insurgency warfare. This is a very significant step, and one that is supported by the facts. This condition—in all its forms—they call the plutocratic insurgency. This podcast discusses some of their conclusions, and asks readers to ponder the implications of this insidious form of warfare on the social health of Western nations.

Contains a <u>28:15 minute podcast</u>.

Notes

1. <u>https://qcurtius.com/2017/03/15/the-rise-of-the-plutocratic-insurgency/</u>.

Reading 13

Plutocratic Insurgency Note No. 5: The Techno-Palaces of the Global Elite

Robert J. Bunker and Pamela Ligouri Bunker

First Published 12 July 2017 in Small Wars Journal [1]

Key Information: David McManus, "One57 Tower New York City, Manhattan Skyscraper, The Billionaire Building Apartments." *e-Architect.* 5 July 2016 (Updated: 6 June 2017), https://www.e-architect.co.uk/new-york/one57-tower-new-york-city:

… Upon completion in 2014, it stood at 1,005 feet (306 m) tall, making it the tallest residential building in the city for a few months until 432 Park Avenue was constructed.

"The 73-floor supertall skyscraper in midtown Manhattan has been crowned the new most expensive building in New York City as of 2015, according to a report by CityRealty", reports Business Insider. "The building's average price per square foot for the year was $6,010, while last year's most expensive, 15 Central Park West, came in at only $5,726.

One57's average price increased 18.5% from last year, while 15 CPW's average decreased 10%. One of the penthouses in the 1,004-foot-tall residence closed this year for $100.5 million, making it the most expensive apartment ever sold in NYC, as well as the first to surpass $100 million."…

Authors' Note—Numerous images are contained in this source.

Key Information: Alyssa Newcomb, "Inside the Tallest Residential Building in the Western Hemisphere." *ABC News.* 14 October 2014, http://abcnews.go.com/US/inside-tallest-residential-building-western-hemisphere/story?id=26186476:

Bragging rights for the tallest residential building in the Western Hemisphere now belong to a luxury skyscraper in New York City that's even taller than the Empire State Building.

Construction has topped out on the luxury tower at 432 Park Ave. in Midtown Manhattan. The building stands 1,396 feet, making it even taller than 1 World Trade Center without the spire.

The 96-story building will welcome its first residents next year, giving them a breathtaking view stretching from Central Park to the Atlantic Ocean and from Lower Manhattan, where the Freedom Tower is located, to Connecticut…

…Among the extras residents can purchase are climate-controlled wine cellars and staff apartments. It comes as no surprise that such a prestigious address isn't cheap. A place in the 104-unit building starts at $16.95 million.

Authors' Note—Numerous images are contained in this source.

Key Information: Mark Cooper, "Svelte Density: Needle Towers Puncture the Sky." *Urban Land*. 14 March 2016, https://urbanland.uli. org/planning-design/svelte-density-needle-towers-puncture-sky/:

Following the 2014 completion of the dramatic One57 tower by Extell Development, a raft of new tall and slender buildings is set to change the midtown Manhattan skyline in New York City. Many are above the 984-foot (300 m) measure used by the Council on Tall Buildings and Urban Habitat to qualify as a supertall building, and most are designed to take advantage of Central Park views.

The 1,000-foot-tall (305 m) One57, on West 57th Street, was the first of this new wave and was briefly New York's tallest residential building, but it has been surpassed by the 1,428-foot-tall (435 m) 432 Park Avenue building. Estimated to be completed by 2018, both will be surpassed by the 1,522-foot (464 m) Nordstrom Tower as well as by the not-quite-as-supertall—but superslim—111 West 57th Street building, which will rise to 1,438 feet (438 m) tall with a tiny floor plate of 60 by 80 feet (18 by 24 m).

Ming Wu, design principal at architect Perkins Eastman, says, "In New York real estate terms, the appearance of needle towers on the skyline is a very recent phenomenon. At present, in Manhattan, there are easily a dozen or so needle towers being planned or under construction—and ranging in height from 900 to 1,500 feet [274 to 457 m], so this phenomenon is significant and will dramatically alter the city's image. Many will surpass the Empire State Building in height, and will rival the [1,776-foot/541-m] Freedom Tower in prominence…

…The final key to unlock these projects is the price that people will pay to acquire a view over Central Park.

One57 has 90 stories and only 94 apartments, plus a Park Hyatt hotel. In January 2015, the top-floor duplex at One57 sold for $100.47 million—the first New York City apartment property to break the $100 million level. The even more willowy 111 West 57th Street has only 45 apartments in its tower section, some of which will be duplexes and are expected to fetch more than $100 million when sold.

The pricing of these apartments—units in 111 West 57th Street are expected to start at $14 million—means they are aimed squarely at the world's richest people, the 40,000 people worldwide who are worth more than $100 million each as tallied by WealthInsight, a research company specializing in ultra-high-net-worth and high-net-worth individuals.

Such developments have been particularly popular with buyers from Asia, the home of many high-rise luxury developments. But the developments have appealed to ultra-high-net-worth buyers from all over the world….

Global Precedent

In Sydney, a city that a decade ago had no high-rise luxury apartment buildings, Chinese state-owned developer Greenland Group is building a 771-foot-tall (235 m) residential tower in the central business district. When completed in 2019, it will be the city's tallest residential building. It is being developed to a higher specification than earlier developments because Greenland wanted to be the market leader in Australia and the building is being marketed primarily to an Asian clientele.

In London, Dalian Wanda is developing the 42-story River Tower near the new U.S. embassy site in Vauxhall. As well as being tall for London, the tower will offer hotel concierge services to its residents—an acknowledgment that many of them will be international buyers with multiple homes, looking for a significant level of service…

Key Information: "Inside The World's First Billion-Dollar Home." *Forbes.* 30 April 2008, https://www.forbes.com/2008/04/30/home-india-billion-forbeslife-cx_mw_0430realestate.html:

While visiting New York in 2005, Nita Ambani was in the spa at the Mandarin Oriental New York, overlooking Central Park. The contemporary Asian interiors struck her just so, and prompted her to inquire about the designer.

Nita Ambani was no ordinary tourist. She is married to Mukesh Ambani, head of Mumbai, India-based petrochemical giant Reliance Industries, and the fifth richest man in the world. (Lakshmi Mittal, ranked fourth, is an Indian citizen, but a resident of the U.K.)

In Pictures: Tour The World's First Billion-Dollar Home

Forbes estimated Ambani's net worth at $43 billion in March. Reliance Industries was founded by Mukesh's father, Dhirubhai Ambani, in 1966, and is India's most valuable firm by market capitalization. The couple, who have three children, currently live in a 22-story Mumbai tower that the family has spent years remodeling to meet its needs.

Like many families with the means to do so, the Ambanis wanted to build a custom home. They consulted with architecture firms Perkins + Will and Hirsch Bedner Associates, the designers behind the Mandarin Oriental, based in Dallas and Los Angeles, respectively. Plans were then drawn up for what will be the world's largest and most expensive home: a 27-story skyscraper in downtown Mumbai with a cost nearing $2 billion, says Thomas Johnson, director of marketing at Hirsch Bedner Associates. The architects and designers are creating as they go, altering floor plans, design elements and concepts as the building is constructed.

<u>Video: World's Most Expensive Home</u>

The only remotely comparable high-rise property currently on the market is the <u>$70 million triplex penthouse</u> at the Pierre Hotel in New York, designed to resemble a French chateau, and climbing 525 feet in the air. When the Ambani residence is finished in January, completing a four-year process, it will be 550 feet high with 400,000 square feet of interior space.

The home will cost more than a hotel or high-rise of similar size because of its custom measurements and fittings: A hotel or condominium has a common layout, replicated on every floor, and uses the same materials throughout the building (such as door handles, floors, lamps and window treatments).

The Ambani home, called Antilla, differs in that no two floors are alike in either plans or materials used. At the request of Nita Ambani, say the designers, if a metal, wood or crystal is part of the ninth-floor design, it shouldn't be used on the eleventh floor, for example. The idea is to blend styles and architectural elements so spaces give the feel of consistency, but without repetition.

Antilla's shape is based on Vaastu, an Indian tradition much like Feng Shui that is said to move energy beneficially through the building by strategically placing materials, rooms and objects.

Pricey Pad

Atop six stories of parking lots, Antilla's living quarters begin at a <u>lobby</u> with nine elevators, as well as several storage rooms and <u>lounges</u>. Down dual stairways with silver-covered railings is a large <u>ballroom</u> with 80% of its ceiling covered in crystal chandeliers. It features a retractable showcase for pieces of art, a mount of LCD monitors and embedded speakers, as well as stages for entertainment. The hall opens to an indoor/outdoor bar, green rooms, powder rooms and allows access to a nearby "entourage room" for security guards and assistants to relax...

Who: The global elite of the world. Only about 40,000 extra-sovereign individuals are able to afford the ten-million dollar plus price of the units in the more prestigious of these residential towers.[2]

What: The building of techno-palaces (e.g. 'needle-towers' and other post-modernist architectural forms) that provide full amenities and are guarded 24-hours by private security personnel.

When: These new urban residences of a transnational plutonomy began to be completed in 2014 and are now spreading to key nodal global city hubs.

Where: This phenomenon initially took place in New York City due to its concentration of global financial capital and limited building space, however, concentrations of global elites in other key cities of the world are also now moving into similar residences though they presently tend to be less expensive.

Why: These residences are likely being purchased due to a combination of factors including their locations in major global financial centers, luxury appointments, high-technology feel, secure nature, and the networking environments they provide to the world's richest families for business facilitation and marriage alliances between their offspring.

Analysis: One of the authors became aware of the existence of what are, essentially, the new 'techno-palaces' of the global elite when travelling to New York City earlier this year. At the time, the One57 ("The Billionaire Building"—Image 2), 432 Park Ave ("Tallest Residential Tower in the Western Hemisphere"—Image 3), and 56 Leonard ("Jenga Skyscraper"—Image 4) high rise residences—while quite amazing—made little sense. These post-modern architectural structures seemed like they had been erected in the city as part of a bad B movie 'alien colonization' story line which it turns out—tragically for the American middle and lower classes—is not too far off the mark. It turns out that they are being marketed to the global elite—comprised of about 40,000 extra-sovereign citizens (representing about .000005% of the world's 7.5 billion population)—who are buying them up in what has quickly developed into a seller's market. The New York City abodes have an average price in the +$10 million range and represent a component of what we term 'Dark Globalization.' Living in high tech skyscraper enclaves guarded by 24-hour private security forces has become another visible road sign on the way to that dystopian future in which a few 'haves' possess massive wealth well beyond the rest of the world's population combined—with an unbridgeable gap in between.

The first of these structures began appearing in New York City with the completion of the One57 building in May 2014 along with the growing number of such completed structures now beginning to drastically alter the city skyline (See Images 2-7, 9). Their erection is due to a combination of factors including the desirability of living in a global hub that generates great financial wealth, a shortage of buildable land within key sections of the city, and an excess of disposable wealth accumulated by the world's elite. Recent advances in construction techniques have further allowed for the building of very thin 'needle' structures that are extremely tall in size—rivaling that of the world's tallest buildings, even such as One World Trade Center—yet are very narrow at their base.

A precursor to these techno-palaces may be the $1 billion dollar 'Antilla' residence of Mukesh Ambani—an industrial, technology, and property magnate—built in Mumbai and completed in November 2010 (See image 1). While only 568 feet tall, it is technically a single unit residence, as opposed to the more typical 1,000 feet tall skyscrapers containing dozens of global elite palatial suites. For less affluent billionaires than Ambani, bargain penthouses (singles up to quads) are going at more affordable prices ranging in the $50 through $250 million range with about $90-100 million now appearing to be a popular price for the most elite among them.

The expectation is that—now that these 'techno palaces' are becoming the *de facto* global elite residences in New York City—they will begin to emerge across the globe in its major financial centers. This is already seemingly the case with their construction being mimicked in a number of other major financial cities worldwide such as Sydney, Hong Kong, and Tokyo and, with more sensible height limits of course placed upon them, in London (See Image 8). One architect interviewed in 2016 already noted that in the United States "San Francisco, Miami, and Boston already have mini–needle towers underway," and "Other cities such as Seattle and Atlanta will follow."[3]

Following that bad alien colonization storyline, the projection is that in the coming decades the new extra-sovereign masters of humanity will raise up many more such gleaming towers to look down from as they further separate themselves from the rest of us. Like master puppeteers, these scions of predatory capitalism are engaged in a sustained global insurgent campaign that is neither understood nor recognized by lesser political elites, the middle strata, or the masses. Instead, we simply marvel at the pretty new shimmering needle-like structures arising in our cities, quite blissfully unaware of the dystopian socio-economic futures they may represent for our children and our children's children.

Table 1. Urban Techno-Palaces of the Global Elite

[Entry]; Date	*Name; City*	*Height; Stories*	*Units; Price*
[1]; November 2010	"Antilla" (Private Residence of Mukesh Ambani), Mumbai, India	568 Feet; 27 Stories (Extra-High Ceilings; Equivalent to 60 Stories)	1 Unit; Appx. $1 Billion
[2]; May 2014	One57 ("The Billionaire Building"), Manhattan, New York, USA	1,005 Feet; 90 Stories (Includes Park Hyatt Hotel on site)	94 Units; $5.825 Million Starting; Penthouse $100.47 Million
[3]; October 2014	432 Park Ave ("Tallest Residential Tower in the Western Hemisphere"), Manhattan, New York, USA	1,396 Feet; 96 Stories	104 Units; $16.95 Million Starting Price; Penthouse $87.7 Million
[4]; December 2016	56 Leonard ("Jenga Skyscraper"), Tribeca, New York, USA	821 Feet; 60 Stories	145 Units; $8 Million Average; Penthouse $47 Million
[5]; Est. 2017	220 Central Park South, Manhattan, New York, USA	950 Feet; 66 Stories	118 Units; $10+ Million; Quadraplex-Penthouse $250 Million (Offered)
[6]; Est. 2018	111 West 57th Street ("Steinway Tower"), Manhattan, New York, USA	1,438 Feet; 82 Stories	60 Units; Sales Information Pending
[7]; Est. 2018	53W53; 53 West 53 ("The Lipstick Building"), Manhattan, New York, USA	1,050 Feet; 82 Stories	160 Units; Currently Available from $2.95 to $50.75 Million
[8]; Est. 2018/2019	One Nine Elms ("River and City Towers"), Vauxhall, London, UK	525 Feet; 42 Stories (River) 654 Feet; 58 Stories (City)	487 Units; Sales Information Not Disclosed. 1 Bd Unit $1.5 Million; Penthouses Appx. $80 Million

[9]; Est. 2020	225 West 57th Street ("Central Park Tower"), Manhattan, New York, USA	1,775 Feet; 95 Stories (Mixed Use)	179 Units; Sales Information Pending

Source: Online Newspaper Articles and Real Estate Information

Refer to the original article for these images: https://smallwarsjournal. com/jrnl/art/plutocratic-insurgency-note-no-5-the-techno-palaces-of-the-global-elite.

Image Links:

Image [1]; Billion Dollar House of Mukesh Ambani, Mumbai, India

https://www.youtube.com/watch?v=MOw-0_7CtDw.

Image [2]; One57 ("The Billionaire Building"), Manhattan, New York, USA

https://www.e-architect.co.uk/new-york/one57-tower-new-york-city.

Image [3]; 432 Park Avenue ("Tallest Residential Tower in the Western Hemisphere"), Manhattan, New York, USA

https://www.forbes.com/sites/aliciaadamczyk/2014/10/16/inside-new-yorks-95-million-penthouse-432-park-avenue/#303837b4a862.

Image [4]; 56 Leonard ("Jenga Skyscraper"), Tribeca, New York, USA

https://www.dezeen.com/2017/02/01/jenga-like-56-leonard-skyscraper-tribeca-new-york-herzog-de-meuron-photographs-hufton-crow/.

Image [5]; 220 Central Park, Manhattan, New York, USA

https://ny.curbed.com/2017/4/14/15299910/220-central-park-south-nyc-luxury-condo-for-sale.

Image [6]; 111 West 57th Street ("Steinway Tower"), Manhattan, New York, USA

https://urbanland.uli.org/planning-design/svelte-density-needle-towers-puncture-sky/.

Image [7]; 53W53; 53 West 53 ("The Lipstick Building"), Manhattan, New York, USA

https://therealdeal.com/2016/08/26/how-gerald-hines-built-an-89b-real-estate-empire/.

Image [8]; One Nine Elms ("River and City Towers"), Vauxhall, London, UK

http://www.onenineelms.com.

Image [9]; 225 West 57th Street ("Central Park Tower"), Manhattan, New York, USA

https://www.cityrealty.com/nyc/midtown-west/central-park-tower-225-west-57th-street/58211.

Notes

All opinions are strictly those of the authors and in no way reflect the viewpoints of any U.S. Governmental, academic, or corporate entity.

1. http://smallwarsjournal.com/jrnl/art/plutocratic-insurgency-note-no-5-the-techno-palaces-of-the-global-elite.
2. Mark Cooper, "Svelte Density: Needle Towers Puncture the Sky." *Urban Land*. 14 March 2016, https://urbanland.uli.org/planning-design/svelte-density-needle-towers-puncture-sky/.
3. Ibid.

Further Reading

Robert J. Bunker and Pamela Ligouri Bunker, Eds., *Global Criminal and Sovereign Free Economies and the Demise of the Western Democracies: Dark Renaissance*. London: Routledge, 2014.

Mike Davis and Daniel Bertrand Monk, Eds., *Evil Paradises: Dreamworlds of Neoliberalism*. New York: The New Press, 2008.

Chrystia Freeland, *Plutocrats: The Rise of the New Global Super-Rich and the Fall of Everyone Else*. New York: Penguin Books, 2013.

Nils Gilman, Jesse Goldhammer, and Steven Weber, Eds., *Deviant Globalization: Black Market Economy in the 21st Century*. New York: Continuum, 2011.

David Rothkopf, *Superclass: The Global Power Elite and the World They Are Making*. New York: Farrar, Straus, and Giroux, 2009.

Joseph E. Stiglitz, *The Price of Inequality: How Today's Divided Society Endangers Our Future*. New York: W.W. Norton & Company, 2013.

Reading 14

Plutocratic Insurgency Note No. 6: Privatizing Urban Public Spaces

John P. Sullivan and Robert J. Bunker

First Published 5 August 2017 in Small Wars Journal [1]

Privately owned public spaces (Pops) are becoming key fixtures in cities around the world. This privatization of public space creates corporately controlled spaces governed by obscure private rules and policed by private security entities with minimal state control. A lack of transparency (as the rules governing policing of these spaces are not always made public) challenges free movement and liberties in these 'pseudo-public spaces' that are reminiscent of feudal enclaves. This situation removes public spaces from the commons and places this territory in the hands of corporate or plutocratic elite rather than under state control.

Key Information: Chris Michael, Jack Shenker, Naomi Larsson, Athlyn Cathcart-Keays, Julie Cox, Chloe Smith, Nick Van Mead, and Pablo Gutierrez, "Revealed: the insidious creep of pseudo-public space in London." *The Guardian* (*Guardian Cities*). 24 July 2017, https://www.theguardian.com/cities/2017/jul/24/revealed-pseudo-public-space-pops-london-investigation-map:

Pseudo-public spaces – large squares, parks and thoroughfares that appear to be public but are actually owned and controlled by developers and their private backers – are on the rise in London and many other British cities, as local authorities argue they cannot afford to create or maintain such spaces themselves.

Although they are seemingly accessible to members of the public and have the look and feel of public land, these sites – also known as privately owned public spaces or "Pops" – are not subject to ordinary local authority bylaws but rather governed by restrictions drawn up the landowner and usually enforced by private security companies…

Private control over large open spaces in the city is not without historical precedent. In the 19th century many areas of central London, including stretches of Belgravia, Marylebone and Pimlico, were effectively gated communities, sealed off from the general public and policed by private entities. Throughout the late 19th and 20th centuries public struggles were waged to force open land and ensure streets, squares and parks were adopted by local authorities over whom Londoners of all backgrounds – not just the influential or wealthy – could exert a measure of democratic control.

In the past few decades, however, the creation of corporate-owned urban areas like Canary Wharf and the Broadgate development around Liverpool Street Station began to reverse this trend, and by 2007 the Royal Institution of Chartered Surveyors was describing the growing private ownership and management of spaces that appeared to be in the public realm as a "quiet revolution in land ownership".

Since then, the acute budgetary pressures placed on local authorities by successive governments have encouraged municipal planners to cede control of almost all new open spaces in the city to developers; some academics now refer to a new era of 'urban enclosure', echoing the fencing and enclosing of Britain's rural commons that took place during the 17ᵗʰ and 18ᵗʰ centuries…

Unsanctioned behavior

Public space campaigners point out that Pops appear unrestricted to the average person as long as they are behaving in ways that corporate landowners approve of, such as passing through on the way to work or using the area for spending and consumption. It is only by exhibiting unsanctioned behaviour – holding a political demonstration, for example, or attempting to sleep rough in the area – that citizens are able to discover the limitations on these seemingly public sites…

Huge variations exist in how clearly land ownership is signposted, as well as in the number of amenities provided by the landowners and the level of security in operation. Many of the newest sites feature similar types of landscaped gardens and water features, free wi-fi and big screens showing summer sport, as well as activities like table tennis, climbing walls and outdoor gyms. Alongside these conveniences, and just as omnipresent, are signs of private surveillance and what experts refer to as 'defensive' architecture – from CCTV cameras to benches specially designed to prevent homeless people from sleeping there.

Key Information: Robert Gottlieb and Simon Ng, "Privatizing the city — in San Francisco and urban China." *San Francisco Chronicle.* 20 June 2017, http://www.sfchronicle.com/opinion/openforum/article/Privatizing-the-city-in-San-Francisco-and-11234510.php:

Are there lessons from China's extraordinary urban transformation and rapid-fire expansion for the Bay Area, and, specifically, for San Francisco? After all, San Francisco has long prided itself as a city of scale, a multiracial, multiethnic urban oasis that is at once tolerant and livable. However, rapid gentrification that has swept neighborhoods has eroded that reputation and extended growing class and racial divides. San Francisco is increasingly becoming privatized, where public spaces are privately operated and where Uber and Lyft rides and Google buses claim the streets.

China's cities, too, are becoming more privatized, where public goods are turned into private acquisitions and what seems old and traditional is being demolished. For example, China has established its own version of gated communities, or "sealed residential quarters." These include huge residential and commercial developments as large as 30 to 50 acres, with populations ranging from 200,000 to 300,000. These resemble more of a "city within a city," with buildings ranging from six to 10 stories. One benefit of this privatized space is exclusive parking with controlled access and a closed perimeter, an enormous premium as roads become congested and parking becomes scarce and contested.

In China, privatization is an outgrowth of a government development philosophy that emphasizes urbanization, marketization and modernization. China's megacities have been created nearly overnight. Onetime fishing village Shenzhen and its surrounding areas have grown from a population of 50,000 to 18 million in just 35 years. At the same time, these megacities have developed enormous class divides, China's version of the tale of two cities…

As a result of this urbanization, the historical character of cities such as Shanghai is being undermined and transformed. Shanghai's famous alleyways are now seen as places that need to be "cleaned" and remade "smooth and quiet" into passageways for cars and for shopping enclaves.

Key Information: Justin Glick, "Privatizing the Streets." *Next City.* 28 December 2009, https://nextcity.org/daily/entry/privatizing-the-streets:

> Some grim news from London: apparently there's a growing trend toward selling developers entire chunks of the city, streets and all, leading to archipelago of private neighborhoods within the city with their own security guards and rules regarding appropriate behavior:
>
> [Privatized streets] raise a challenge to the kind of public life, culture and democracy that has been taken for granted in British cities for the last 150 years. A host of seemingly innocuous activities – skateboarding, rollerblading, even eating in some places – are routinely banned, along with filming and, of course, taking photographs. So is begging, homelessness, selling the Big Issue, handing out political leaflets, and holding political demonstrations. It's a very different and far less democratic idea of the city and citizenship. In place of the diversity of high streets we are creating sterile, high-security enclaves, policed by private security and CCTV. And rather than making us feel safer, the emphasis on security is a reminder of ever-present danger, fuelling fear of crime.

Analysis

Psuedo-public spaces—also known as Pops: privately owned public spaces—complicate governance and territorial control within cities.

Inventories and maps of privately held public spaces are increasingly valuable tools in understanding urban terrain and urban social-spatial relationships (essentially geo-social intelligence). Maps and datasets for urban Pops are now available for London, New York, San Francisco, and Toronto.[2]

Privately owned public spaces (Pops) include small plazas, atriums, arcades, gardens, terraces, and small parks, squares, snippets (micro-parcels) and other indoor and outdoor spaces on private land open for public use through an easement or zoning concession. In some cases, developers were allowed to build taller or denser structures if they provided public access to public space. Over time, some of the property owners reverted to sole private use by denying public access, limiting operating hours or allowing adjacent tenants (like cafés) to usurp the space and violate public use provisions.[3] In San Francisco, they are known as Privately-Owned Public Open Spaces (POPOS), emphasizing outdoor venues.[4]

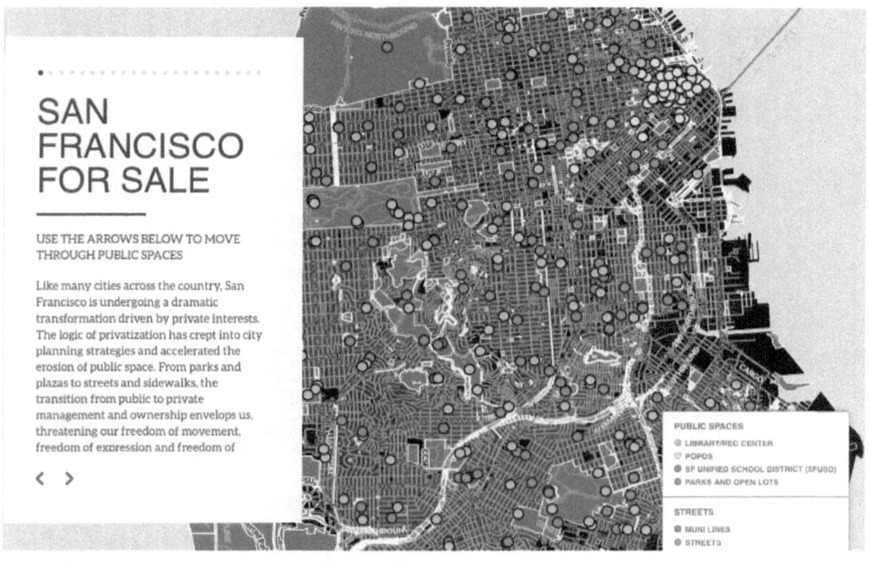

Source: "San Francisco For Sale" Anti-Eviction Mapping Project at http://www.antievictionmappingproject.net/publicspace.html.

In addition to private spaces developed for public use, there is a trend for existing public spaces to be 'adopted' by private corporations or public-private partnerships (P3) essentially privatizing public space. These "sales' of public goods for limited public use or private use have the potential to be abused and deny the public their traditional right to the commons. In New York City, for example, over half (182 of 333) of the Pops were violating their usage requirements agreements with the City.[5] In San Francisco, the diversion of public space to private use has increased civic tensions in as many components of San Francisco's urban spaces (bus stops, parks, plazas, streets, and sidewalks) are limiting public access. These limits threaten freedom of movement, recreation, speech, and expression through increased privatization, policing, and reduction of public spaces.[6] This denial of access to the urban commons is similar to the wealthy denying access to beaches,[7] waterways and rivers such as the Thames.[8]

In London centuries of tradition are being erased as cash-strapped local councils[9] sell off public squares and parks to corporations and foreign landholders. As the *Guardian* has observed:

> "The public spaces of London, the collective assets of the city's citizens, are being sold to corporations – privatised – without explanation or apology. The process has been strategically engineered to seem necessary, benign and even inconsequential, but behind the veil, the simple fact is this: the United Kingdom is in the midst of the largest sell-off of common space since the enclosures of the 17th and 18th century, and London is the epicentre of the fire sale."[10]

The new pseudo-private spaces are creating an opportunity for open, accessible public space in economic hard times, but this potential is often short-changed by exclusion and limitation of the traditional freedom of the commons. In London, the beneficiaries of many of these spaces are sovereign wealth funds and the regulations governing their use are secret or the enforcement arms of the Pops won't share their contents (or don't know of their existence) making these ostensibly public spaces essentially private in nature. Examples of this type of space include:

> "major areas of open land around Paddington Station (encompassing both Merchant Square and Paddington Central), nearly seven acres of open space owned by Arsenal Football Club in Islington, busy shopping and dining plazas in Covent Garden and Victoria, and the pseudo-public area around one of London's most iconic attractions, the London Eye."[11]

Such usurpation of public space often yields conflict. Such conflicts have been long recognized as features of the urban 'power-counterpower' struggle. Urbanist Jane Jacobs identified early manifestations of the contest for urban land use when describing the negative effects of urban renewal and displacing people (often the urban poor) from neighborhoods to build expressways and refined (or gentrified) public spaces.[12] Mike Davis echoed those concerns when he described urban apartheid in Los Angeles' spatial segregation, gated communities, and militarized security of privatized spaces in *City of Quartz*. The culmination of this plutocratic land use paradigm is seen in *Bladerunner*-like scenarios of wealthy enclave outposts like Dubai and the geographically distributed micro-enclaves known as Pops, and their alter ego the competing global slums.[13]

In London, these struggles came to the forefront during the Occupy Protests. The exclusion of the public from Pops also raises concerning about the plutocratic domination of property, especially since "nearly half the country is already owned by 0.06% of the population and furthering that trend is exacerbating social inequality."[14] According to the *Guardian*:

> "In 2011, the consequences of privatising public land came into sharp focus when Occupy protesters were forced out of Paternoster Square by a court order

that revealed that the space was owned by the Mitsubishi Estate Company. It seemed, at the time, too dystopian to be true, that the rules imposed by a corporation could supersede the law of the land.

Soon after, we began hearing about confrontations in other pseudo-public spaces, such as on the land of More London, where City Hall is a public island in a sea of privatised open air space owned by Kuwaiti land barons. It transpires that for the past few decades almost every major redevelopment in London has resulted in the privatisation of public space, including areas around the Olympic Stadium, King's Cross and Nine Elms."[15]

A similar situation occurred when Occupy protesters were evicted from Zuccotti Park, New York City—a highly visible privately owned park that raised First Amendment concerns.[16] Policing privatized spaces (Pops) or mass private property raises a number of concerns including fragmenting provision of public safety services and the distribution of rights and authority among public and private actors with private concerns often outweighing public liberty interests as the promotion of corporate interest outweighs concerns for public justice.[17] Concerns about the outsourcing of accountability and lack of transparency complicate the public-private interaction on these quasi-public spaces.[18] The quest for maintaining public order has resulted in conflicting views over security and access as historically public squares started to restrict access and install ubiquitous CCTV monitoring on private streets and in public places with private security essentially acting in lieu of public police. Among the actions banned in these spaces are begging, homelessness, skateboarding, busking (street music), and a range of typically protected speech: handing out political leaflets, soliciting signatures for petitions, and political demonstrations.[19]

Concerns over privatization and urban land use also complicate the security situation and are evident in São Paulo where squatters have occupied spaces.[20] They have also been voiced in Barcelona where squatters from the *Indignodos* (15-M) movement occupy public spaces to protest economic and social exclusion.[21]

Rising urban crime and instability have led some to consider privatizing public streets so that persons frequenting 'public' gathering spaces can be subject to searches and weapons screening. Such a proposal is currently being considered in Kansas City that seeks to privatize portions of the public streets in the Westport Entertainment District.[22]

Calls to curtail public space and liberties are fuelled by insecurity and fear of street gangs and crime. They also inhibit security by 'over fortifying' public spaces in a manner that restricts legitimate use which itself would help contain crime.[23] This manipulation of the spatial dynamics of the city contributes to "the architecture of dissent" where design and land use influences urban protest, crime, and conflict.[24] This contest is being fueled by two interconnected trends playing out in the global network of cities: criminal insurgency and plutocratic insurgency. These 'Twin Insurgencies" are changing the distribution of power and profit in the licit, illicit, and grey markets.[25] The contest for spatial domination in cities is long standing, ranging from the Classical era through the Middle Ages to today's emerging global network states.[26] Preserving access to public spaces fills an essential role in ensuring access to the political realm—that is, ensuring the physical space and transactions necessary to promote the free flow of ideas in the *Agora*.

Sources

Bradley L. Garrett, "These squares are our squares: be angry about the privatisation of public space." *The Guardian*. 25 July 2017, https://amp.theguardian.com/cities/2017/jul/25/squares-angry-privatisation-public-space.

Justin Glick, "Privatizing the Streets." *Next City*. 28 December 2009, https://nextcity.org/daily/entry/privatizing-the-streets.

Chris Michael, Jack Shenker, Naomi Larsson, Athlyn Cathcart-Keays, Julie Cox, Chloe Smith, Nick Van Mead, and Pablo Gutierrez, "Revealed: the insidious creep of pseudo-public space in London." *The Guardian (Guardian Cities).* 24 July 2017, https://www.theguardian.com/cities/2017/jul/24/revealed-pseudo-public-space-pops-london-investigation-map.

GiGL (Greenspace Information for Greater London CIC), "Privately Owned Public Spaces." 2017, http://www.gigl.org.uk/open-spaces/privately-owned-public-spaces/; Dataset (UK Open Government License, OGL v3) available at *London Datastore,* https://data.london.gov.uk/dataset/privately-owned-public-spaces.

Robert Gottlieb and Simon Ng, "Privatizing the city — in San Francisco and urban China." *San Francisco Chronicle.* 20 June 2017, http://www.sfchronicle.com/opinion/openforum/article/Privatizing-the-city-in-San-Francisco-and-11234510.php.

Notes

All opinions are strictly those of the authors and in no way reflect the viewpoints of any U.S. Governmental, academic, or corporate entity.

1.   http://smallwarsjournal.com/jrnl/art/plutocratic-insurgency-note-no-6-privatizing-urban-public-spaces.
2. An inventory of London's Pops is available at Guardian Cities/GiGL. See "Pseudo-public space: explore the map – and tell us what we're missing." *The Guardian (Guardian Cities).* 24 July 2017, https://www.theguardian.com/cities/2017/jul/24/pseudo-public-space-explore-data-what-missing. For Pops in New York, see "Privately Owned Public Space in New York City," https://apops.mas.org/find-a-pops/. For Toronto, see "Privately-Owned Publicly Accessible Spaces (POPS)," https://www1.toronto.ca/wps/portal/contentonly?vgnextoid=98d4c5181ee5c510VgnVCM10000071d60f89RCRD. San Francisco's POPOS are listed at "Map: POPOS (Privately Owned Public Open Spaces) Of San Francisco." *SFist.* 29 January 2010, http://sfist.com/2010/01/29/map_secret_popos_privately_owned_pu.php and an open data set is found at DATASF, https://data.sfgov.org/Culture-and-Recreation/Privately-Owned-Public-Open-Spaces/65ik-7wqd/data.

3. "How Privatization Impacts Public Spaces and Infrastructure." *WBUR*. Interview with Jerold Kayden. 11 May 2017, http://www.wbur.org/hereandnow/2017/05/11/privately-owned-public-space.

4. "San Francisco's "Hidden" Public Places, Public Art." *Tales Told From the Road*. 10 February 2015, http://talestoldfromtheroad.com/2015/02/10/san-franciscos-hidden-public-places-public-art/.

5. Nathan Tempy, "Report: More Than Half The City's Privately Owned, Allegedly Public Spaces Aren't Playing By The Rules." *Gothamist*. 19 April 2017, http://gothamist.com/2017/04/19/pops_balderdash.php.

6. Marke B., "A map of our vanishing public space." *Anti-Eviction Mapping Project's latest interactive visualization details the attack on SF's fragile common, 48 Hills. 10 July 2015,* http://48hills.org/2015/07/10/map-vanishing-public-space/.

7. The denial of beach access by the wealthy has a long and contested history, especially in California. Despite being against state law, several wealthy land owners persisted in denying access to beaches—often posting no trespassing signs, installing fences, gates, and barriers, and hiring security guards to deny access. The California Coastal Commission has levied large fines (over $5.1 million) against property owners for diverting public easements and denying access in violation of state law. See Dan Weikel, "Two Malibu property owners fined $5.1 million for blocking access to public beach." *Los Angeles Times*. 09 December 2016, http://www.latimes.com/local/lanow/la-me-headlines-coastal-fines-20161208-story.html; and Mary O'Hara, "Get off my beach! How the wealthy are laying claim to California's coast." *The Guardian*. 02 October 2015, https://www.theguardian.com/us-news/2015/oct/02/california-wealthy-public-beaches-private-security.

8. See Jack Shenker, "Privatised London: the Thames Path walk that resembles a prison corridor." *The Guardian (Guardian Cities)*. 24 February 2015, https://www.theguardian.com/cities/2015/feb/24/private-london-exposed-thames-path-riverside-walking-route.

9. Harry Smith, "Public spaces are going private – and our cities will suffer." *The Conversation*. 06 July 2016, http://theconversation.com/public-spaces-are-going-private-and-our-cities-will-suffer-60460.

10. Bradley L. Garrett, "These squares are our squares: be angry about the privatisation of public space." *The Guardian (Guardian Cities)*. 25 July 2017, https://amp.theguardian.com/cities/2017/jul/25/squares-angry-privatisation-public-space.

11. Chris Michael, et al, "Revealed: the insidious creep of pseudo-public space in London," *The Guardian*.

12. Jane Jacobs, *The Death and Life of Great American Cities*. New York: Vintage, 1992.

13. See Mike Davis, *City of Quartz: Excavating the Future in Los Angeles*. London: Verso, 1990; Mike Davis, "Dubai: Sinister Paradise; From the Archives: Does

the road to the future end here?" *Mother Jones.* 14 July 2005, http://www.motherjones.com/environment/2005/07/dubai-sinister-paradise/; and Mike Davis, *Planet of Slums,* London: Verso, 2007.

14. Bradley L. Garrett, "These squares are our squares: be angry about the privatisation of public space." *The Guardian.*

15. Ibid.

16. See Raymond Vasvari, "Occupying the First Amendment." *Slate.* 15 November 2011, http://www.slate.com/articles/news_and_politics/jurisprudence/2011/11/occupy_wall_street_police_raid_what_zuccotti_park_teaches_us_about_public_spaces_and_citizen_protest.html. Similar concerns have been raised by the American Civil Liberties Union. See Sarah Goomar, "The Threat of Privatized-Public Spaces on Free Speech." ACLU Michigan. 29 January 2015, http://www.aclumich.org/article/threat-privatized-public-spaces-free-speech.

17. See Mark Button, "Private security and the policing of quasi-public space." *International Journal of the Sociology of Law.* 31:3, September 2003; 227-237, https://doi.org/10.1016/j.ijsl.2003.09.001; and Steven Hutchinson, "Security Governance on a Mass Private Property in Canada." *Policing and Society*, 15:2, 19 August 2006; 125-144, http://dx.doi.org/10.1080/10439460500071739.

18. Candice Bernd, "The Rise of Privatized Policing: How Crisis Capitalism Created Crisis Cops." *Truthout.* 28 April 2015, http://www.truth-out.org/news/item/30467-the-rise-of-privatized-policing-in-the-us-how-crisis-capitalism-created-crisis-cops.

19. Anna Minton, "These cities within cities are eating up Britain's streets." *The Guardian.* 15 December 2009, https://www.theguardian.com/commentisfree/2009/dec/15/public-space-private-property-companies.

20. Sarah DiLorenzo, "Battle for downtown Sao Paulo pits squatters against mayor." *San Francisco Chronicle.* 12 July 2017, http://www.sfchronicle.com/news/world/article/Battle-for-downtown-Sao-Paulo-pits-squatters-11283078.php.

21. See Charlotte Vorms (Oliver Waine, Trans), "Barcelona: local mobilisation or global desperation?" *Metropolitics.eu.* 08 February 2012, http://www.metropolitiques.eu/Barcelona-local-mobilisation-or.html; and Manuel Castells, *Networks of Outrage and Hope: Social Movements in the Internet Age.* Cambridge: Polity, 2012.

22. See Lynn Horsely, "Privatize Westport streets? Proposal has supporters, detractors." *Kansas City Star.* 02 June 2017, http://www.kansascity.com/news/politics-government/article154151404.html.

23. See, for example, Saskia Sassen, *Territory, Authority, Rights: From Medieval to Global Assemblages.* Princeton: Princeton University Press, 2006.

24. See, for example, Ryan Lee Anderson, "The Effect of Urban Fortification on Public Space." University of Wisconsin-Milwaukee, Theses and Dissertations. Paper 655; Simone Tulumello, *Fear, Space and Urban Planning: A Critical*

Perspective from Southern Europe. Berlin: Springer, 2016; and Jordon Cosby, "In defense of public space: Why planners should protect the right to occupy public space during the Trump Administration." *The Wagner Review Online.* March 2017, http://www.thewagnerreview.org/2017/03/in-defense-of-public-space-why-planners-should-protect-the-right-to-occupy-public-space-during-the-trump-administration/.

25. Jathan Sadowski, "The architecture of dissent." *Al Jazeera America.* 28 December 2014, http://america.aljazeera.com/opinions/2014/12/urban-design-architectureprotests.html#.

26. Nils Gilman, "The Twin Insurgencies: Plutocrats and Criminals Challenge the Westphalian State." Chapter 2 in Hilary Matfess and Michael Miklaucic, Eds., *Beyond Convergence: World Without Order.* Washington, DC: National Defense University Press, 2016; http://cco.ndu.edu/BCWWO/Article/980714/2-the-twin-insurgencies-plutocrats-and-criminals-challenge-the-westphalian-state/.

Additional Reading

Robert J. Bunker and Pamela Ligouri Bunker, "Plutocratic Insurgency Note No. 5: The Techno-Palaces of the Global Elite." *Small Wars Journal.* 12 July 2017, http://smallwarsjournal.com/jrnl/art/plutocratic-insurgency-note-no-5-the-techno-palaces-of-the-global-elite.

Mike Davis, *City of Quartz: Excavating the Future in Los Angeles.* London: Verso, 1990.

Mike Davis and Daniel Bertrand Monk, Eds., *Evil Paradises: Dreamworlds of Neoliberalism.* New York: The New Press, 2008.

Margaret Kohn, *Brave New Neighborhoods: The Privatization of Public Space.* London: Routledge, 2004.

Reading 15

The Continued Progress of the Plutocratic Insurgency

George Thomas

First Published 15 August 2017 at Quintus Curtius: Fortress of the Mind [1]
Reprinted with permission.

This podcast accompanies my <u>most recent article.</u> In it, we explore two additional dimensions of the "plutocratic insurgency": (1) the techno-palaces of the global elite, and (2) the creeping confiscation of public lands by private actors. The end result of these two trends is to accelerate the already destabilizing wealth imbalances in societies across the globe.
Contains a <u>26:50 minute podcast.</u>

Notes

1. <u>https://qcurtius.com/2017/08/15/the-continued-progress-of-the-plutocratic-insurgency-podcast/</u>.

Reading 16

The Plutocratic Insurgency and the LSI

Carlos Fazio (Alma Keshavarz, Trans.)

First Published 31 de Diciembre de 2017 as "La insurgencia plutocrática y la LSI" in La Jornada [1] *(Translation 8 November 2018)*

In 2011, Robert J. Bunker noted that "the plutocratic insurgency (…) involves global elites and lacks the traditional traits of an insurgency; that is, an armed struggle. It is a counterpart to the criminal insurgency concept initially developed by John Sullivan. However, instead of being based on illicit economies and bottom up in nature, it is derived from sovereign free economies and top down in nature."

According to Bunker, a Strategic Studies Institute professor, United States Army War College, "the winners of globalization"—represented by multi-national corporations and the transnational capitalist class—seek to withdraw from the regulatory and fiscal authorities, and—ultimately—the politics of the states (while using their coercive tactics by excellence: the armed forces, police and espionage, as well as the powers of the executive, legislative, and judicial branches to transform and instrumentalize it in their favor).

The mechanisms used for this is to promote an economy beyond the sovereignty of the nation state (extra-sovereign) using foreign tax havens; becoming non-resident citizens in order to avoid paying taxes, and employing a group of lawyers and lobbyists within the states to obtain special privileges and beneficial economic considerations.

At the same time, as Nils Gilman points out, one of the most important global tendencies of previous decades has been the proclivity of the wealthy elites to get entangled in private enclaves. For them, the primary function of society is to serve as a source of cheap, subservient labor; as a resource to be exploited.

On the other hand, gated communities are a more extensive patter of economic enclaves drawn from the nation state and enabled to play according to a set of rules that are fundamentally different from those prevailing in a surrounding territory. By themselves, Gilman adds, these private communities are not equivalent to a plutocratic insurgency; but they emerge where you see the financial and economic elites using such enclaves as a strategic base from which to wage war against public goods.

This is the defining political-economic attribute of a plutocratic insurgency: the attempt by the rich to leave the provisioning of public goods without funds for the purpose of "leaving without teeth" a state that threatens its prerogatives, but use as a policing-security instrument in defense of their interests.

Unlike a kleptocracy, which involves the institutions of the state to plunder the population, a plutocratic insurgency wants to create a state to facilitate widespread dispossession or dispossession (using even hybrid warfare). Although in practice, both modalities can intermingle.

There currently is no sovereign authority capable of dealing with the plutocratic insurgency, the unintended consequence of predatory and criminal capitalism resulting in growing economic inequalities in western states. During the last 11 years, an insurgency was disguised as a war on drugs in Mexico and now in its new phase could legally use the "forces of order" to suppress protests and anti-plutocratic demonstrations.

Within this context, it is convenient to take into account the declarations of Joseph Mark Mobius, a German-American based in Singapore and CEO of Templeton Emerging Markets Group—a division of Franklin Templeton Investment, that largest investment fund in the world for emerging markets, Mexico included—in the sense that "the best time to buy is when there is blood on the streets (…) even if it's your own blood," because typically, when there is war, revolution or political and economic problems, "stocks go down and those who bought them as they bottomed out, make a lot of money."

Another facet of the same phenomenon, Emir Sader said that "the governments on the right, all neoliberals, are dedicated to looking after the rich." It's not enough for them to be rich, they have to be careful not to leave their countries for some tax haven in the Virgin Islands, Panama, Luxembourg, Nevada or Delaware (in the US), or any of the 30 shell companies of Barclays Bank of London.

Mexico is no exception: the interests of local plutocrats must also be taken care of in their old and new hydrocarbon, electric, mining, agroindustry and maquiladora economic enclaves, including those that will soon enter the Exclusive Economic Zones (EEZ) of the south-southwest of the country.

Additionally, the wardens of the plutocracy must also be taken care of. That is what the Homeland Security Law (Law of Internal Security) (LSI) of Enrique Peña Nieto response is, who will go down in history as the intellectual author of an ugly law under pressure by the secretariats of Defense and Navy by some of the administration's civil and military members.

Even though Peña Nieto now intends to use the Supreme Court of the nation as a cover and accomplice to his unconstitutional initiative, it is the historical responsibility of the new punitive paradigm of the state that regulates the state and subordinates the civil authorities to military commanders indefinitely and without the obligation of the latter to render an account to anyone.

Every security decision will institutionally integrate the armed forced in the informative, deliberative and executive process. As the law itself states, the rule of the military will not be to supplant the police, but to solve the internal security problems in military terms.

Seen in this way, the LSI is an extraordinary success from the plutocratic perspective and from investment funds. Expanding the application of war logics as a preponderant instrument of government will lead to a greater perpetration of crimes against humanity. With this, Peña will have closed the tragic cycle of absolutism, state violence, corruption, simulation and impunity imposed by Felipe Calderón since 2006.

Notes

1. http://www.jornada.com.mx/2017/12/31/estados/016a2pol.

Reading 17

Plutocratic Insurgency Note No. 8: Rotten at the Core— Apple Incorporated's Stateless Tax Avoidance Strategies & Subsequent Cash Hoard

Pamela Ligouri Bunker and Robert J. Bunker

First Published 3 January 2018 in Small Wars Journal [1]

> *Apple Inc. is an American multinational technology company headquartered in Cupertino, California that designs, develops, and sells consumer electronics, computer software, and online services.*
>
> —*Wikipedia* [2]

Much like the fictional account of the *Strange Case of Dr. Jekyll and Mr. Hyde*, Apple Incorporated is a beloved 'American' company by day when it sells its innovative and sleek technology products such as iMacs and iPhones to our people and those of other nations and a 'stateless' revenue-maximizing multinational behemoth after hours when it comes time to pay the tax bill. Humble garage start-up origins and intense brand loyalty aside, this free multinational corporation's darker underbelly focuses on profit maximization for its shareholders and executive officers at the expense of sovereign state revenues contributing to the public good of the American citizenry.

Key Information: United States Senate PERMANENT SUBCOMMITTEE ON INVESTIGATIONS, Committee on Homeland Security and Governmental Affairs, "EXHIBITS Hearing On Offshore Profit Shifting and the U.S. Tax Code Part 2 (Apple Inc.) May 21, 2013." https://www.hsgac.senate.gov/download/?id= B2F27D33-856B-4B2A-8B55-D045DC285978:

I. EXECUTIVE SUMMARY

On May 21, 2013, the Permanent Subcommittee on Investigations (PSI) of the U.S. Senate Homeland Security and Government Affairs Committee will hold a hearing that is a continuation of a series of reviews conducted by the Subcommittee on how individual and corporate taxpayers are shifting billions of dollars offshore to avoid U.S. taxes. The hearing will examine how Apple Inc., a U.S. multinational corporation, has used a variety of offshore structures, arrangements, and transactions to shift billions of dollars in profits away from the United States and into Ireland, where Apple has negotiated a special corporate tax rate of less than two percent. One of Apple's more unusual tactics has been to establish and direct substantial funds to offshore entities in Ireland, while claiming they are not tax residents of any jurisdiction. For example, Apple Inc. established an offshore subsidiary, Apple Operations International, which from 2009 to 2012 reported net income of $30 billion, but declined to declare any tax residence, filed no corporate income tax return, and paid no corporate income taxes to any national government for five years. A second Irish affiliate, Apple Sales International, received $74 billion in sales income over four years, but due in part to its alleged status as a non-tax resident, paid taxes on only a tiny fraction of that income.

In addition, the hearing will examine how Apple Inc. transferred the economic rights to its intellectual property through a cost sharing agreement with its own offshore affiliates, and was thereby able to shift tens of billions of dollars offshore to a low tax jurisdiction and avoid U.S. tax. Apple Inc. then utilized U.S. tax loopholes, including the so-called "check-the-box" rules, to avoid U.S. taxes on $44 billion in taxable offshore income over the past four years, or about $10 billion in tax avoidance per year. The hearing will also examine some of the weaknesses and loopholes in certain U.S. tax code provisions, including transfer pricing, Subpart F, and related regulations, that enable multinational corporations to avoid U.S. taxes...

Key Information: Lee Sheppard, "How Does Apple Avoid Taxes?" *Forbes*. 28 May 2013, https://www.forbes.com/sites/leesheppard/2013/05/28/how-does-apple-avoid-taxes/#12c343d720a7:

Apple's brand halo is slipping. Silicon Valley's well-known vanity and contempt for government are amply displayed in Apple's tax figures. Apple, a consumer products company that sells beautifully designed gadgets, pays very little tax anywhere in the world, including the United States.

Apple AAPL +0.01% is playing fast and loose with consumers' affection for its highly discretionary products, especially in Europe. It is ill-advised for any consumer products company not to pay tax where it sells products. Equally important, Apple's tax avoidance is also testing the patience of strapped European governments that are looking for ways to get American multinationals to pay tax.

The Senate Homeland Security Permanent Subcommittee on Investigations laid out Apple's tax planning in a May 20 report. The report concluded that Apple's tax arrangements have nothing to do with its business. Even for a jaded tax lawyer used to hokey schemes to avoid taxation, Apple's arrangements were surprising...

Key Information: Nellie Bowles, "Cupertino's mayor urges Apple to pay more tax: 'Where's the fairness?'" *The Guardian.* 5 May 2016, https://www.theguardian.com/technology/2016/may/05/apple-taxes-cupertino-mayor-infrastructure-plan:

Barry Chang is stuck between Apple on one side not paying for his infrastructure proposal and frustrated citizens on the other who see their roads too crowded.

The last time the mayor of Cupertino walked into Apple—the largest company in his small Californian town and, it so happens, the most valuable company in the world—he hoped to have a meeting to talk about traffic congestion.

Barry Chang barely made it into the lobby when Apple's security team asked him to leave, he said.

"They said 'you cannot come in, you're not invited'. After that I left and have not gone back," said an exasperated Chang, who's been mayor since December 2015 and had approached the computing firm when he was serving on the city council three years ago.

Many people in Cupertino, a 60,000-person town in the heart of Silicon Valley, are beginning to organize around their overburdened city. They claim the region is struggling with aging infrastructure and booming companies whose effective tax rate is often quite low. Frustrated by traffic and noise, some in Cupertino are trying to put a stop to more development, which they argue brings more congestion on the roads, parking and train system. But Chang says limiting new development would damage the regional economy and that the real solution should be higher taxes on the wealthy and companies such as Apple…

Apple is building a new headquarters in Cupertino that some have called the Death Star. Photograph: Handout

Key Information: Tripp Mickle, "Apple's Mountain of Cash Is Set to Top $250 Billion." *The Wall Street Journal.* 1 May 2017, A1, A6, https://www.wsj.com/articles/apples-250-billion-cash-pile-enlivens-hopes-fuels-expectations-1493566748 (Original). Via Dow Jones Newswires: http://www.foxbusiness.com/features/2017/05/01/apples-mountain-cash-is-set-to-top-250-billion-wsj.html:

Apple Inc. is expected to report Tuesday that its stockpile of cash has topped a quarter of a trillion dollars, an unrivaled corporate hoard that is greater than the market value of both Wal-Mart Stores Inc. and Procter & Gamble Co. and exceeds the combined foreign-currency reserves held by the U.K. and Canada combined.

The money, more than 90% of which is stockpiled outside of the U.S., has drawn fresh attention as President Donald Trump has proposed slashing business taxes and a one-time tax holiday on corporate cash brought home. That could ratchet up pressure on the tech giant to make splashy acquisitions or dole out more money to shareholders.

Apple's quarterly results will show the company has doubled its cash pile in just over 4 1/2 years. In the last three months of 2016, it racked up new cash at a rate of about $3.6 million an hour.

As of December, the company had $246.09 billion total cash, cash equivalents, and securities. Apple, like many big American companies, parks most of that cash offshore rather than paying U.S. taxes on its overseas profits...

Key Information: Rita Barrera and Jessica Bustamante, "The Rotten Apple: Tax Avoidance in Ireland." *The International Trade Journal.* 2 August 2017, http://www.tandfonline.com/doi/full/10.1080/08853908.2017.1356250?scroll=top&needAccess=true:

ABSTRACT

The European Commission found that Ireland gave Apple preferential tax treatment which amounted to $14.5 billion in unpaid taxes between 2003 and 2014. Due to Apple's tax havens in Ireland, they have taken advantage of U.S. and Irish tax regulations. However, the issue in controversy is whether there was, in fact, a special deal between Apple and Ireland, and whether the European Commission has the authority to make such claims. To answer this question, we explore the legal and ethical issues of using tax havens and how

Apple's stakeholders are affected by Apple's complex organizational structure…

Tax avoidance has become a major concern for the U.S. Congress due to multinational companies such as Apple, Starbucks, Amazon, and several other firms shifting their profits to offshore subsidiaries, which allows them to violate and abuse U.S. tax laws. The drastic downturn in U.S. tax revenue and an increase in the practice of U.S. corporations investing significant amounts of their earnings in their foreign subsidiaries was a result of tax havens and tax shelters. Numerous studies indicate that global companies are moving their income to tax havens such as Ireland, Bermuda, and the Cayman Islands to pay little or no taxes…

Key Information: "Apple and Google U.S. Treasury Holdings Soar in 2017." *Smaulgld.* 8 August 2017, https://smaulgld.com/apple-google-u-s-treasury-holdings-soar-2017/:

Apple and Alphabet (Google) Boost U.S. Treasury Security Holdings to Nearly $100 billion at June 30, 2017.

Combined Apple and Google US Treasury Security holdings top holdings of Canada, France and Germany.

At the end of the second quarter large U.S. Corporations held growing and substantial amounts of U.S. Treasury Securities…

According to recent SEC filings at the end of the second quarter:

Apple owned $52.6 billion in US Treasuries up 28.3% from $41 billion in the third quarter of 2016.

Apple's holdings were about $20.1 short term U.S. Treasury Notes (2, 3, 5, 7, or ten year maturities) and $31.4 in long term U.S. Treasury Bonds (30 year maturity) with the remainder in Treasury bills.

Alphabet (Google) held $44.8 billion in US Treasury Notes (with maturities of 2, 3, 5, 7, or ten years) up 19.1% from $37.6 billion at the end of 2016…

Key Information: "Paradise Papers: Apple's secret tax bolthole revealed." *BBC News*. 6 November 2017, http://www.bbc.com/news/world-us-canada-41889787:

> The world's most profitable firm has a secretive new structure that would enable it to continue avoiding billions in taxes, the Paradise Papers show.
>
> They reveal how Apple sidestepped a 2013 crackdown on its controversial Irish tax practices by actively shopping around for a tax haven.
>
> It then moved the firm holding most of its untaxed offshore cash, now $252bn, to the Channel Island of Jersey…
>
> Up until 2014, the tech company had been exploiting a loophole in tax laws in the US and the Republic of Ireland known as the "double Irish".
>
> This allowed Apple to funnel all its sales outside of the Americas— currently about 55% of its revenue— through Irish subsidiaries that were effectively stateless for taxation purposes, and so incurred hardly any tax…

Who: Apple Incorporated (Nasdaq, AAPL; Website; https://www.apple.com), a multinational technology company founded in 1976 with ±117,500 employees and headquartered in Cupertino, CA.

What: Complicated corporate tax avoidance strategies devised by top international law firms that focus on exploiting loopholes in national tax codes. By utilizing these tax avoidance strategies, Apple Incorporated has become a 'free corporation,' essentially an extra-sovereign entity nearly immune to U.S. taxes, resulting in its being able to create an ever-growing cash hoard.

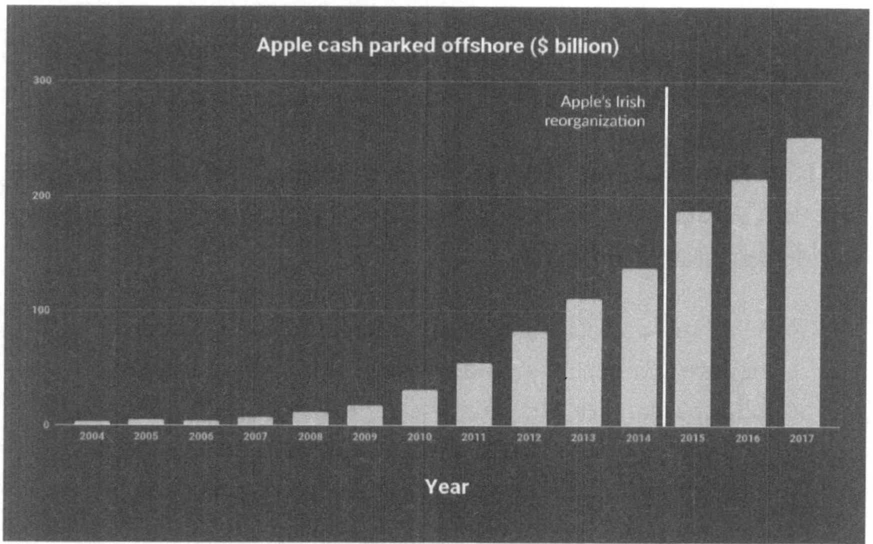

Apple's Offshore Cash Hoard 2004-2017
https://www.icij.org/investigations/paradise-papers/
apples-secret-offshore-island-hop-revealed-by-paradise-papers-leak-icij/

When: These corporate tax avoidance strategies have existed since at least 2003 per the European Commission findings and have been in the public spotlight beginning in the mid-2012 to early-2013 time period.

Where: This is taking place at a global level for Apple Incorporated sales of goods and services and specifically in the United States, the European Union, Ireland, Holland, and Jersey related to taxation and tax avoidance measures.

Why: To maximize profit for Apple shareholders and executive officers—a rational and legal multinational corporate approach just not an ethical one, given the blatant nature of twisting the 'tax rules' and playing sovereign states against each other for profit seeking purposes.

Analysis: In what should be a public relations disaster for Apple, Inc.—engaging in tax avoidance activities at the tens-of-billions of dollars level and then being caught red handed by U.S. and EU investigators and subsequently written up by liberal democratic press—their corporate image remains relatively untarnished. This is partially due to "Silicon Valley's well-known vanity and contempt for government…amply displayed in Apple's tax figures"[3] as well as the fact that other U.S. headquartered multinational corporations—and the elite who are their major shareholders—are engaging in similar tax avoidance schemes as evidenced in the millions of documents leaked in *The Panama Papers* in 2015[4] and *The Paradise Papers* in November 2017.[5]

Apple's tax avoidance strategies, which in the past have centered on creating Irish and Dutch shell companies to exploit U.S. tax regulations[6] and now due to EU pressure have migrated to Jersey (a crown dependency of the United Kingdom and a well-known tax haven with no corporate taxes[7]) for similar purposes, have resulted in its building up an unprecedented amount of cash on hand which includes over $50 billion in U.S Treasuries. The overall amount, as of May 2017, "… has swelled to over $250bn (£194bn), a sum greater than the combined foreign reserves of the British government and Bank of England."[8] This sum is also larger than the cash reserves of the United Kingdom and Canada combined.[9]

A bullet listing of Apple's offshore profits and tax dodging strategy highlighted in a November 2017 Institute on Taxation and Economic Policy (ITEP) fact sheet is as follows:

- Apple has booked $252.3 billion[iv] in profits offshore on which it has not paid a dime in U.S. taxes. It's offshore sum is greater than any other company.[v] This is nearly 10 percent of the total $2.6 trillion in profits that U.S. Fortune 500 companies disclose holding offshore.
- By keeping these profits offshore, Apple is avoiding $78.5 billion in U.S. taxes.[vi]
- A repatriation rate of 12 percent, as proposed by the GOP, would generate at least $51.6 billion in tax savings for Apple.
- Between 2008 and 2015, Apple earned $305 billion before taxes, and paid a foreign tax rate of only 5.8% during this time. [vii]

- Apple was able to achieve this low foreign rate by shifting a large portion of its profits into its three Irish subsidiaries.[viii]
- A Senate investigation in 2013 found that two of Apple's Irish subsidiaries were structured so that, for tax purposes, they weren't "residents" of either Ireland or the U.S., allowing them to pay almost nothing to either country.[ix]
- Last year, European authorities charged Ireland with illegally cutting a special tax deal with Apple that gave the company a tax rate as low as 0.005%, lowering its Irish tax bill by over $14 billion.[x]
- Much of the profits that Apple has assigned to its Irish subsidiaries is actually held in U.S. bank accounts and government bonds, but it can avoid S. taxes on these amounts because for tax purposes, the profits are under "foreign control."[xi][10]

The preceding statistics are rather sobering and show that tens-of-millions dollars invested in assembling a world class team of tax lawyers and accountants, political consultants and lobbyists, and more than a few shady overseas officials for 'strategic tax mitigation purposes' can reap massive benefits for multinational corporations, their executive officers, and well heeled shareholders.

To add insult to such corporate thievery, Apple has recently built a shiny new 2,800,000 sq ft 'spaceship-like' headquarters in Cupertino at an estimated cost of $5 billion[11] which, in essence, has been funded by the American public from lost U.S. Treasury revenues. The square footage of this headquarters is slightly larger than that of the 104-floor One World Trade Center and the 102-floor Empire State Building in New York City, respectively. This monument to plutocratic capitalism, contrasted with Cupertino's underfunded and aging public infrastructure[12], is illustrative of not only the corporation's ongoing hubris but the expectation that it will continue to reap the fruits of its tens-of-billions of dollars stateless tax avoidance strategies well into the foreseeable future, even with the occasional governmental fines and sanctions as a minor cost of engaging in this form of business being thrown into the mix.[13]

Notes

All opinions are strictly those of the authors and in no way reflect the viewpoints of any U.S. Governmental, academic, or corporate entity.

1. http://smallwarsjournal.com/jrnl/art/plutocratic-insurgency-note-no-8-rotten-core-apple-incorporateds-stateless-tax-avoidance.

2. "Apple Inc." *Wikipedia*. 26 November 2017 (Last edited), https://en.wikipedia.org/wiki/Apple_Inc.

3. Lee Sheppard, "How Does Apple Avoid Taxes?" *Forbes*. 28 May 2013, https://www.forbes.com/sites/leesheppard/2013/05/28/how-does-apple-avoid-taxes/#12c343d720a7.

4. "The Panama Papers: Politicians, Criminals and the Rogue Industry that Hides Their Cash." Washington, DC: The International Consortium of Investigative Journalists, 2017, https://panamapapers.icij.org

5. "The Paradise Papers: Secrets of the Global Elite." Washington, DC: The International Consortium of Investigative Journalists, 2017, https://www.icij.org/investigations/paradise-papers/.

6. See "Double Irish With A Dutch Sandwich." *The New York Times*. 28 April 2012, http://www.nytimes.com/interactive/2012/04/28/business/Double-Irish-With-A-Dutch-Sandwich.html.

7. Chris Welch, "Apple chose Jersey as new offshore tax haven after Ireland crackdown." *The Verge*. 6 November 2017, https://www.theverge.com/2017/11/6/16614158/apple-jersey-offshore-tax-shelter-ireland.

8. James Titcomb, "Apple's cash reserves swell to $250bn." *The Telegraph*. 1 May 2017, http://www.telegraph.co.uk/technology/2017/05/01/apples-cash-reserves-swell-250bn/.

9. Joe Mullin, "Apple has a record $250 billion in the bank." *Ars Technica*. 1 May 2017, https://arstechnica.com/gadgets/2017/05/apple-has-a-record-250-billion-in-the-bank/.

10. "Fact Sheet: Apple and Tax Avoidance." Institute on Taxation and Economic Policy (ITEP). November 2017, https://itep.org/wp-content/uploads/applefactsheet1117.pdf.

11. Patrick May, "Apple Park: How many cafes, parking spaces, bicycles …" *The Mercury News*. 21 April 2017, http://www.mercurynews.com/2017/04/21/apple-park-by-the-numbers/.

12. Nellie Bowles, "Cupertino's mayor urges Apple to pay more tax: 'Where's the fairness?'" *The Guardian*. 5 May 2016, https://www.theguardian.com/technology/2016/may/05/apple-taxes-cupertino-mayor-infrastructure-plan.

13. Or, as the Apple CEO has called it, "total political crap." See, Connor Humphries and Alastair Macdonald, "EU ruling on Apple's Irish tax is 'total

political crap': CEO." *Reuters*. 31 August 2016, https://www.reuters.com/article/us-eu-apple-cook/eu-ruling-on-apples-irish-tax-is-total-political-crap-ceo-idUSKCN1173Q2.

Further Reading

Simon Bowers, "Leaked Documents Expose Secret Tale Of Apple's Offshore Island Hop." The International Consortium of Investigative Journalists. 6 November 2017, https://www.icij.org/investigations/paradise-papers/apples-secret-offshore-island-hop-revealed-by-paradise-papers-leak-icij/.

Sean Farrell and Henry McDonald, "Apple ordered to pay €13bn after EU rules Ireland broke state aid laws." *The Guardian*. 30 August 2016, https://www.theguardian.com/business/2016/aug/30/apple-pay-back-taxes-eu-ruling-ireland-state-aid.

Nigar Hashimzade and Yuliya Epifantseva, eds., *The Routledge Companion to Tax Avoidance Research*. Abingdon: Routledge, 2017.

Reading 18

Vanguard of the Plutocratic Insurgency: Apple Inc. Plies Its Trade

George Thomas

First Published 5 January 2018 at Quintus Curtius: Fortress of the Mind [1]
Reprinted with permission.

Previous articles here have described in detail a phenomenon called the "plutocratic insurgency." The term was coined by Robert J. Bunker and Pamela L. Bunker in a series of articles that have appeared in *Small Wars Journal*. I have discussed the Bunkers' conclusions in my own articles here:

The Rise Of The Plutocratic Insurgency

"Dark Globalization": The New Dimensions And Continued Progress Of The Plutocratic Insurgency

Simply stated, the term "plutocratic insurgency" describes a feature of modern Western society whereby the moneyed elites withdraw themselves further and further from the rest of society, aggregating more and more wealth into their own hands, while at the same time dodging any duty or responsibility that comes with being a member of the societies they parasitically exploit. This is not just a matter of wealth concentration. It goes far beyond that. *What we are talking about here is the wholesale pillage of social resources for the sake of a tiny elite that is becoming more and more untouchable with every passing year.* The only way that this trend could be reversed would be through the muscular intervention of a progressive reformer who could attack the plutocrats directly, as Theodore Roosevelt and Franklin Roosevelt did in the twentieth century. But such courageous leadership is not a feature of the current American political landscape.

While many writers have taken note of the incredible income disparities that now characterize most of the Western world, only the Bunkers have drawn the necessary and inescapable conclusions from the data. Their work is extremely important: putting the finger on those responsible for society's ills is the first step in correcting the problem. *They have correctly identified what is going on as a form of insurgency warfare conducted by the moneyed elites against the rest of society. This is economic warfare, pure and simple, and must be understood as such.*

No other writers have made this connection to insurgency warfare; yet if one follows the evidence, there is no way to draw any other conclusion. We are under attack by the elites, and they are slowly but deliberately eroding what little is left of the economic pie to complete their subjugation of the states of the West. If you think this is an exaggeration, I suggest you read the articles identified in the first paragraph above.

In the <u>most recent installment of their "plutocratic insurgency"</u> <u>series</u>, the Bunkers focus on the corrupt practices of Apple Inc., the celebrated technology company. Apple likes to portray itself as a "down home," friendly, local company that is just here to make your life better. The cult of Steve Jobs is peddled as if he were some kind of secular saint. The reality is quite different:

> Apple Incorporated is a beloved 'American' company by day when it sells its innovative and sleek technology products such as iMacs and iPhones to

our people and those of other nations and a 'stateless' revenue-maximizing multinational behemoth after hours when it comes time to pay the tax bill. Humble garage start-up origins and intense brand loyalty aside, this free multinational corporation's darker underbelly focuses on profit maximization for its shareholders and executive officers at the expense of sovereign state revenues contributing to the public good of the American citizenry.

Relentless Tax Avoidance

Apple's tax avoidance games would be shocking to the average American, were they more widely known. But they are not widely known, primarily because no one wants to talk about them. The media colludes with the plutocratic players, since they themselves are playing the same tax-dodging games. Meanwhile, the middle classes are stuck with financial responsibility for funding the US's imperialistic wars abroad:

> One of Apple's more unusual tactics has been to establish and direct substantial funds to offshore entities in Ireland, while claiming they are not tax residents of any jurisdiction. For example, Apple Inc. established an offshore subsidiary, Apple Operations International, which from 2009 to 2012 reported net income of $30 billion, but declined to declare any tax residence, filed no corporate income tax return, and paid no corporate income taxes to any national government for five years. A second Irish affiliate, Apple Sales International, received $74 billion in sales income over four years, but due in part to its alleged status as a non-tax resident, paid taxes on only a tiny fraction of that income.

In addition, the hearing will examine how Apple Inc. transferred the economic rights to its intellectual property through a cost sharing agreement with its own offshore affiliates, and was thereby able to shift tens of billions of dollars offshore to a low tax jurisdiction and avoid U.S. tax. Apple Inc. then utilized U.S. tax loopholes, including the so-called "check-the-box" rules, to avoid U.S. taxes on $44 billion in taxable offshore income over the past four years, or about $10 billion in tax avoidance per year.

Just your average, friendly, down-home technology company, founded by the avuncular, quirky Steve Jobs. Meanwhile, Apple stockpiles cash at a frantic pace. A war-chest is always a good idea in a "democracy" where influence and votes can be purchased by the highest bidder:

> Apple Inc. is expected to report Tuesday that its stockpile of cash has topped a quarter of a trillion dollars, an unrivaled corporate hoard that is greater than the market value of both Wal-Mart Stores Inc. and Procter & Gamble Co. and exceeds the combined foreign-currency reserves held by the U.K. and Canada combined.

> The money, more than 90% of which is stockpiled outside of the U.S., has drawn fresh attention as President Donald Trump has proposed slashing business taxes and a one-time tax holiday on corporate cash brought home. That could ratchet up pressure on the tech giant to make splashy acquisitions or dole out more money to shareholders.

> Apple's quarterly results will show the company has doubled its cash pile in just over 4 1/2 years. In the last three months of 2016, it racked up new cash at a rate of about $3.6 million an hour.

> As of December, the company had $246.09 billion total cash, cash equivalents, and securities. Apple, like many big American companies, parks most of that cash

offshore rather than paying U.S. taxes on its overseas profits...

Becoming An Extra-Sovereign Entity

Having reaped the fruits of its tax avoidance, Apple has launched plans to build a new "corporate headquarters" in Cupertino that some have derisively called the "Death Star." But we would be wrong to think that Apple's stockpile of cash was designed simply to buy influence from favorable political figures. The plutocratic insurgency is way beyond this level of simplicity. The goal now is to become an extra-sovereign entity, to become literally above national governments and institutions, to be unregulated and untouchable. And the US government permits this:

> By utilizing these tax avoidance strategies, Apple Incorporated has become a 'free corporation,' essentially an extra-sovereign entity nearly immune to U.S. taxes, resulting in its being able to create an ever-growing cash hoard...
>
> **Why:** To maximize profit for Apple shareholders and executive officers—a rational and legal multinational corporate approach just not an ethical one, given the blatant nature of twisting the 'tax rules' and playing sovereign states against each other for profit seeking purposes.
>
> **Analysis:** In what should be a public relations disaster for Apple, Inc.—engaging in tax avoidance activities at the tens-of-billions of dollars level and then being caught red-handed by U.S. and EU investigators and subsequently written up by liberal democratic press— their corporate image remains relatively untarnished. This is partially due to "Silicon Valley's well-known vanity and contempt for government...amply displayed in Apple's tax figures" as well as the fact that other U.S.

headquartered multinational corporations—and the elite who are their major shareholders—are engaging in similar tax avoidance schemes as evidenced in the millions of documents leaked in *The Panama Papers* in 2015 and *The Paradise Papers* in November 2017.

Apple's tax avoidance strategies, which in the past have centered on creating Irish and Dutch shell companies to exploit U.S. tax regulations and now due to EU pressure have migrated to Jersey (a crown dependency of the United Kingdom and a well-known tax haven with no corporate taxes) for similar purposes, have resulted in its building up an unprecedented amount of cash on hand which includes over $50 billion in U.S Treasuries...

A bullet listing of Apple's offshore profits and tax dodging strategy highlighted in a November 2017 Institute on Taxation and Economic Policy (ITEP) fact sheet is as follows:

- Apple has booked $252.3 billion in profits offshore on which it has not paid a dime in U.S. taxes. It's offshore sum is greater than any other company. This is nearly 10 percent of the total $2.6 trillion in profits that U.S. Fortune 500 companies disclose holding offshore.
- By keeping these profits offshore, Apple is avoiding $78.5 billion in U.S. taxes.
- A repatriation rate of 12 percent, as proposed by the GOP, would generate at least $51.6 billion in tax savings for Apple.
- Between 2008 and 2015, Apple earned $305 billion before taxes, and paid a foreign tax rate of only 5.8% during this time.

- Apple was able to achieve this low foreign rate by shifting a large portion of its profits into its three Irish subsidiaries.
- A Senate investigation in 2013 found that two of Apple's Irish subsidiaries were structured so that, for tax purposes, they weren't "residents" of either Ireland or the U.S., allowing them to pay almost nothing to either country.
- Last year, European authorities charged Ireland with illegally cutting a special tax deal with Apple that gave the company a tax rate as low as 0.005%, lowering its Irish tax bill by over $14 billion.
- Much of the profits that Apple has assigned to its Irish subsidiaries is actually held in U.S. bank accounts and government bonds, but it can avoid S. taxes on these amounts because for tax purposes, the profits are under "foreign control."

The preceding statistics are rather sobering and show that tens-of-millions dollars invested in assembling a world-class team of tax lawyers and accountants, political consultants and lobbyists, and more than a few shady overseas officials for 'strategic tax mitigation purposes' can reap massive benefits for multinational corporations, their executive officers, and well-heeled shareholders.

To add insult to such corporate thievery, Apple has recently built a shiny new 2,800,000 sq ft 'spaceship-like' headquarters in Cupertino at an estimated cost of $5 billion which, in essence, has been funded by the American public from lost U.S. Treasury revenues. The square footage of this headquarters is slightly larger than that of the 104-floor One World Trade Center and the 102-floor Empire State Building in New York City, respectively. This monument to plutocratic capitalism, contrasted with Cupertino's underfunded and aging public infrastructure, is illustrative of not only the corporation's ongoing hubris but the expectation that it will continue to reap the fruits of its tens-of-billions of dollars stateless tax avoidance strategies well into the foreseeable future, even with the occasional governmental fines and sanctions as a minor cost of engaging in this form of business being thrown into the mix.

The Collusion Of Western "Leaders"

Apple Inc. is not the only multinational corporation engaging in this kind of activity, of course. It is a feature of the modern business climate. The super-rich get away with this kind of looting because the leadership in the US allows them to get away with it. "Leaders" are elected who are nothing more than spokesmen for the plutocratic elites, men whose job is only to read the teleprompter and intone sanctimoniously about their love for freedom and equality, while at the same time engaging in avaricious spoliation of the most venal kind. Meanwhile, a hypnotized, distracted public sits hunched over its iPhones, frantically pressing buttons on the machine that its masters provided them for entertainment.

One way or another—if history is any guide—this picture is going to change in the years ahead. No political or social system can long last if the vast majority of resources are concentrated at the top in the hands of a very few. The effect is profoundly destabilizing. But windows of opportunity for reform do not stay open indefinitely; and the time for taking action is narrowing with each passing year. History shows that either peaceful reform is instituted from the top by enlightened leadership, or a revolutionary redistribution of wealth takes place from the bottom. Which of these outcomes takes places is something each nation must decide for itself.

Notes

1. https://qcurtius.com/2018/01/05/vanguard-of-the-plutocratic-insurgency-apple-inc-plies-its-trade/.

Reading 19

Plutocratic Insurgency Note No. 7: Artificial Intelligence (AI) Pricing Software— Profit Optimization Beyond 'The Invisible Hand'

Robert J. Bunker and Pamela Ligouri Bunker

First Published 7 January 2018 in Small Wars Journal [1]

> *The travel site Orbitz made headlines when it was revealed to have calculated that Apple Mac users were prepared to pay 20-30% more for hotel rooms than users of other brands of computer[s], and to have adjusted its pricing accordingly.*
>
> —*The Guardian* [2]

Artificial intelligence (AI) algorithms built into business applications software is increasingly changing how multinational corporations interface with their customer base. Such 'learning software'—when combined with massive data sets tracking hundreds of individual (i.e. client specific) and group purchasing, life style, and socio-economic variables—allows for corporate profit optimization to take place when goods and services are offered to the consumer by means of 'dynamic' and 'algorithmic' pricing strategies. While such AI derived profit optimization may represent an additional revenue stream to big business shareholders, it also means that the consumer shopping experience is increasingly becoming like that of extended casino gambling—with the house taking small wins hand after hand—rather than a free and fair market exchange between buyers and sellers.

Key Information: Kevin Kelleher, "How Artificial Intelligence Is Quietly Changing How You Shop Online." *Time.* 1 March 2017, http://time.com/4685420/artificial-intelligence-online-shopping-retail-ai/:

> The writer William Gibson once said that the future is here, just not evenly distributed. That was the case with the World Wide Web 20 years ago, when some business models—notably e-commerce and new media—took off faster than others. Now a similar trend is happening with artificial intelligence, or AI.
>
> The promise of AI has seemingly been just on the horizon for years, with little evidence of change in the lives of most consumers. A few years ago, buzzwords like "big data" hinted at the potential, but ending up generating little actual impact. That's now changing, thanks to advancements in AI like deep learning, in which software programs learn to perform sometimes complex tasks without active oversight from humans.
>
> Deep learning algorithms have been powering self-driving cars and making quick progress in tasks like facial recognition. Now these innovations are beginning to find their way into the daily lives of consumers as well…

Key Information: Sam Schechner, "Why Do Gas Station Prices Constantly Change? Blame the Algorithm." *The Wall Street Journal.* 8 May 2017, https://www.wsj.com/articles/why-do-gas-station-prices-constantly-change-blame-the-algorithm-1494262674?mod=e2tw:

ROTTERDAM, the Netherlands—One recent afternoon at a Shell-branded station on the outskirts of this Dutch city, the price of a gallon of unleaded gas started ticking higher, rising more than 3½ cents by closing time. A little later, a competing station 3 miles down the road raised its price about the same amount.

The two stations are among thousands of companies that use artificial-intelligence software to set prices. In doing so, they are testing a fundamental precept of the market economy.

In economics textbooks, open competition between companies selling a similar product, like gasoline, tends to push prices lower. These kinds of algorithms determine the optimal price sometimes dozens of times a day. As they get better at predicting what competitors are charging and what consumers are willing to pay, there are signs they sometimes end up boosting prices together...

Key Information: Tim Adams, "Surge pricing comes to the supermarket." *The Guardian.* 4 June 2017, https://www.theguardian.com/technology/2017/jun/04/surge-pricing-comes-to-the-supermarket-dynamic-personal-data:

Online retailers are increasingly using your personal data to decide how much to charge you. And high-street shops are about to get in on the act...

...The notion of "dynamic pricing" has long been familiar to anyone booking a train ticket, a hotel room or holiday (Expedia might offer thousands of price changes for an overnight stay in a particular location in a single day). We are used to prices fluctuating hour by hour, apparently according to availability. Uber, meanwhile, has introduced—and been criticised for—"surge pricing", making rapid adjustments to the fares on its platform in response to changes in demand. During the recent tube strikes in London, prices for cab journeys 'automatically" leapt 400%. (The company argued that by raising fares it was able to encourage more taxi drivers to take to the streets during busy times, helping the consumer.)

What we are less aware of is the way that both principles have also invaded all aspects of online retailing—and that pricing policies are not only dependent on availability or stock, but also, increasingly, on the data that has been stored and kept about your shopping history. If you are an impulse buyer, or a full-price shopper or a bargain hunter, online retailers are increasingly likely to see you coming. Not only that: there is evidence to suggest that calculations about what you will be prepared to pay for a given product are made from knowledge of your postcode, who your friends are, what your credit rating looks like and any of the thousands of other data points you have left behind as cookie crumbs in your browsing history…

Key Information: Sven Brodmerkel, "Dynamic pricing: Retailers using artificial intelligence to predict top price you'll pay." *ABC.Net.* 26 June 2017, http://www.abc.net.au/news/2017-06-27/dynamic-pricing-retailers-using-artificial-intelligence/8638340:

…Prices already fluctuate online for certain products and services like airline fares, hotel rooms and ride-sharing services like Uber. One day you score a great deal, the next you end up paying a bit more than you wanted.

Most people focus on the positive—the bargain they got. But what if such flexibility and uncertainty was a feature of all your shopping?

Until now, those variations have been dictated by the laws of supply and demand: a price surge algorithm detects a spike in demand and ups the charge—following the fundamental logic of the market.

But new developments in artificial intelligence are radically changing the relationship between retailers and customers.

Besides supply and demand, what's also now becoming important is the maximum price you're willing to pay. And that calculation is made not by you, but by an algorithm…

Who: Thousands of major corporations across business sectors including Amazon, Google, Orbitz Uber, Walmart, Shell, Staples, and Home Depot.

What: The use of artificial intelligence (AI) linked to 'big data' pools of information on individual customer spending behaviors, lifestyle choices, and socio-economic profiles cross-linked to seller and competitor real time product and service pricing as well as to sales and transactions.

When: Increasingly over the last decade with heightened media interest within the last year.

Where: Not only within the United States and Europe but increasingly transnationally across liberal democracies as well as throughout the online global web.

Why: For multinational corporate profit optimization for e-business and brick-and-mortar stores products and services.

Analysis: Thousands of large businesses and multinational corporations are now getting a 'helping hand' from the use of artificial intelligence (AI) algorithms linked to big data pools that draw upon customer tracking software and real time market pricing and sales updates. These algorithms allow for corporations to engage in the additional extraction of anywhere from a few pennies a gallon for gasoline through to hundreds of dollars for large consumer goods or airline flights during each customer transaction, as a component of dynamic and algorithmic pricing strategies that result in hundreds of billions of additional dollars added to their yearly revenue streams.

Artificial intelligence employed as a form of 'subtle e-market strong arming' that squeezes additional profits out of unsuspecting consumers represents a far cry from the spirit of free market capitalism discussed in Adam Smith's 1776 work *The Wealth of Nations*. A 21st century revision of the work would now be more in line with the concept of the wealth of corporations benefiting their plutocratic elite shareholders. In the predatory—extra-sovereign—capitalist economy that is emerging, individual consumers have become 'marks' to be shaken down by transnational corporations for the last pennies in their pockets as part of their initiatives towards profit optimization.

The corporate shakedown process begins with creating individual consumer profiles on not only their past spending habits but also on their lifestyle specifics and socio-economic level as well as arcane data such as the type of computer they use, preferred routes to work, vacation spots, favorite ice cream, and the online movies that they watch. The detailed consumer picture that can now be created far exceeds anything a Stasi analyst would have ever hoped for:

> Facebook has about 100 data points on each of its 2 billion users, generally including the value of your home, your regular outgoings and disposable income— the kind of information that bazaar owners the world over might have once tried to intuit. Some brokerage firms offering data to retailers can provide more than 1,500 such points on an individual.[3]

Once a consumer's 'intelligence file' has been assembled, it resides in the world of online big data which is accessed by corporate AI systems that implement optimization strategies during each and every consumer interaction that takes place. The AI as a learning system— much like the old IBM Deep Blue chess-playing computer but now many magnitudes more powerful and advanced[4]—utilizing predictive analytics determines the appropriate product 'transaction approach,' drawing upon those individual intelligence files as well as the up-to-the-second demand and supply of the specific goods in question for market contextualization purposes.

Hence, the revenue streams generated by commodities—such as all the seats for an airline flight—are now being approached by AI systems as 'games' that can be maximized against a few hundred consumers for every iteration of play over and over again. Rather than open information games such as chess, with known rules and complete game-board awareness provided to both players, corporate and consumer interactions are now looking a lot more like a never ending poker game with the house constantly changing the rules and possessing complete awareness of all the cards held by those playing at their tables. What makes this ongoing game so insidious is that the consumer a) is not a willing participant like a gambler who knowingly places their bets, b) can't walk away from the table like they would in a casino after they have lost their money, and c) doesn't even know that they are in a game in the first place, much less that they have AI systems implementing strategies against them during each and every online transaction that they are involved in to extract as much money as possible from their wallets.

With the outcome of such seller and buyer transactions preordained—humans cannot compete with AI invested with "almost superhuman insight into market dynamics"[5]—another indicator of the eclipse of state-moderated capitalism has taken place. States, especially liberal democratic ones, have a social contract with the governed to protect them from predatory market forces such as multinational (and increasingly stateless) corporations. What is possibly most astounding about this situation is that, while much recent and vocal consternation exists about artificial intelligence someday being deployed on the battlefield, similar capabilities have already been unleashed in the online—and increasingly brick-and-mortar—global marketplaces with little to no protest by the representatives of states or non-governmental organizations.

Notes

All opinions are strictly those of the authors and in no way reflect the viewpoints of any U.S. Governmental, academic, or corporate entity.

1. http://smallwarsjournal.com/jrnl/art/plutocratic-insurgency-note-no-7-artificial-intelligence-ai-pricing-software-profit.
2. Tim Adams, "Surge pricing comes to the supermarket." *The Guardian*. 4 June 2017, https://www.theguardian.com/technology/2017/jun/04/surge-pricing-comes-to-the-supermarket-dynamic-personal-data. For the original article breaking this story see Dana Mattioli, "On Orbitz, Mac Users Steered to Pricier Hotels." *The Wall Street Journal*. 23 August 2012, https://www.wsj.com/articles/SB10001424052702304458604577488822667325882.
3. Tim Adams, "Surge pricing comes to the supermarket." *The Guardian*.
4. AI pricing optimization services include *Perfect Price* (https://www.perfectprice.com) and *Blue Yonder* (https://www.nanalyze.com/2017/04/blue-yonder-ai-optimize-inventory/). For more information on AI in commerce with eleven categories defined, see "Beyond Chatbots: 40+ Commerce Startups Using AI To Style Shoppers, Adjust Pricing, Track Behavior, And More." *CB Insights*. 16 June 2017, https://www.cbinsights.com/research/ai-retail-smart-shop-startups/.
5. Sam Schechner, "Why Do Gas Station Prices Constantly Change? Blame the Algorithm." *The Wall Street Journal*. 8 May 2017, https://www.wsj.com/articles/why-do-gas-station-prices-constantly-change-blame-the-algorithm-1494262674?mod=e2tw.

Further Reading

Danny Asling, "19 Powerful Ways To Use Artificial Intelligence In Ecommerce." *Linnworks Blog*. 11 April 2017, http://blog.linnworks.com/artificial-intelligence-in-ecommerce.

Robert L. Phillips, *Pricing and Revenue Optimization*. Stanford: Stanford University Press, 2005.

David Simchi-Levi, "The New Frontier of Price Optimization." *MIT Sloan Management Review*. Fall 2017. 7 September 2017, https://sloanreview.mit.edu/article/the-new-frontier-of-price-optimization/.

Reading 20

How the Plutocratic Insurgency Targets You Personally: The Use of AI for Targeted Shakedowns

George Thomas

First Published 7 January 2018 at Quintus Curtius: Fortress of the Mind [1]
Reprinted with permission.

In our <u>discussions on the "plutocratic insurgency" here</u>, we have focused on the malfeasance and corrupt practices of the moneyed elites, their political lackeys, and a few of the major corporations. Some people, reading these pages, may be tempted to think, "Well, so what? It doesn't affect me personally! What do I care!" *But the insurgency does, in fact, affect all of us on an individual basis.* When your society is being attacked, you come into the cross-hairs. It makes no difference whether the attack is prolonged or sudden; it is an attack nonetheless.

You will recall that we have taken special care to <u>highlight the term "insurgency" in this discussion</u>. By insurgency we mean just that: the moneyed elites are waging economic warfare against the host societies in which they operate, to an extent that threatens the very foundations of civilized life. This is not your grand-daddy's war: there is no "front line," no identifiable leaders, and no cease-fire negotiations. But it is a war nonetheless. *It is a war that is taking place in the shadows, out of sight, and it is going on with the connivance and encouragement of the highest levels of national "leadership." It is a conspiratorial war, one that is being waged without quarter against all of us.* Its boundaries are debt slavery, the plundering of national resources for the benefit of the few, the creeping theft of public spaces, and the slowly narrowing boundaries of personal freedoms.

In the latest installment of their vitally-important series of articles in the *Small Wars Journal*, Dr. Robert Bunker and Pamela Bunker explain a disturbing new dimension of the insurgency: the use of artificial intelligence (AI) algorithms to extract the maximum resources possible from unsuspecting citizens. The <u>full story can be found here</u>.

Have you noticed how nearly every company now wants personal information about you? Have you noticed how they love to badger you with surveys, questionnaires, and similar intrusive requests? This is all being done for a reason. And the reason is for their benefit, not yours. The Bunkers <u>explain it in greater detail here:</u>

> Artificial intelligence (AI) algorithms built into business applications software is increasingly changing how multinational corporations interface with their customer base. Such 'learning software'—when combined with massive data sets tracking hundreds of individual (i.e. client specific) and group purchasing, life style, and socio-economic variables—allows for corporate profit optimization to take place when goods and services are offered to the consumer by means of 'dynamic' and 'algorithmic' pricing strategies. While such AI derived profit optimization may represent an additional revenue stream to big business shareholders, it also means that the consumer shopping experience is increasingly becoming like that of extended casino gambling—with the house taking small wins hand after

hand—rather than a free and fair market exchange between buyers and sellers.

Need more specific information? According to a June 7, 2017 article in the publication *The Guardian*, "The travel site Orbitz made headlines when it was revealed to have calculated that Apple Mac users were prepared to pay 20-30% more for hotel rooms than users of other brands of computer[s], and to have adjusted its pricing accordingly."

Here is the entire breakdown, which I can do no better than to quote in full from the Bunkers' article. It is worth reading very carefully:

Who: Thousands of major corporations across business sectors including Amazon, Google, Orbitz Uber, Walmart, Shell, Staples, and Home Depot.

What: The use of artificial intelligence (AI) linked to 'big data' pools of information on individual customer spending behaviors, lifestyle choices, and socio-economic profiles cross-linked to seller and competitor real time product and service pricing as well as to sales and transactions.

When: Increasingly over the last decade with heightened media interest within the last year.

Where: Not only within the United States and Europe but increasingly transnationally across liberal democracies as well as throughout the online global web.

Why: For multinational corporate profit optimization for e-business and brick-and-mortar stores products and services.

Analysis: Thousands of large businesses and multinational corporations are now getting a 'helping hand' from the use of artificial intelligence (AI) algorithms linked to big data pools that draw upon customer tracking software and real time market pricing and sales updates. These algorithms allow for corporations to engage in the additional extraction of anywhere from a few pennies a gallon for gasoline through to hundreds of dollars for large consumer goods or airline flights during each customer transaction, as a component of dynamic and algorithmic pricing strategies that result in hundreds of billions of additional dollars added to their yearly revenue streams.

Artificial intelligence employed as a form of 'subtle e-market strong arming' that squeezes additional profits out of unsuspecting consumers represents a far cry from the spirit of free market capitalism discussed in Adam Smith's 1776 work *The Wealth of Nations*. A 21st century revision of the work would now be more in line with the concept of the wealth of corporations benefiting their plutocratic elite shareholders. In the predatory—extra-sovereign—capitalist economy that is emerging, individual consumers have become 'marks' to be shaken down by transnational corporations for the last pennies in their pockets as part of their initiatives towards profit optimization.

The corporate shakedown process begins with creating individual consumer profiles on not only their past spending habits but also on their lifestyle specifics and socio-economic level as well as arcane data such as the type of computer they use, preferred routes to work, vacation spots, favorite ice cream, and the online movies that they watch. The detailed consumer picture that can now be created far exceeds anything a Stasi analyst would have ever hoped for:

Facebook has about 100 data points on each of its 2 billion users, generally including the value of your home, your regular outgoings and disposable income—the kind of information that bazaar owners the world over might have once tried to intuit. Some brokerage firms offering data to retailers can provide more than 1,500 such points on an individual.

Once a consumer's 'intelligence file' has been assembled, it resides in the world of online big data which is accessed by corporate AI systems that implement optimization strategies during each and every consumer interaction that takes place. The AI as a learning system—much like the old IBM Deep Blue chess-playing computer but now many magnitudes more powerful and advanced—utilizing predictive analytics determines the appropriate product 'transaction approach,' drawing upon those individual intelligence files as well as the up-to-the-second demand and supply of the specific goods in question for market contextualization purposes.

Hence, the revenue streams generated by commodities—such as all the seats for an airline flight—are now being approached by AI systems as 'games' that can be maximized against a few hundred consumers for every iteration of play over and over again. Rather than open information games such as chess, with known rules and complete game-board awareness provided to both players, corporate and consumer interactions are now looking a lot more like a never ending poker game with the house constantly changing the rules and possessing complete awareness of all the cards held by those playing at their tables. What makes this ongoing game so insidious is that the consumer a) is not a willing participant like a gambler who knowingly places their bets, b) can't walk away from the table like they would in a casino after they have lost their money, and c) doesn't even know that they are in a game in the first place, much less that they have AI systems implementing strategies against them during each and every online transaction that they are involved in to extract as much money as possible from their wallets.

With the outcome of such seller and buyer transactions preordained—humans cannot compete with AI invested with "almost superhuman insight into market dynamics"—another indicator of the eclipse of state-moderated capitalism has taken place. States, especially liberal democratic ones, have a social contract with the governed to protect them from predatory market forces such as multinational (and increasingly stateless) corporations. What is possibly most astounding about this situation is that, while much recent and vocal consternation exists about artificial intelligence someday being deployed on the battlefield, similar capabilities have already been unleashed in the online—and increasingly brick-and-mortar—global marketplaces with little to no protest by the representatives of states or non-governmental organizations.

As we have said before, awareness is the first step in self-protection. All of us need to be aware of what is going on right under our noses, and not be distracted by the demagoguery and charlatanry of our "political leaders." These people care little or nothing about the people they were appointed to serve, so the burden is on us not to participate in immoral or corrupt practices of these business entities. Understand what is going on, and do not allow yourself to be distracted by fake enemies or emotional nonsense. The great challenge of this century will be the development of an appropriate counter-insurgency strategy.

Notes

1. https://qcurtius.com/2018/01/07/how-the-plutocratic-insurgency-targets-you-personally-the-use-of-ai-for-targeted-shakedowns/.

Reading 21

Plutocratic Insurgency Note No. 7: Artificial Intelligence (AI) Pricing Software— Profit Optimization Beyond 'The Invisible Hand' (Critique)

Naimisha Forest

First Published 9 January 2018 at Naimisha Forest Blog [1]
Reprinted with permission.

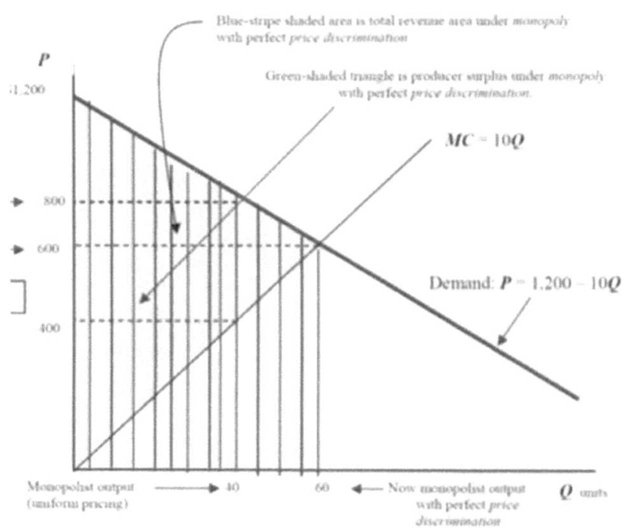

There is an enjoyably agitated article in the online 'Small Wars Journal,' with the title <u>"Plutocratic Insurgency Note No. 7: Artificial Intelligence (AI) Pricing Software - Profit Optimization Beyond 'the Invisible Hand."'</u> The subject is the growing ability of corporations to squeeze more profit out of online customers, by using 'big data' to charge different people different prices for the same product, according to their ability to pay.

"Thousands of large businesses and multinational corporations are now getting a 'helping hand' from the use of artificial intelligence (AI) algorithms linked to big data pools that draw upon customer tracking software and real time market pricing and sales updates. These algorithms allow for corporations to engage in the additional extraction of anywhere from a few pennies a gallon for gasoline through to hundreds of dollars for large consumer goods or airline flights during each customer transaction..."

"Artificial intelligence employed as a form of 'subtle e-market strong arming' that squeezes additional profits out of unsuspecting consumers represents a far cry from the spirit of free market capitalism discussed in Adam Smith's 1776 work *The Wealth of Nations*. A 21st century revision of the work would now be more in line with the concept of the wealth of corporations benefiting their plutocratic elite shareholders. In the predatory—extra-sovereign—capitalist economy that is emerging, individual consumers have become 'marks' to be shaken down by transnational corporations for the last pennies in their pockets as part of their initiatives towards profit optimization."

Perfect price discrimination

Although the authors do not use the term, the monopolistic behavior they describe is well known to economists as 'perfect' or '<u>first-degree price discrimination.</u>' In the model of a competitive market, firms charge a single price. Many customers enjoy a consumer surplus, because, at that price, they pay less than what they would have been willing. A perfectly price discriminating monopolist, on the other hand, knows enough about each customer to charge them a different price, according to their maximum willingness to pay. In theory, the level of output will be the same as in a competitive market, but the distributional outcome is different: the monopolist drains off the consumer surplus. Shareholders, managers and other 'stakeholders' in the monopoly gain at the expense of consumers.

Hal Varian's 'Intermediate Microeconomics' textbook is reassuring that perfect price discrimination is an idealized concept, with few real-life examples. But Professor Varian, who is the chief economist at Google, oddly omits to mention that the growth of internet e-commerce multiplies the opportunities for perfect price discrimination.

Adam Ozimek at Bloomberg notes: "The more information we have, the more profitable first degree price discrimination will be. As big data and online buying increases the information that business have on us, the ease and profitability of first degree price discrimination will become difficult to resist."

Felix Salmon at Reuters says that: "the obvious place for this kind of price discrimination is newspaper paywalls. The FT [Financial Times] already does it: there's no real list price for an FT subscription, and the paper basically just charges whatever it thinks it can get away with, given what it knows about you…. And here's the thing: newspapers know a *lot* about their readers—and especially the regular readers who come back often enough to hit paywalls. To take a simple example, they know if those readers are looking at local sports reports, or whether they're looking at general entertainment news. The former group will be much more willing to pay than the latter. But they're also quite likely to know a lot more about you than that, including—if you're someone who's ever had a print subscription—exactly where you live." Grrrr! *I* subscribe to the FT. I'm annoyed I probably got suckered.

Here's a 2015 paper on Measuring price discrimination and steering on e-commerce websites: "we use the accounts and cookies of over 300 real-world users to detect price steering and discrimination on 16 popular e-commerce sites. We find evidence for some form of personalization on nine of these e-commerce sites. Third, we investigate the effect of user behaviors on personalization. We create fake accounts to simulate different user features including web browser/OS choice, owning an account, and history of purchased or viewed products. Overall, we find numerous instances of price steering and discrimination on a variety of top e-commerce sites."

Here's an 'Econsultancy' piece with some thoughts on how you might try to combat online price discrimination. Try clearing your cookies and browsing data or swapping browsers and computers. But I have a hapless feeling these Mickey Mouse defenses will probably be as nothing before the sophisticated algorithms of the internet moguls.

Antitrust?

So what about antitrust regulation by the government? There's a good 2017 paper by Ramsi Woodcock arguing for just this: "Price discrimination as a violation of the Sherman Act." To show that online perfect price discrimination violates U.S. antitrust law, you'd need to show, first, that it harms consumers—which seems easy enough—and, second, that the company is a dominant firm which is acting to exclude competitors from its market.

Here's where things get interesting. For a perfect price discriminator its most effective competitors would be some of its own customers. Suppose that less wealthy readers get low price subscriptions to the FT, and can turn around and sell those subscriptions on an online secondary market. Any price discrimination scheme would collapse.

To stop such arbitrage, online price discriminators have to stop customers from reselling the product, for example by writing a promise into the contract of sale— and that would be exclusionary conduct, coming under the ambit of the antitrust laws.

Here's what you read on the FT's *'Terms and Conditions'* web page, for example: "Each registration is for a single user only. On registration, you will choose a user name smd password ("ID")... You are not allowed to share your ID or give access to FT Content through your ID to anyone else... You may not create additional registration or subscription accounts for the benefit of others or with the aim of avoiding our use of IDs to control access to and use of FT.com."

Ramsi Woodcock discusses several remedies, such as enforcing freedom to resell the product, but concludes that the best remedy would be a uniform pricing rule: the firm can choose any price it likes, but it must be one price for all customers.

We'll have to see if the putatively populist Trumpians get any tougher on anti-competitive conduct than the Obama administration. But here's a 2015 report by the Obama White House on "Big Data and Differential Pricing" that is remarkable for its generally sunny lack of concern over these phenomena, and emphasis that existing consumer protection laws will be quite enough to handle any future difficulties. The term 'antitrust' is used not once! No worries there for our good friends in Silicon Valley.

Notes

1. https://naimisha_forest.silvrback.com/plutocratic-insurgency-note-no-7-profit-optimization-beyond-the-invisible-hand.

Reading 22

Plutocratic Insurgency Note No. 9: Tax Cuts and Jobs Act— Class Warfare 'Red Line' Crossed

Robert J. Bunker, Nils Gilman, John P. Sullivan
and Pamela Ligouri Bunker

First Published 11 January 2018 in Small Wars Journal [1]

> *"There's class warfare, all right,"* Mr. Buffett said, *"but it's my class, the rich class, that's making war, and we're winning."*
>
> Warren Buffett, November 2006[2]

> *"Actually, there's been class warfare going on for the last 20 years, and my class has won. We're the ones that have gotten our tax rates reduced dramatically."*
>
> Warren Buffett, September 2011[3]

The prophetic words of Warren Buffett—of Berkshire Hathaway fame and one of the richest persons in the United States—resound like a 'double-tap' to the skull of the American middle class after the recent *Tax Cuts and Jobs Act* has now passed in the US Senate.[4] The social contract between the governed and the government, which is derived from the consent of the people and conveys legitimacy to our political system, is becoming increasingly imperiled. Not only in this Bill have the taxes of the rich once again been reduced but to offset this plutocratic economic boon the taxes of the middle class have been brazenly raised to subsidize it:

> By 2027, people making $40,000 to $50,000 would pay a combined $5.3 billion more in taxes, while the group earning $1 million or more would get a $5.8 billion cut, according to the <u>Joint Committee on Taxation and the Congressional Budget Office.</u>[5]

The vast majority of the US populace—the proverbial 99%—just witnessed the blatant crossing of a *class warfare* 'red line' to the benefit of the American plutocracy—that other 1% (or .01% depending on your metrics) which increasingly holds most of the wealth in our society. The 'pluto-populist' political rhetoric concerning how this tax plan really benefits the other 99% of US citizens ranks as one of Western history's worst class relations marketing campaigns—possibly only surpassed by the *Ancien Régime's* disastrous cake-making tips series offered up to late 18th century French peasants.

Key Information: Katrina vanden Heuvel, "Republican tax bills would be paradise for plutocrats." *Washington Post.* 14 November 2017, <u>https://www.washingtonpost.com/opinions/republican-tax-bills-would...f9f8-c8e7-11e7-b0cf-7689a9f2d84e_story.html?utm_term=.70bd42e8c122</u>:

> The Paradise Papers—the trove of 13.4 million documents leaked largely from the files of Appleby, a Bermuda-based law firm—detail the many ways the biggest corporations and richest individuals use tax havens to avoid taxes, obscure ownership and hide financial transactions. Reporters have only just begun to comb through the documents, but two things are

already clear: First, Leona Helmsley was right when she famously said, "Only the little people pay taxes." Second, the Republican tax bills are built around a very big and shameless lie.

The revelations show once again that the very wealthy of many countries—particularly the United States—and the largest global corporations don't pay taxes like the rest of us. They use sophisticated law firms and accountants to set up shell companies, private trusts and other dodges to avoid high taxes. Millionaires and billionaires of all ideological stripes—reactionaries like the Koch brothers and Robert Mercer, major Republican donors like Steve Wynn and Sheldon Adelson, liberal donors like George Soros and Penny Pritzker, Trump officials like Secretary of State Rex Tillerson and economic adviser Gary Cohn, Russian oligarchs like Leonid Mikhelson, celebrities like Bono and Madonna and even Queen Elizabeth II—use offshore companies, obscure ownership arrangements and elaborate trusts to avoid taxes. Global companies like Apple, Nike, Citibank, JPMorgan Chase and Uber avoid literally billions in taxes...

Key Information: Derek Thompson, "Why the GOP Tax Bill Is So Unpopular." *The Atlantic.* 25 November 2017, https://www.theatlantic.com/business/archive/2017/11/gop-tax-bill-unpopular/546668/:

President Donald Trump says he doesn't want to cut taxes on the rich. His Treasury Secretary Steven Mnuchin said he doesn't want to cut taxes on the rich. The Democratic Party says they don't want to cut taxes on the rich. Americans say they don't want to cut taxes on the rich.

The House and Senate Republican tax bills are taking a different approach: They are cutting taxes on the rich—significantly. Their plans would slash the corporate tax rate by almost half, cut taxes on pass-through income for smaller businesses, eliminate the Alternate Minimum Tax, and erode the estate tax, all of which disproportionately help rich families. This comes at a time when post-tax corporate profits as a share of GDP have hovered at a record-high level for the last seven years, and the top 1 percent's share of total income is higher than any time in the second half of the 20th century…

Key Information: Heather Long, "As tax bill evolved, benefits for corporations and the wealthy grew." *Standard-Examiner.* 1 December 2017, http://www.standard.net/Business/2017/12/02/As-tax-bill-evolved-benefits-for-corporations-and-the-wealthy-grew-1:

When Senate Republicans introduced their tax bill in mid-November, they faced competing interests: Some senators thought it wasn't generous enough for working-class families. Others thought it didn't deliver enough to business owners.

By late Friday evening, as the Senate headed toward a vote on the bill, it had undergone a series of transformations. The bill had fewer benefits for working-class families than the original version. And it had new benefits for business owners.

The disparate treatment underlined how the legislation—a massive rewrite of the individual and corporate tax code—has evolved since its first incarnation: What began as an effort that would favor the wealthy and corporations became, in many ways, even more tilted in their favor as the legislation.

When lawmakers needed a way to limit the legislation's impact on the deficit to make it comply with Senate rules, they made the bill's tax cuts affecting individuals temporary—ending in 2025—while leaving in place ones that benefit corporations. The move would lead to a tax hike on many Americans in the middle of the next decade…

Key Information: Martin Wolf, "A Republican tax plan built for plutocrats." *Financial Times*. 2 December 2017, https://www.ft.com/content/e494f47e-ce1a-11e7-9dbb-291a884dd8c6:

How does a political party dedicated to the material interests of the top 0.1 per cent of the income distribution win and hold power in a universal suffrage democracy? That is the challenge confronting the Republican party. The answer it has found is "pluto-populism". This is a politically successful, but dangerous, strategy. It has brought Donald Trump to the presidency. His failure might bring someone more dangerous, more determined, to power. This matters to the US and, given its power, to the wider world.

The tax bills going through Congress demonstrate the party's primary objectives. According to the Center on Budget and Policy Priorities, in the House version of the bill, about 45 per cent of the tax reductions in 2027 would go to households with incomes above $500,000 (fewer than 1 per cent of filers) and 38 per cent to households with incomes over $1m (about 0.3 per cent of filers). In the more cautious Senate version, households with incomes below $75,000 would be worse off. This simply is reform for plutocrats…

Key Information: The Editorial Board, "A Historic Tax Heist." *New York Times*. 2 December 2017, https://www.nytimes.com/2017/12/02/opinion/editorials/a-historic-tax-heist.html:

With barely a vote to spare early Saturday morning, the Senate passed a tax bill confirming that the Republican leaders' primary goal is to enrich the country's elite at the expense of everybody else, including future generations who will end up bearing the cost. The approval of this looting of the public purse by corporations and the wealthy makes it a near certainty that President Trump will sign this or a similar bill into law in the coming days.

The bill is expected to add more than $1.4 trillion to the federal deficit over the next decade, a debt that will be paid by the poor and middle class in future tax increases and spending cuts to Medicare, Social Security and other government programs. Its modest tax cuts for the middle class disappear after eight years. And up to 13 million people stand to lose their health insurance because the bill makes a big change to the Affordable Care Act.

Yet Republicans somehow found a way to give a giant and permanent tax cut to corporations like Apple, General Electric and Goldman Sachs, saving those businesses tens of billions of dollars…

Key Information: David Weigel, Robert Costa and Paul Kane, "'This is class warfare': Tax vote sparks political brawl over populism that will carry into 2018 elections." *Washington Post.* 2 December 2017, https://www.washingtonpost.com/powerpost/this-is-class-warfare-tax-vote-sparks-political-brawl-over-populism-that-will-carry-into-2018-elections/2017/12/02/c8e2ccdc-d762-11e7-b62d-d9345ced896d_story.html?utm_term=.d19a7413bae4:

DAYTON, Ohio—The Senate Republicans' chaotic late-night vote Friday to overhaul the tax system widened the country's partisan divisions Saturday—sparking a political grudge match that lawmakers vowed to carry into next year's midterm elections. Democrats, united in their opposition, attacked the legislation as a "scam" passed to benefit wealthy donors and corporations.

Republicans, promising years of wage and job growth once the bill becomes law, acknowledged that they face a difficult task convincing voters to have faith in a measure that received support from the GOP alone…

Several at-risk Democrats, including Sen. Jon Tester (Mont.), recorded viral videos to dramatize how late the bill had been printed, and how some revisions had been written in hard-to-read pen scratches.

"Take a look at this, folks. This is your government at work," Tester said, slamming his fist on the bill. "It's going to shift money from middle-class families to the rich, and we were given it 20 minutes ago"…

Key Information: John Cassidy, "The Passage of the Senate Republican Bill was a Travesty." *The New Yorker*. 2 December 2017, https://www.newyorker.com/sections/news/the-passage-of-the-senate-republican-tax-bill-was-a-travesty:

When historians write about the broader atrophy of the American system of governance, the passage of the 2017 tax-reform bill will be an illuminating event to dwell upon. Whatever the Founding Fathers had in mind, it surely can't have resembled the unedifying spectacle that played out in the Senate this week. When the delayed vote on the Senate version of the G.O.P's Tax Cuts and Jobs Act finally took place, in the early hours of Saturday morning, the sole Republican to dissent was Senator Bob Corker, of Tennessee…

The last-minute haggling and rewriting resulted in a bill even more skewed toward the rich. To buy the votes of Senators Steve Daines, of Montana, and Ron

Johnson, of Wisconsin, the G.O.P. leadership agreed to further sweeten the pot for owners of unincorporated businesses who declare their profits as "pass through" income on their personal tax returns. Although Daines and Johnson claimed that they were trying to help owners of small businesses, the fact is that the richest one per cent of households receive more than half of all the pass- through income the economy generates. Donald Trump, who owns dozens of pass-through ventures, is a member of this group, and as a result of the bill he could see his marginal tax rate reduced from 39.6 per cent to below thirty per cent.

As tax experts raced through the final text, they discovered other giveaways to the one per cent—indeed, to the 0.001 per cent. They included the retention of the infamous carried-interest deduction, which allows hedge-fund managers and private-equity tycoons to pay a lower tax rate on their profits than the one many middle-class families face...

Who: Components of the US Congress and Senate—essentially, these in the Republican party—emphasizing a free and unregulated market economy, big business, and multinational corporate profits—which are in line with *de facto* plutocratic economic interests.

What: Fiscal Year 2018 <u>*H.R.1 - Tax Cuts and Jobs Act*</u> amendments and repeals to the 1986 Internal Revenue Code. Last minute additions to the Bill were hand written on it and virtually illegible. Further, almost no time was provided for those voting on the Bill to actually read it with the vote passing as a political *fait accompli*—albeit by the slimmest Senate margin possible.

257

1   (b) EFFECTIVE DATE.—The amendment made by

2 this section shall apply to taxable years beginning after

3 December 31, 2017.

4 **SEC. 13543. MODIFICATION OF TREATMENT OF S CORPORA-**

5   **TION CONVERSIONS TO C CORPORATIONS.**

6   (a) IN GENERAL.—Section 1371 is amended by add-

7 ing at the end the following new subsection:

8   "(f) CASH DISTRIBUTIONS FOLLOWING POST-TERMI-

9 NATION TRANSITION PERIOD.—

10   "(1) IN GENERAL.—In the case of a distribu-

11 tion of money by an eligible terminated S corpora-

12 tion after the post-termination transition period, the

13 accumulated adjustments account shall be allocated

14 to such distribution, and the distribution shall be

15 chargeable to accumulated earnings and profits, in

16 the same ratio as the amount of such accumulated

17 adjustments account bears to the amount of such ac-

18 cumulated earnings and profits.

19   "(2) ELIGIBLE TERMINATED S CORPORA-

20 TION.—For purposes of this subsection, the term 'el-

21 igible terminated S corporation' means any C cor-

22 poration—

23   "(A) which—

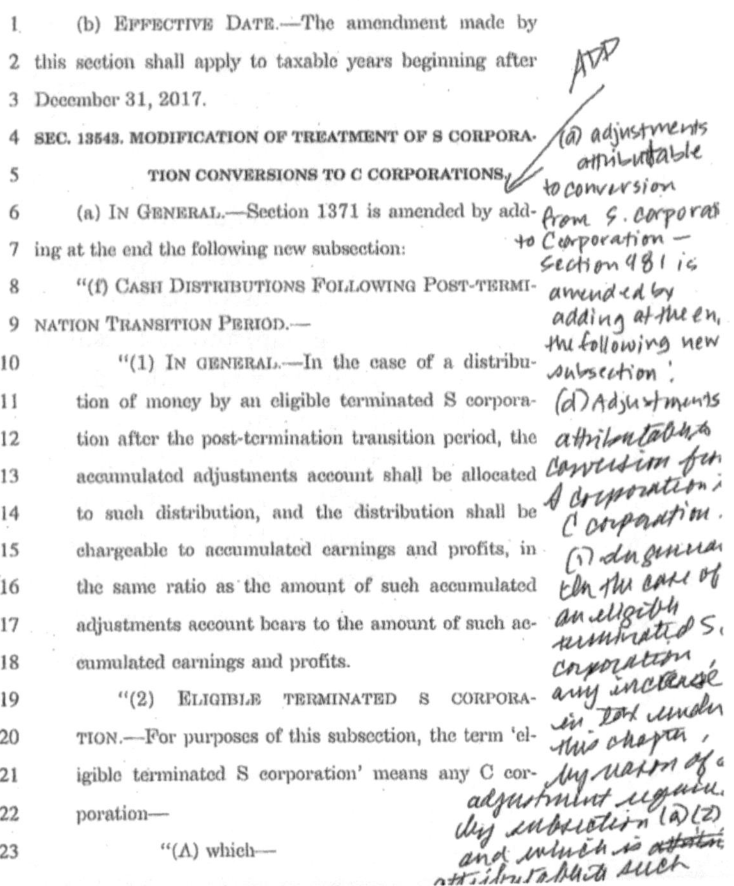

Tax Cuts and Jobs Act

"The final text of the Tax Cuts and Jobs Act was delivered to Democrats on Friday just hours before an expected final vote on the bill. But Democratic lawmakers said it was nearly unreadable, with handwritten notes in the margin outlining some of the tweaks."[6]

When: The time period is primarily from 2 November 2017 with the introduction of the Bill in the House, the House passing of the Bill on 16 November 2017, and through to the passing of the Bill in the Senate on 2 December 2017. The Bill is presently in the resolving differences phase between its House and Senate versions.

Where: Within the United States of America concerning the US Tax Code with direct impact on taxation of overseas individual, trust, and corporate earnings.

Why: The recent co-option of the Republican Party stemming from the emergence of "pluto-populism"[7]—the synthesis of what might be benevolently defined as "A political movement in which a wealthy individual offers ideas and policies that appeal to the common person."[8] Within the contemporary context the application of pluto-populism is far darker and represents a variant of free market authoritarianism—an emerging form of post-World II neo-fascism in which a democratically elected leader views him or herself as 'above the law because they are the law.'[9] Such a position of executive privilege is beginning to become uncomfortably close to the authoritarian approach to governance embodied in Louis XIV—the Sun King of France—when he said *'L'etat c'est moi'* ('I am the state').

Presidential Plutocratic Retreat—Mar-a-Lago. See: https://www.maralagoclub.com/Default. aspx?p=dynamicmodule&pageid=100010&ssid=100032&vnf=1.

"Trump's weekend sojourns, which Politico has estimated cost taxpayers $3 million per trip, have caused Mar-a-Lago membership fees to double from $100,000 to $200,000, as America's wealthy clamors for a seat at, or at least near, the table."[10]

Analysis

The *Tax Cuts and Jobs Act* (aka the 2017 Federal Tax Bill) signals a significant milepost in the analysis of 'plutocratic insurgency" with potential ramifications echoing a return to economic conditions last seen in The Gilded Age with the accelerating prospects of *class warfare.*

The Gilded Age was characterized by unfettered capitalism, conspicuous consumption, extreme income inequality, and rampant corruption. The beneficiaries were a small plutocratic class that benefited from profiteering and a lack of regulation that allowed them to concentrate wealth in hands of a few. Typically, that small class is known as the 1 percent, but within that economic elite a significant proportion of wealth was—and is once again—concentrated in the hands of the top 1 percent (in 2012 that cohort included about 160,000 families with a net worth above $20.6 million.[11] The *Tax Cuts and Jobs Act*, if enacted, will benefit that small class by redistributing a substantial redistribution of wealth from the middle class to the highest income cohorts; and, as Alan Krueger, former chair of the Council of Economic Advisers told the *New York Times*, "the proposal would also deepen and further entrench existing class divisions and reduce economic mobility."[12]

Indeed, currently 40 percent of US wealth is concentrated in the hands of the wealthiest 1 percent of Americans with that cohort owning more wealth than the bottom 90 percent combined. That gap has been growing in recent decades and the 2017 Federal Tax Bill will exacerbate those inequities, giving the greatest tax cuts to the super rich while the poorest will face actual tax increase over the long-term.[13]

The 2017 US Federal Tax Bill, which as of this writing is currently undergoing reconciliation between the House and Senate versions, represents in significant ways the principles of plutocratic insurgency. Or rather, more accurately, it represents an opening volley in what looks likely to be a plutocratic insurgency campaign set to last for as long as the GOP controls both chambers of Congress as well the White House.

While the details remain to be worked out, the bill most certainly does not represent tax "reform" in the way that the term has most usually been used in Washington. "Reform" measures have typically centered on three core ideas: lowering the top rates, broadening the tax base, and simplifying the code. The first two measures are broadly speaking regressive (or at least de-progressive) while the latter mainly entails closing special interest loopholes of one sort or another.

The 2017 tax bill, however, does little of this. While the Senate version of the bill slightly lowers the top marginal personal income (from 39.6 percent to 38.5 percent) tax rate, the main focus of both versions of the bill has been on dramatically lowering the corporate tax rate (from 35 percent to 20 percent), as well as on making it easier for certain kinds of partnerships to constitute themselves as corporations eligible for these rates. The net effect is that many rich individuals will effectively reclassify their earnings as corporate earnings, thus dramatically lowering their marginal tax rates. This is why, over the next ten years, the vast majority of the tax savings (about 80 percent, according to the nonpartisan Tax Policy Center)[14] will go to the top 1 percent of earners—in other words, to plutocrats.

To make up for the shortfall, various alternative revenue enhancing schemes have been proposed, all of which have been carefully targeted to primarily affect blue states and heavily demographic constituencies—for example, targeting private university endowments and graduate students for heavy tax increases, as well as industries and earners concentrated in blue states. On a superficial level, this represents not so much ideology as a kind of political vengeance by way of the tax code.

Political daggers aside, in what sense can this bill be said to represent the plutocratic insurgency in action? We believe there are four elements to this:

- First, this bill represents a dramatic realization of the dream of plutocratic insurgents in United States to shield themselves from having to contribute financially to the country and its public goods. The bill either drastically scales back or abolishes the estate tax, something that only affects the largest 0.2 percent of estates in the United States—i.e. plutocrats.[15] By enabling many more high earners to reclassify their businesses as "pass through corporations," moreover, it will enable many members of the 1 percent to pay only about half of what they would as top individual earners. As such, it represents the further secession of plutocratic insurgents from any sense of shared economic fate with their fellow citizens.
- Second, the tax bill contains a number of new deductions and special interest loopholes which are specifically designed to

benefit the plutocrats. One that has received particular notoriety has been the deduction for maintenance costs on the ultimate symbol of plutocratic insurgency, namely private jets. Likewise, the carried interest loophole survived, allowing private equity managers, hedge fund managers, and real estate investors to pay the lower capital gains rate (20 percent) on their income rather than the top personal income tax rate (38.5 percent). And of course, in a nod to the President, the bill contains plenty of breaks for golf course owners and real estate developers.[16]

- Third, one of the main sources of backfill for the revenues that will be lost by lowering the tax rates that plutocrats pay is the abolition and/or capping of the deduction for state and local taxes (SALT). SALT deductions have been standard ever since the federal income tax was first imposed. However, this measure in effect punishes taxpayers in states where real estate is very expensive (and therefore property taxes are high) as well as states with significant income taxes. States with high income taxes—such as California, New Jersey, Massachusetts, and New York—are, not coincidentally, states that also tend to offer relatively generous social welfare packages to their less fortunate residents. The Republicans have been explicit that the goal in eliminating the SALT deduction is to punish states that choose to tax their citizens. In effect, they are trying to pressure blue states to lower their tax rates—which will all but inevitably force them also to cut the public benefits and social services they offer their residents. In other words, it is an effort by the legislative handmaidens of the plutocratic insurgency to force the blue states become more like the low-tax, low-welfare providing red states.

- But the fourth and most important way in which the tax bill is a representative product of the plutocratic insurgency is that it presages the slashing of the core pillars of the welfare state. While the GOP has gamely claimed that the tax bill would not increase the deficit because of all the growth it was going to create (a claim roundly denied by all nonpartisan experts),[17] if the tax bill in fact ends up creating a huge new set of deficits, from the perspective of plutocratic insurgents, this will be not a bug but a feature, as it will provide the GOP controlled government with the lever they need to cut the entitlement programs they've had in their gun sights for a generation. Indeed, as the *New York Times* has reported, the tax bill seems expressly designed to add to the debt in a manner that will then trigger automatic cuts to Medicare and other entitlement programs.[18] The bottom line is that the 2017 tax bill seems expressly designed to break the fiscal camel's back in a way that will enable and indeed mandate the rollback of the welfare state that the GOP has dreamed about since the 1980s.

That taking a plutocratic machete to the welfare state is the ultimate agenda is not in doubt. Literally, before the scribbles in the margins of the deficit-exploding tax bill were dry, the stewards of the plutocratic insurgency on Capitol Hill were already declaring that the huge deficit to come would require gashing cuts to the welfare state. "You also have to bring spending under control," said Senator Marco Rubio (R-Florida) even before the vote on the tax bill was final. "And not discretionary spending. That isn't the driver of our debt. The driver of our debt is the structure of Social Security and Medicare for future beneficiaries."[19] "We're spending ourselves into bankruptcy," declared Senate Finance Committee Chairman Orrin G. Hatch (R-Utah) the same day. "Let's just be honest about it: We're in trouble. This country is in deep debt. You don't help the poor by not solving the problems of debt, and you don't help the poor by continually pushing more and more liberal programs through."[20]

Clearly, the radical redistribution of income is being accelerated by a concerted effort to enact a revised tax structure that favors the richest at the expense of the middle class and poor. This looks like class warfare to many—especially the political opposition.[21] Many Americans share that view with 52 percent of voters opposing the tax plan and 59 percent viewing it as benefiting the wealthy at the expense of the middle class according to a November Quinnipiac Poll.[22] Redistributing wealth and favoring the interests of the top income cohorts (the 1 percent or the 0.1 percent) relies on a strategy of 'pluto-populism.' That strategy— derived from a bizarre synthesis of cliental from Tiffany and Dollar General (who come from vastly different existences)—replaces income equity with identity politics and a loathing for the regulatory institutions of the state.

As the Federal deficit grows, the pressures to cut government spending and benefits increase the likelihood of a severe backlash. Reducing spending on health and social security is one prospect to sustain this redistribution of income from the lower and middle classes to the hyper-rich (with the top 1 percent through 0.1 to 0.001 percent reaping the greatest increases in annual real income growth).[23] The current tax plan is likely to accelerate economic insecurity for the masses while ensuring hyper-wealth for the gilded, plutocratic elite. Income inequality combined with class and racial tensions are likely to influence political instability if left unchecked. This in turn, challenges the stability of states and can lead to a violent competition for resources characterized by class warfare with a potential for actual insurrection.

Whether the project to roll back Medicare, Social Security, Obamacare, and the other major welfare entitlements succeeds remains to be seen. Both the GOP and the current resident of the White House are plumbing unprecedented depths of unpopularity, perhaps auguring not just a wave election in 2018, but perhaps an even more fundamental realignment of the party system in the United States, whose institutional foundations are crumbling before our eyes. We live in a time of profound political uncertainty. Meanwhile, the plutocratic insurgents seem intent on clearing out the shelves in the store before the hurricane rolls in. Whether they will be able to build their private sea walls high enough to hold back the political storm surge remains to be seen.

Sources

John Cassidy, "The Passage of the Senate Republican Bill was a Travesty." *The New Yorker.* 2 December 2017, https://www.newyorker.com/sections/news/the-passage-of-the-senate-republican-tax-bill-was-a-travesty.

The Editorial Board, "A Historic Tax Heist." *New York Times.* 2 December 2017, https://www.nytimes.com/2017/12/02/opinion/editorials/a-historic-tax-heist.html.

Katrina vanden Heuvel, "Republican tax bills would be paradise for plutocrats." *Washington Post.* 14 November 2017, https://www.washingtonpost.com/opinions/republican-tax-bills-would...f9f8-c8e7-11e7-b0cf-7689a9f2d84e_story.html?utm_term=.70bd42e8c122.

Heather Long, "As tax bill evolved, benefits for corporations and the wealthy grew." *Standard-Examiner.* 1 December 2017, http://www.standard.net/Business/2017/12/02/As-tax-bill-evolved-benefits-for-corporations-and-the-wealthy-grew-1.

Derek Thompson, "Why the GOP Tax Bill Is So Unpopular." *The Atlantic.* 25 November 2017, https://www.theatlantic.com/business/archive/2017/11/gop-tax-bill-unpopular/546668/.

David Weigel, Robert Costa and Paul Kane, "'This is class warfare': Tax vote sparks political brawl over populism that will carry into 2018 elections." *Washington Post.* 2 December 2017, https://www.washingtonpost.com/powerpost/this-is-class-warfare-tax-vote-sparks-political-brawl-over-populism-that-will-carry-into-2018-elections/2017/12/02/c8e2ccdc-d762-11e7-b62d-d9345ced896d_story.html?utm_term=.d19a7413bae4.

Martin Wolf, "A Republican tax plan built for plutocrats." *Financial Times.* 2 December 2017, https://www.ft.com/content/e494f47e-ce1a-11e7-9dbb-291a884dd8c6.

Notes

All opinions are strictly those of the authors and in no way reflect the viewpoints of any US governmental, academic, or corporate entity.

1. http://smallwarsjournal.com/jrnl/art/plutocratic-insurgency-note-no-9-tax-cuts-and-jobs-act-class-warfare-red-line-crossed.
2. Ben Stein, "In Class Warfare, Guess Which Class Is Winning." *New York Times*. 26 November 2006, http://www.nytimes.com/2006/11/26/business/yourmoney/26every.html.
3. Greg Sargent, "'There's been class warfare for the last 20 years, and my class has won.'" *Washington Post*. 30 September 2011, https://www.washingtonpost.com/blogs/plum-line/post/theres-been-class-warfare-for-the-last-20-years-and-my-class-has-won/2011/03/03/gIQApaFbAL_blog.html?utm_term=.d05003b35141.
4. This note was completed in early December prior to the approval of the final version of the bill by the Senate on 20 December 2017. See Deirdre Walsh et. al., "White House, GOP celebrate passing sweeping tax bill." *CNN*. 20 December 2017, http://www.cnn.com/2017/12/20/politics/house-senate-trump-tax-bill/index.html.
5. Peter S. Goodman and Patricia Cohen, "It started as a tax cut, now it could change American life." *New York Times*. 29 November 2017, https://www.nytimes.com/2017/11/29/business/republican-tax-cut.html.
6. Bob Bryan, "The final tax bill Democrats got from Republicans is covered in handwritten notes — and senators are complaining it's unreadable." *Business Insider*. 1 December 2017, http://www.businessinsider.com/gop-senate-tax-reform-bill-final-version-text-trump-2017-12.
7. "Leader: The rise of pluto-populism." *The New Statesman*. 20 July 2016, https://www.newstatesman.com/culture/observations/2016/07/leader-rise-pluto-populism.
8. "Pluto-populism—New Word Suggestion." *Collins Dictionary*. 26 July 2016, https://www.collinsdictionary.com/us/submission/17704/pluto-populism.
9. Sari Horwitz and Philip Rucker, "A bold new legal defense for Trump: Presidents cannot obstruct justice." *Washington Post*. 4 December 2017, https://www.washingtonpost.com/world/national-security/a-bold-new-legal-defense-for-trump-presidents-cannot-obstruct-justice/2017/12/04/b95cb262-d91c-11e7-a841-2066faf731ef_story.html?utm_term=.3a45b96cf187.
10. Christopher Hooton, "Mar-a-Lago: Questions about membership applications since Trump elected are 'inappropriate', says resort." *Independent*. 9 March 2017, http://www.independent.co.uk/news/world/americas/us-politics/mar-a-lago-donald-trump-florida-weekends-membership-members-list-cost-club-a7621051.html.
11. See "Back to a Gilded Era," table detailing share of household wealth in the U.S., 1913-2013 based on data from Emmanuel Saez and Gabriel Zucman, National

Bureau of Economic Research in Thomas B. Edsall, "Republicans Wonder How to Make the Rich Richer." *New York Times*. 9 November 2017, https://www.nytimes.com/2017/11/09/opinion/republican-tax-bill.html.

12. In Thomas B. Edsall, "Republicans Wonder How to Make the Rich Richer." *New York Times*. 9 November 2017, https://www.nytimes.com/2017/11/09/opinion/republican-tax-bill.html.

13. Christopher Ingraham, "The richest 1 percent now owns more of the country's wealth than at any time in the past 50 years." *Washington Post*. 6 December 2017, https://www.washingtonpost.com/news/wonk/wp/2017/12/06/the-richest-1-percent-now-owns-more-of-the-countrys-wealth-than-at-any-time-in-the-past-50-years/?utm_term=.5bd5b5f05548.

14. Jeff Stein, "Ryan says Republicans to target welfare, Medicare, Medicaid spending in 2018." *Washington Post*. 6 December 2017, https://www.washingtonpost.com/news/wonk/wp/2017/12/01/gop-eyes-post-tax-cut-changes-to-welfare-medicare-and-social-security/?utm_term=.6f69cab7c359.

15. Chye-Ching Huang and Chloe Cho, "Ten Facts You Should Know About the Federal Estate Tax." *Center on Budget and Policy Priorities*. 30 October 2017, https://www.vanityfair.com/news/2017/12/with-tax-cuts-on-the-line-flake-suddenly-decides-to-trust-trump.

16. Dan Wilchins and Prashant Gopal, "One Tax Loophole Untouched So Far: The Trump Golf-Course Break." *Bloomberg*. 9 November 2017, https://www.bloomberg.com/news/articles/2017-11-09/one-tax-loophole-untouched-so-far-the-trump-golf-course-break.

17. The nonpartisan Joint Committee on Taxation claimed the Senate version of the bill would increase the debt by \$160B over the next decade. The nonpartisan Congressional Budget Office claimed it would be \$140B. Even with "dynamic scoring"—i.e. modeling the additional revenues that will come from the additional growth which supposedly will materialize as a result of the tax cut—all of the nonpartisan experts expect an increase of at least a trillion dollars in debt over the next decade. "Under Dynamic Scoring, House Tax Bill Still Explodes the Debt." *Committee for a Responsible Federal Budget*. 8 November 2017, http://www.crfb.org/blogs/under-dynamic-scoring-house-tax-bill-still-explodes-debt. There is strong reason to believe that if anything this will be an underestimate, since it is highly likely that some of the additional revenue enhancements that the federal government is expecting, for example from closing the SALT deductions will not materialize, as blue states change their revenue mix away from income taxes and over to payroll taxes, which addition to being regressive and growth-retarding, will also mean less revenues flowing to the federal government.

18. Margot Sanger-Katz, "The Tax Bill's Automatic Spending Cuts." *New York Times*. 29 November 2017, https://www.nytimes.com/interactive/2017/11/29/upshot/paygo-medicare-cuts-tax-bill.

19. Jeff Stein, "Ryan says Republicans to target welfare, Medicare, Medicaid spending in 2018." Note 9.

20. Bess Levin, "With Tax Cuts on the Line, Flake, Suddenly Decides to Trust Trump." *Vanity Fair*. 1 December 2017, https://www.vanityfair.com/news/2017/12/with-tax-cuts-on-the-line-flake-suddenly-decides-to-trust-trump.

21. Alex Roarty, "Dems warn GOP: We're prepared for class war." *Sacramento Bee*. 5 December 2017, http://www.sacbee.com/news/article188065154.html.

22 "Quinnipiac University National Poll Finds; Voters Reject GOP Tax Plan 2-1." *Quinnipiac University/Poll*. 15 November 2017, https://poll.qu.edu/national/release-detail?ReleaseID=2501.

23. The average annual real income growth for all in the US from 1980-2014 is roughly 1.5%, the top 1 percent's growth is roughly 2.2%, the top 0.1 percent's roughly 3.2%, the top 0.01 percent about 4.4%, and the top 0.001 percent's growth 6% according to the table "To those who have" with data from Piketty, Saez & Zucman in Martin Wolf, "A Republican tax plan built for plutocrats." *Financial Times*. 21 November 2017, https://www.ft.com/content/e494f47e-ce1a-11e7-9dbb-291a884dd8c6.

Additional Reading

Larry M. Bartels, *Unequal Democracy: The Political Economy of the New Gilded Age*. Princeton: Princeton University Press, 2016.

Ronald F. Formisano, *Plutocracy in America*. Baltimore: Johns Hopkins University Press, 2015.

Chrystia Freeland, *Plutocrats*. New York: The Penguin Press, 2012.

Denis L. Gilbert, *The American Class Structure in an Age of Growing Inequality*. Thousand Oaks: Sage Publications, 2014.

Thomas Piketty (Arthur Goldhammer, Trans.), *Capital in the Twenty-First Century*. Harvard: Belknap Press, 2014.

Thomas Piketty (Arthur Goldhammer, Trans.), *The Economics of Inequality*. Harvard: Belknap Press, 2015.

David Rothkopf, *Superclass*. New York: Farrar, Straus, and Giroux, 2008.

Reading 23

Research Guide:
Plutocratic Insurgency—
The Gilded Age Redux

Robert J. Bunker

First Published 15 May 2018 in Small Wars Journal [1]

Plutocratic insurgency represents an emerging form of insurgency not seen since the late 19th century Gilded Age. It is being conducted by high net worth globalized elites allowing them to remove themselves from public spaces and obligations—including taxation—and to maximize their ability to generate profits transnationally. It utilizes 'lawyers & lobbyists' and corruption, rather than armed struggle—though mercenaries may be employed—to create shadow governance in pursuit of plutocratic policy objectives. Ultimately, this form of insurgency is representative of the challenge of 21st century predatory and sovereign-free capitalism to 20th century state moderated capitalism and its ensuing public welfare programs and middle class social structures. It can be viewed as a component of 'Dark Globalization' that, along with the emergence of

criminal insurgency, is now actively threatening the public institutions and citizenry of the Westphalian state form.
 —Plutocratic Insurgency Notes, *Small Wars Journal*

This research guide has been created for *Small Wars Journal* readers to aid in their understanding of the plutocratic insurgency construct and explain how it is related to the earlier criminal insurgency construct which has been the focus of numerous *El Centro* works over the last decade. The plutocratic insurgency concept dates back to 2011 and has been influenced by earlier work done by John Robb (*Onward to a Hollow State*, 2008) and Nils Gilman (*Deviant Globalization*, 2010). As a theoretical construct, it was further inspired by the global street protests and demonstrations of the Occupy movement taking place during that period. Research on this topical area for its U.S. national security threat potentials has been conducted related to U.S. Department of Defense and Army programs, with a number of works produced or derivative of these efforts; *Op-Ed: Not Your Grandfather's Insurgency* (2014), *Global Criminal and Sovereign Free Economies and the Demise of the Western Democracies* (2014), and *Old and New Insurgency Forms* (2016). Of these works, the "Foreword: The twin insurgency—facing plutocrats and criminals" written by Nils Gilman for the derivative 2014 edited book project—and reprinted online as *The Twin Insurgency* in *The American Interest*—is by far the best known and eloquent of these writings:

> The defining feature of the plutocratic insurgency is its goal: to defund or de-provision public goods in order to defang a state that its adherents see as a threat to their prerogatives. (Note that, conceptually, plutocratic insurgencies differ from kleptocracies; the latter use the institutions of state to loot the population, whereas the former wish to neutralize those institutions in order to facilitate private-sector looting. In practice, these may overlap or co-mingle.) Practically speaking, plutocratic insurgency takes the form of efforts to lower taxes, which necessitates cutting spending on public goods;

reducing regulations that restrict corporate action or protect workers; and defunding or privatizing public institutions such as schools, health care, infrastructure, and social space.

The rise of a new plutocratic class in American society, as well as growing economic inequality in our country, and the increasing power of multinational corporations to the detriment of sovereign states have all been identified and commented upon by numerous scholars including David Rothkopf (*Superclass*, 2008 and *Power, Inc.*, 2012), Chrystia Freeland (*Plutocrats*, 2012), David Grusky and Tamar Kricheli-Katz, eds., (*The New Gilded Age*, 2012), Dennis L. Gilbert (*The American Class Structure in an Age of Growing Inequality*, 2014), Thomas Piketty (*Capital in the Twenty-First Century*, 2014 and *The Economics of Inequality*, 2015), and Ronald Formisano (*Plutocracy in America*, 2015 and *American Oligarchy*, 2017).

Such a new class of powerful economic elites has not been witnessed since the historical Gilded Age and in some ways can be likened to the smart and talented winners of a large Monopoly™ game—one that has taken place not only within American society but also transnationally within the larger global economy that has developed. Major differences, of course, are that, unlike a traditional Monopoly™ game, this one never ends. The participants who lost do not get a restart and—since the stakes are exceedingly high, with individual and family livelihoods and futures on the line—cheating and other underhanded tricks are commonly used to ensure success. The new class of plutocrats that has emerged has moved 'beyond the state' and does not need or require public goods or services such as education, health services, or police protection, preferring to purchase such commodities on the open market. They seek economic impunity of action with no obligations to the state including paying taxes and, at times, even suffering the burdens of citizenship and would rather live separate (and unequal) lives to those of the common lower socio-economic members of the public.

It took the full weight of the U.S. Federal government, the muckrakers (reformist journalists), and engaged citizens to eventually tame the historical Gilded Age plutocrats. This was done over some decades through a process of trust-busting (initiated during the Roosevelt and Taft presidential administrations), newspaper exposes and shaming, anti-corruption campaigns, and ultimately robust income tax and estate tax levees to ensure that a network of aristocratic families did not come to dominate all aspects of American society. From the 1930s well into the 1970s, the plutocratic class had been relatively contained with it once again beginning to slowly emerge and then build in strength from the 1990s and beyond. This time around, however, the newly ascendant plutocratic class may not be as easy to tame, for it now exists well beyond the domestic U.S. economy and has powerful criminal confederates as allies.

Plutocratic insurgency can be placed 'in strategic context' when juxtaposed with John Sullivan's criminal insurgency concept which dates back to 2008. Both concepts, in turn, draw upon Steve Metz's brilliant postulation of the commercial insurgency form in 1993—although as a bi-furcation of that proposed form into the lower (criminal) and upper (plutocratic) socio-economic components of the burgeoning global political economy. The fusion of these two concepts—which yielded Nils Gilman's before-mentioned twin insurgency work as a descriptive introduction to the post-modern epochal transition now taking place—provides a powerful lens into evolving elements of early 21st century dark (i.e. deviant) globalization.

A visual representation of the compression effect of the underworld of criminality pushing up into the "Goldilocks Zone" inhabited by the Western Democracies—one defined by a strong middle class, a viable legitimate (state-moderated) economy, conventional warfare, and sovereign rights—and the upper-world of sovereign free entities pushing down on it can be viewed in Figure 1. Variations on this figure have existed since 2011 and have been utilized in various briefings and presentations to diverse academic, governmental, and military and law enforcement audiences. As we increasingly enter into the epochal transition from the modern to the post-modern era, it is projected that the compression effect will become increasingly pronounced. Loss of liberal democratic leadership in the world along with a concurrent rise in non-state radicalism and state authoritarianism will progress. As the Westphalian state form perceives itself besieged, it will likely over-centralize its decision-making functions and institutional processes, exacerbating this cycle.

Fig 1. Compression Effect on the Western Democracies

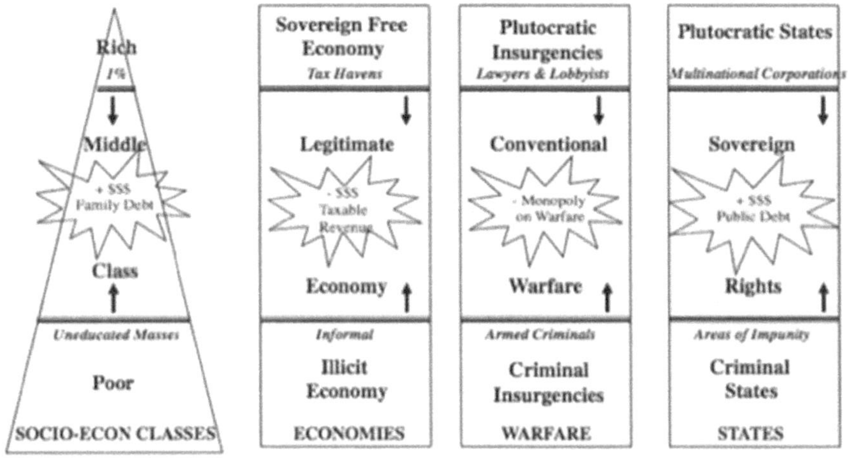

For the Westphalian state—and its socio-economic class structure founded on a strong, vibrant, and politically engaged middle class—the threat represented by the twin insurgencies (and sometimes collusion between these insurgent plutocrats and criminals) cannot be overstated. Contemporary state moderated capitalism has in the past functioned as a bulwark, protecting not only the middle class from predatory economic exploitation but also serving as a means to extract tax revenues from wealthy corporations and individuals (e.g. the 1%). This has been done in order to help fund state programs that provide goods and services to its citizenry and to help mitigate the economic gulf between the very rich and very poor in society thus preventing the emergence of aristocratic family dynasties which would not only threaten the integrity of the middle class but also, in the process, destroy the social mobility potentials of the underclasses.

With state moderated capitalism now increasingly becoming extinct, the economics of the Westphalian state and most of it citizenry are slowly becoming untenable. This has resulted in massive U.S. public (<u>20 trillion USD</u>) and household (<u>12.7 trillion USD</u>) debt levels, with real wealth now being concentrated at the criminal and plutocratic (as well as the hybrid autocratic) extremes where high profit levels and little-to-no sovereign taxation (other than informal bribes, kickbacks, and political contributions to co-opted officials) exist. Old adages like "What's good for the country is good for General Motors…" and the "Horatio Alger" rags-to-riches mythos have pretty much faded away. They are being replaced with a dystopian world that looks strikingly like a Gilded Age 'redux' wherein the major multinational corporation shareholder families place profit over the needs of their national brethren while their scions born of a new plutocratic class enjoy rank and privilege most of society cannot imagine. Alarmingly, in American politics, no serious reform movement in the tradition of Teddy Roosevelt and other federal 'trust busters' has as of yet emerged from either the conservatives (Republicans), liberals (Democrats) or unaligned and opted-out center (Independents) willing to stand up to the plutocratic insurgency now in full force within our society. Rather, if the new administration's <u>tax cut plan</u> is any indication, co-optation of political interests at the highest levels has now taken place, with significant tax breaks for high-income individuals and tax increases for middle class earners ensuing:

> By 2027, people making $40,000 to $50,000 would pay a combined $5.3 billion more in taxes, while the group earning $1 million or more would get a $5.8 billion cut, according to the <u>Joint Committee on Taxation and the Congressional Budget Office</u>.

Given such a stark and disingenuous reality, the fiduciary duty of national governance for elected and appointed U.S. officials requires that some sort of federal counter-plutocratic insurgency program—enacted by governmental leaders from across the political spectrum—be established to protect the economic viability of a threatened American middle class. Failure to do so may well result in the rise of a 'sham democracy,' catering only to the needs of the economic elite, and the eventual fragmentation of large segments of both the middle and lower classes, that would fall even further into financial insolvency and poverty. The development of such a chilling future over the coming decades could result in increased social unrest on America's streets that would make the relatively bloodless Occupy movement protests of 2011 seem like a walk in the park.

Plutocratic Insurgency Notes Guide

Since early 2017, a new series of research notes has been published at *Small Wars Journal* focusing on this topical area. These provide state-moderated capitalism scholar perspectives on the dangers of increasing wealth concentration and polarization between the 'haves' and 'have nots' not only in contemporary American society but throughout the Western liberal democracies. Present authors in this series are Robert J. Bunker, Pamela Ligouri Bunker, John P. Sullivan, and Nils Gilman with note topics including:

Note No. 1: Eight Individuals are Now as Wealthy as the Poorest Half of the World

The eight richest individuals in the world have a combined net worth of $426 billion dollars, equivalent to that of the economic bottom half of humanity—3.6 billion people. It is resulting in dystopian futures for large segments of humanity.

Note No. 2: 69% of Americans Don't Even Have $1,000 in Savings

Google Consumer Surveys conducted by *GoBankingRates.com* concerning how much money respondents had in their savings accounts. In 2015, of those surveyed, 62% have less than a $1,000.00 in savings while, in 2016, this number rose to 69% of the respondents.

<u>Note No. 3: No Shoring: Job Obsolescence Via Artificial Intelligence</u>
<u>(AI) and Robotics</u>

The no shoring concept—articulated by Ian Barkin (in *The Wall Street Journal*)—is the process of taking off-shored American jobs and bringing them back to the U.S. for artificial intelligence programs and robotic lines to perform.

<u>Note No. 4: Silencing the Middle Class—The Gradual Extinction of</u>
<u>Tenure in American Universities</u>

The gradual demise of tenure and concurrent reduction in full-time faculty on American college campuses mirrors the thinning of other sectors of the middle-class workforce no longer required for 20th century based mass industrial production and conventional warfare utilizing large standing armies. Further, the gradual silencing of the middle class in U.S. public debate due to the increasing elimination of tenured faculty is a little-recognized systemic phenomenon.

<u>Note No. 5: The Techno-Palaces of the Global Elite</u>

Techno-palaces (e.g. the 'needle-towers') emerging in New York and other global financial centers provide full amenities and are guarded 24-hours by private security personnel. Units in these towers are only affordable to about 40,000 extra-sovereign individuals who can pay for the ten-million dollar-plus price in the more prestigious of these residential complexes.

<u>Note No. 6: Privatizing Urban Public Spaces</u>

Privately owned public spaces (Pops) are becoming key fixtures in cities around the world. This privatization of public space creates corporately controlled spaces governed by obscure private rules and policed by private security entities with minimal state control. These 'pseudo-public spaces' are reminiscent of feudal enclaves.

Note No. 7: Artificial Intelligence (AI) Pricing Software—Profit Optimization Beyond 'The Invisible Hand'

Artificial intelligence (AI) algorithms built into business applications software are increasingly changing how multinational corporations interface with their customer base. Such 'learning software'—when combined with massive data sets tracking hundreds of individual (i.e. client specific) and group purchasing, life style, and socio-economic variables—allows for corporate profit optimization to take place by means of 'dynamic' and 'algorithmic' pricing strategies.

Note. No. 8: Rotten at the Core—Apple Incorporated's Stateless Tax Avoidance Strategies & Subsequent Cash Hoard

Much like the fictional account of the *Strange Case of Dr. Jekyll and Mr. Hyde*, Apple Incorporated is a beloved 'American' company by day when it sells its innovative and sleek technology products such as iMacs and iPhones to our citizens and those of other nations and a 'stateless' revenue maximizing multinational behemoth after hours when it comes time to pay the tax bill, resulting in a $250 billion cash hoard being accumulated.

Note. No. 9: Tax Cuts and Jobs Act—Class Warfare 'Red Line' Crossed

The prophetic plutocratic class warfare warnings of Warren Buffett (of Berkshire Hathaway fame and one of the richest persons in the United States) resound like a 'double-tap' to the skull of the American middle class after the recent *Tax Cuts and Jobs Act* has now passed in the U.S. Senate. In this bill, not only have the taxes of the rich once again been reduced but, to offset this plutocratic economic boon, the taxes of the middle class have been brazenly raised to subsidize it.

The first six of these research notes—with additional and articulate commentary—have since been rebroadcasted in two podcasts by Quintus Curtis at his *Fortress of the Mind* site:

<u>The Rise Of The "Plutocratic Insurgency"</u> (28:15 minutes)

<u>The Continued Progress Of The Plutocratic Insurgency</u> (26:50 minutes)

The readers of *Small Wars Journal* may expect to see additional plutocratic insurgency notes written in the future—in addition to more standard fare such as the ongoing criminal insurgency essays—as well as combined works which discuss the strategic level effects of the twin insurgencies as a component of the epochal transition underway.

Notes

All opinions are strictly those of the author and in no way reflect the viewpoints of any U.S. governmental, academic, or corporate entity.

1. <u>http://smallwarsjournal.com/jrnl/art/research-guide-plutocratic-insurgency-gilded-age-redux</u>.

Reading 24

Henry David Thoreau Versus
the Plutocratic Insurgency

Bryan T. Baker

First Published 28 March 2018 in Small Wars Journal [1]

Introduction [2]

"...the 'winners of globalization,' represented by multinational corporations and global elites, are seeking to remove themselves from the regulatory, taxation, and, ultimately, political authority of states. This is done by promoting an extra-sovereign economy: using foreign tax havens, playing states off against each other to maximize profit, being a nonresident citizen so as not to pay taxes, and employing a bevy of lawyers and lobbyists within states to gain special privileges and economic considerations. This is very much representative of a Gilded Age (1870-1900) redux, but at a globalized level. No sovereign authority presently exists to contend with such an insurgent form; one that is an unintended consequence of globalized capitalism

*and is resulting in growing economic inequalities in
Western states, yet has been relatively violence free.*"[3]
                                        —Dr. Robert J. Bunker

Athens was in crisis in 594 B.C. The aristocracy had become increasingly
rich to the detriment of the lower classes. Countless Athenians had lost
their land to the aristocrats or been forced into slavery to pay their debts.
Immigrants had few political rights. As tensions mounted between
the rich and poor, the rich did exactly what Louis XVI failed to do in
1789—they agreed to radical change that would ensure greater wealth
equality. To achieve this, they gave a poet named Solon special powers
to change Athens' laws. Solon used these powers to free slaves, restore
ancestral lands to their rightful owners, and increase political rights for
immigrants. Civil war was averted, while the groundwork was laid for
Athens' eventual transition to democracy.[4]-[5]-[6]

In the world today, eight men control as much wealth as the poorest
half of the globe—that's around 3.5 billion people.[7] Those 3.5 billion
people live in abject poverty and face horrifying human security issues
despite over seven decades of "expert" development advice from the
West and trillions of dollars in foreign aid.[8] This profound inequality
has existed in the developing world for most of the modern era, but
it is increasingly found in the developed world as well. In the United
States, the middle class has been in decline for nearly five decades.[9]
By 2015, nearly twenty-five percent of all income in the US was earned
by the wealthiest one percent of the population—and this elite group
controlled forty percent of the nation's wealth. As recently as 1990,
however, these numbers had been twelve percent and thirty-three
percent, respectively.[10]

Some might argue that these successes of the ultra-rich have trickled
down to the middle and working classes; the data simply does not
support such notions. Nobel Prize-winning economist Joseph Stiglitz
finds that from 2005 to 2015 the income of the ultra-rich increased by
eighteen percent, while the middle class saw slight declines in income
and men with high school degrees experienced *precipitous* falls in income.
This income inequality is similar to the levels seen today in Russia and

Iran. The brutal truth is that most citizens in the United States are doing worse economically year after year, and our income disparity is now on par with authoritarian regimes.[11] What should be concerning to all Americans is the likelihood that this situation continues to worsen given recent developments in the republic.[12]

The Storming of the Bastille, by Jean-Pierre Houel,
watercolor, 1789 [Public Domain]

In 2010, the Supreme Court dealt a serious blow to democracy, while giving a boost to the burgeoning plutocratic insurgency. The Court's decision in *Citizens United v. FEC*, "...enshrined the right of corporations to buy government, by removing limitations on campaign spending."[13] According to Stiglitz, this is partly the reason why, "... virtually all US senators, and most of the representatives in the House, are members of the top 1 percent when they arrive, are kept in office by money from the top 1 percent, and know that if they serve the top 1 percent well they will be rewarded by the top 1 percent when they leave office."[14] This is plutocracy–government by the wealthy.

While this essay may seem like an attempt to vilify the rich, that is not my purpose. Some of those at the top—like Bill Gates—are extremely generous people who are striving to resolve these issues. Others, like Warren Buffet, have publicly recognized the problem:

"There's class warfare, all right...but it's my class, the rich class, that's making war, and we're winning."[15]

Those at the top who are not generous or have not recognized the problem are simply human. To desire to hold on to as much of one's money as possible is human nature. Most citizens would do the same thing if they had been born into the upper classes. Therefore, while I would call on the upper classes to do their part to bring about change in America, I am a firm believer that this *Great Divide*[16] can and should be bridged by middle and working-class Americans.

Thoreau Versus the Insurgency

It is said that when Benjamin Franklin emerged from Independence Hall on the last day of deliberations at the Constitutional Convention, he was asked what type of government had been created. The ailing statesman, who had only three more years to live, famously replied: "a republic, if you can keep it."[17] Franklin knew that republics were fragile. A republic could easily become a monarchy, oligarchy, or an empire—as the Roman Republic had. The American people had to remain vigilant, lest some modern-day Caesar take the reins of government and institute tyranny.

I will argue that the reason the plutocratic insurgency has been so successful is because the middle and working classes in American have neglected to *keep the republic*; they have fallen asleep. My idea is not original, however. In the 1840s, a somewhat aloof man living alone on the shores of Walden Pond made similar observations:

"The millions are awake enough for physical labor; but only one in a million is awake enough for effective intellectual exertion, only one in a hundred million to a poetic or divine life. To be awake is to be alive."[18]

Portrait of Henry David Thoreau, by Benjamin Maxham, 1856 [Public Domain]

For Thoreau,[19] to be awake one had to overcome the monotony of daily existence and connect with the poetic and divine. While this may sound overly transcendental, this poetic and divine existence was a search for truth, justice and virtue. Thoreau very practically turned his search into a scathing critique of slavery and the Mexican-American War—the the two great injustices of his time. Americans today must wake up and genuinely search for truth and virtue so that we can recognize current injustices. There are, however, two major obstacles in their way—materialism, and a deeply flawed education system.

Rejecting Materialism

Materialism prevented Americans from seeking truth, justice and virtue in Thoreau's day. He derided his fellow man's willingness to give the better part of their lives to work so that they could gain ever bigger houses, farms, and always be up on the latest fashions. According to Thoreau, these men were literally plowing their own lives into the soil in exchange for these material possessions:

> *"But men labor under a mistake. The better part of the man is soon ploughed into the soil for compost. By a seeming fate, commonly called necessity, they are employed, as it says in an old book, laying up treasures which moth and rust will corrupt and thieves break through and steal. It is a fool's life, as they will find when they get to the end of it, if not before."* [20]

The average American today has fallen into this same trap. We enter into mortgages we cannot afford, we keep up with the latest fashions–and go into credit card debt to do so–and we spend $1,000 to get the latest cell phone model, all while sixty-nine percent of Americans do not even have $1,000 in savings.[21] We aren't plowing ourselves into the soil anymore, but we are exchanging our time–our lives–for material possessions all the same. The result, of course, is we have very little time to search for truth, justice and virtue; we have very little time to keep the republic. Materialism must be rejected in order to defeat the plutocratic insurgency.

Embracing Classical Education

> *"For what are the classics but the noblest recorded thoughts of man? They are the only oracles which are not decayed, and there are such answers to the most modern inquiry in them as Delphi and Dodona never gave."*[22]

A lack of interest in learning from the great books of old prevented Americans in Thoreau's day from taking action to end injustice in their society. Instead of learning from these classic authors—such as Plato, Aristotle, or Augustine—people in Thoreau's time were satisfied with newspapers and simple novels that did not rise to the poetic or divine. Thoreau responded to this with a challenge that is still relevant today:

> *"...shall I hear the name of Plato and never read his book? ... His Dialogues, which contain what was immortal to him, lie on the next shelf, and yet I never read them. We are under-bred and low-lived and illiterate; and in this respect I confess I do not make any very broad distinction between the illiterateness of my townsmen who cannot read at all, and the illiterateness of him who has learned to read only what is for children and feeble intellects."[23]*

A deep study of classical literature used to be a hallmark of an American education. Our founders—nearly all of whom received a classical liberal arts education—believed that it was essential for Americans to understand ancient Greece, Rome and the Western Canon in order for the republic to be maintained.[24] America, however, has since rejected this sort of education for more utilitarian training. Instead of imbuing our youth with the collective wisdom of the ages—the wisdom that set the West apart politically, economically, and socially—we have skipped ahead and focused on making mechanics, accountants, bankers, and medical technicians. We have produced a population that is highly skilled and poorly educated. This must be reversed. I would have a classical liberal arts education for every American. It may sound ridiculous to think of an auto mechanic or a bartender well-versed in Plato. But why? Are these citizens not intelligent? Do they not have a stake in truth, justice and virtue? Are they not voters?

Cultivating Philosophers

Three years ago, this author left the Army and became a teacher at a classical liberal arts academy (which happens to be a charter school). I have seen students from every socioeconomic background engage with and learn from the classics. My ninth-grade students engage in in-depth studies (we read and discuss works in their entirety) of the writings of Jefferson, Adams, Madison, Hamilton, Tocqueville, Thoreau, Douglass, Melville, Twain, Cather, Shakespeare, Fitzgerald, Hemingway, and King–in Socratic seminars. In these seminars we strive to understand truth, justice and virtue–and what it means to keep the republic. I do not tell my students what to think regarding these writings. Instead, I teach them to think critically by asking them questions. I am–I hope–helping them become philosophers as Thoreau would understand the term:

> *"To be a philosopher is not merely to have subtle thoughts, nor even to found a school, but so to love wisdom as to live according to its dictates, a life of simplicity, independence, magnanimity, and trust. It is to solve some of the problems of life, not only theoretically, but practically."*[25]

In their next three years my students will engage with Rousseau, Locke, Dostoevsky, Thucydides, Herodotus, Augustine, Plato, Aristotle, and countless others. They will graduate, in my opinion, much better educated than the vast majority of Americans. They are awake. They will keep the republic–but will enough of their fellow Americans do so?

I fear that the average American will not engage with the classics. They will not wake up. Not because they are unintelligent, but because they are distracted by the trivial things of life. This must be reversed in the ascendant generation. In his dystopian warning, *1984*, George Orwell describes exactly what will happen to a working class–which he calls the proletariat, or 'proles'—that refuses to wake up:

"Heavy physical work, the care of home and children, petty quarrels with neighbors, films, football, beer, and, above all, gambling filled up the horizon of their minds. To keep them in control was not difficult...The Lottery, with its weekly pay-out of enormous prizes, was the one public event to which the proles paid serious attention. It was probable that there were some millions of proles for whom the Lottery was the principle if not the only reason for remaining alive. It was their delight, their folly, their anodyne, their intellectual stimulant. Where the Lottery was concerned, even people who could barely read and write seemed capable of intricate calculations and staggering feats of memory."[26]

Could we not replace Orwell's "Lottery" with "professional sports," "reality television," or "social media" in America today? No wonder the plutocrats are taking over.

I am well aware that this essay has lacked in more practical steps that can be taken to tackle the plutocratic insurgency. I hope to follow this essay with one that will do just that. I believe the foundation for any change will be, however, a re-awakening of the average American. It is unlikely the top one percent in America today will be as wise as the aristocrats in Solon's time.

Bibliography

"Benjamin Franklin (1706-90). Respectfully Quoted: A Dictionary of Quotations." Bartleby. 1989. Accessed February 17, 2018. http://www.bartleby.com/73/1593.html.

Bunker, Robert J. "Not Your Grandfather's Insurgency - Criminal, Spiritual, and Plutocratic." Strategic Studies Institute. February 20, 2014. Accessed February 12, 2018. http://ssi.armywarcollege.edu/index.

cfm/articles/Not-Your-Grandfathers-Insurgency-Criminal-Spiritual-and-Plutocratic/2014/02/20.

Bunker, Robert J., and Pamela Ligouri Bunker. "Plutocratic Insurgency Note No. 2: 69% of Americans Don't Even Have $1,000 in Savings." *Small Wars Journal.* February 14, 2017. http://smallwarsjournal. com/jrnl/art/plutocratic-insurgency-note-no-2-69-of-americans-don%E2%80%99t-even-have-1000-in-savings.

Cartledge, Paul. "History - Ancient History in depth: The Democratic Experiment." *BBC.* February 17, 2011. Accessed February 18, 2018. http://www.bbc.co.uk/history/ancient/greeks/greekdemocracy_01.shtml.

Easterly, William. *The Tyranny of Experts: Economists, Dictators, and the Forgotten Rights of the Poor.* New York: Basic Books, a member of the Perseus Book Group, 2016.

Hardoon, Deborah. "An Economy for the 99%: It's time to build a human economy that benefits everyone, not just the privileged few." *OXFAM Briefing Paper*, January 16, 2017. doi:10.21201/2017.8616. https://policy-practice.oxfam.org.uk/publications/an-economy-for-the-99-its-time-to-build-a-human-economy-that-benefits-everyone-620170.

Howe, Daniel Walker. "Classical Education in America." *The Wilson Quarterly.* December 19, 2014. Accessed February 17, 2018. https://www.wilsonquarterly.com/quarterly/spring-2011-the-city-bounces-back-four-portraits/classical-education-in-america/.

Martin, Thomas R. "The Reforms of Solon." An Overview of Classical Greek History from Mycenae to Alexander. Accessed February 18, 2018. http://www.perseus.tufts.edu/hopper/text?doc=Perseus%3Atext%3A1999.04.0009%3Achapter%3D6%3Asection%3D25.

Orwell, George. *1984.* New York, NY: Signet Classics, 2015.

Stein, Ben. "In Class Warfare, Guess Which Class Is Winning." *The New York Times*. November 25, 2006. Accessed February 23, 2018. http://www.nytimes.com/2006/11/26/business/yourmoney/26every.html.

Stiglitz, Joseph E. *The Great Divide: Unequal Societies and What We Can Do About Them*. New York, NY: W. W. Norton and Company, 2016.

"The American Middle Class Is Losing Ground." Pew Research Center's Social & Demographic Trends Project. December 09, 2015. Accessed February 15, 2018. http://www.pewsocialtrends.org/2015/12/09/the-american-middle-class-is-losing-ground/.

The Editors of Encyclopædia Britannica. "Solon's laws." *Encyclopædia Britannica*. February 09, 2018. Accessed February 18, 2018. https://www.britannica.com/topic/Solons-laws.

Thoreau, Henry David. *Walden and Civil Disobedience*. New York, NY: Penguin Books, 1986.

Notes

1. http://smallwarsjournal.com/jrnl/art/henry-david-thoreau-versus-plutocratic-insurgency.
2. I am extremely grateful for the editing and insights that Ryan Adkins and Elisabeth Baker provided during the development of this paper. Any remaining errors are my own. This paper does not represent the views of the aforementioned individuals or any organizations with which they are associated.
3. The Plutocratic Insurgency was first conceptualized by Dr. Bunker. This quotation was taken from: Bunker, Robert J. "Not Your Grandfather's Insurgency - Criminal, Spiritual, and Plutocratic." Strategic Studies Institute. February 20, 2014. Accessed February 12, 2018. http://ssi.armywarcollege.edu/index.cfm/articles/Not-Your-Grandfathers-Insurgency-Criminal-Spiritual-and-Plutocratic/2014/02/20.
4. Martin, Thomas R. "The Reforms of Solon." An Overview of Classical Greek History from Mycenae to Alexander. Accessed February 18, 2018. http://www.perseus.tufts.edu/hopper/text?doc=Perseus%3Atext%3A1999.04.0009%3Achapter%3D6%3Asection%3D25.

5. The Editors of Encyclopædia Britannica. "Solon's laws." *Encyclopædia Britannica*. February 09, 2018. Accessed February 18, 2018. https://www.britannica.com/topic/Solons-laws.

6. Cartledge, Paul. "History - Ancient History in depth: The Democratic Experiment." *BBC*. February 17, 2011. Accessed February 18, 2018. http://www.bbc.co.uk/history/ancient/greeks/greekdemocracy_01.shtml.

7. Hardoon, Deborah. "An Economy for the 99%: It's time to build a human economy that benefits everyone, not just the privileged few." *OXFAM Briefing Paper*, January 16, 2017. doi:10.21201/2017.8616. https://policy-practice.oxfam.org.uk/publications/an-economy-for-the-99-its-time-to-build-a-human-economy-that-benefits-everyone-620170.

8. Easterly, William. *The Tyranny of Experts: Economists, Dictators, and the Forgotten Rights of the Poor*. New York: Basic Books, a member of the Perseus Book Group, 2016.

9. "The American Middle Class Is Losing Ground." Pew Research Center's Social & Demographic Trends Project. December 09, 2015. Accessed February 15, 2018. http://www.pewsocialtrends.org/2015/12/09/the-american-middle-class-is-losing-ground/.

10. Stiglitz, Joseph E. *The Great Divide: Unequal Societies and What We Can Do About Them*. New York, NY: W. W. Norton and Company, 2016. 88.

11. Stiglitz 88-89.

12. *The Storming of the Bastille*, by Jean-Pierre Houel, watercolor, 1789. This painting is in the public domain: https://commons.wikimedia.org/wiki/File:Prise_de_la_Bastille.jpg.

13. Stiglitz 92.

14. Stiglitz 92.

15. Stein, Ben. "In Class Warfare, Guess Which Class Is Winning." *The New York Times*. November 25, 2006. Accessed February 23, 2018. http://www.nytimes.com/2006/11/26/business/yourmoney/26every.html.

16. This is the title of Joseph Stiglitz's book that is cited extensively in this essay. I highly recommend that you pick up a copy: https://www.amazon.com/Great-Divide-Unequal-Societies-About/dp/0393352188.

17. "Benjamin Franklin (1706-90). Respectfully Quoted: A Dictionary of Quotations." Bartleby. 1989. Accessed February 17, 2018. http://www.bartleby.com/73/1593.html.

18. Thoreau, Henry David. *Walden and Civil Disobedience*. New York, NY: Penguin Books, 1986. 134.

19. Portrait of Henry David Thoreau, by Benjamin Maxham, 1856. This image is in the public domain: https://commons.wikimedia.org/w/index.php?curid=10285.

20. Thoreau 47-48.

21. Bunker, Robert J., and Pamela Ligouri Bunker. "Plutocratic Insurgency Note No.

2: 69% of Americans Don't Even Have $1,000 in Savings." *Small Wars Journal*. February 14, 2017. http://smallwarsjournal.com/jrnl/art/plutocratic-insurgency-note-no-2-69-of-americans-don%E2%80%99t-even-have-1000-in-savings.

22. Thoreau 146.

23. Thoreau 152.

24. Howe, Daniel Walker. "Classical Education in America." *The Wilson Quarterly*. December 19, 2014. Accessed February 17, 2018. https://www.wilsonquarterly.com/quarterly/spring-2011-the-city-bounces-back-four-portraits/classical-education-in-america/.

25. Thoreau 57.

26. Orwell, George. *1984*. New York, NY: Signet Classics, 2015. 71 and 85.

Reading 25

AMLO vs The Dictatorship of the Market

Carlos Fazio (Alma Keshavarz, Trans.)

First Published 7 de noviembre de 2018 as "AMLO
vs la dictadura del Mercado" in Mira [1]
(Translation 8 November 2018)

The decision of president-elect Andrés Manuel López Obrador (AMLO) to cancel the construction for the airport in Texcoco escalated the plutocratic insurgency (Robert J. Bunker) and placed the dispute over hegemony and the exercise of political power on the agenda. With this, and beyond the myths coined by neoliberal ideology and its media parrots, the contradiction between the shell of a formal Mexican democracy and the private dictatorship of capital has resurfaced.

AMLO and Moreno won the elections overwhelmingly, but the new hegemon is implicit in Mexico's transformation will not materialize in power if there is no political, social, and economic change that restores the republic; if the society does not place limits and rules on the plutonomy (Citicorp).

Although the reform project of López Obrador does not want to break with capitalism, it will mitigate a little of its predatory voracity and manage it from a redistributive prism, and to materialize it will require creating a strong popular power; this is of a social majority that prevails over the markets and not vice versa, but that in its beginnings will operate within a concrete social formation, with its subordinates and its structure, and its material relations constituted and overdetermined by the existence of a specific, neoliberal capitalism model, which works at the service of a rapacious oligarchy under the protection of a militarized nanny state.

Any modification of the current social formation will go through to overpower the possibility of doing politics; to transform the reality. Hence, the fourth transformation involves modifying the current correlation of forces, with the exception that the relationship of material forces does not always correspond to the relationship of forces at the political level. And you cannot reform neoliberalism without touching the institutions that provide support. That is, without reconstituting the State, without endowing it with a new democratic institutional architecture. So, regime change is not reduced to the triad of corruption-impunity-simulation.

Within this context, the conflicts surrounding the new airport is a backdrop to the situation, the bidding among those seeking to perpetuate the capitalism of clientelist friends (crony capitalism) and those who want to separate transnational corporate power from political power intensified. Between an amoral corporatocracy, which is not in the humanitarian business but to extract benefits and maximize its actions, and those who seek to file the roughest edges of class domination and exploitation.

Given the flood of ideological distortion and apocalyptic ads (investment collapse, stock market debacle, devaluation, serious economic uncertainty, injunctions, claims before international tribunals) propagated by those who have the pulse of representing markets, it should be noted that they respond to the individual or group of decision makers—almost always awful—of powerful family clans (Slim, Larrea, Baillères, Hank, Salinas de Gortari, Vázquez, Azcárraga, Tricio, Salinas Pliego, Ramírez, Coppel, González el al.); from a small group of shareholders of large corporate corporations (for example, in Mexico, the group of 10 in Monterrey, the Carso Group, Hermes, México Group, ICA, Peñoles Group, etc); bank managers like JP Morgan, Citigroup, Bank of America, HSBC, Santander, BBVA Bancomer,

Banorte, UBS and others; the investment funds type like Black Rock, AXA, Capital and Goldman Sachs; risk qualifiers like Moody's, Fitch Ratings, Morgan Stanley and Standard and Poor's; hedge funds (hedge fund, the sharks of the markets raging sea), and the bosses/guard dogs of the imperial power: the International Monetary Fund and the World Bank, who depend on the Department of Treasury in the United States.

Thus, they manipulate, threaten, and insert fear in the markets and investment—described as if they were forces of nature or entities with their own will, and not the result of economic and political decisions made by powerful corporate groups based on cost-benefit analysis—only seeks to perpetuate the power of elites (Acemoglu/Robinson) that have historically attacked democracy, the state's rights, and citizenship and human rights.

Interest groups in the current framework of the current phase of the financial and speculative capitalism—also known as casino capitalism, with their gamblers, rent seekers, influence traffickers and beneficiaries of corruption—and by theologizing the market as in Mexico, in the last 35 years, to an absolutist regime that combines plutocracy with kleptocracy. That old regime, which 30 million Mexicans voted against, is the one that has to be disbanded and dismantled. But it will not be easy. The plutocratic insurgency (a class war and my class is winning it, said Warren Buffet) will intensify its offensive; happening now is just a warning. Hence, the need for a conscious and organized people.

Notes

1. http://mirahechosyrealidades.mx/nacional/amlo-vs-la-dictadura-del-mercado/.

Reading 26

Plutocratic Insurgency Note 10: Increasing Global Wealth Concentration, Record Private Jets at Davos, and the Demise of the American Dream

Pamela Ligouri Bunker and Robert J. Bunker

First Published 25 January 2019 in Small Wars Journal [1]

This plutocratic trifecta focuses upon the increasing global wealth concentration of the world's billionaires—as well as the falling tax income tax rates on the rich and their corporations—discussed in a new Oxfam report, the fact that a record number of private (multi-million dollar+ jets) are ferrying global elites to the Davos meeting this year, and that a majority of the U.S. poor (per a World Economic Forum commissioned poll) now recognize that they and their children have little hope of working hard and, as a result, ever becoming rich in American society.

Key Information: Laura Paddison, "26 Billionaires Own The Same Wealth As The Poorest 3.8 Billion People." *Huffington Post*. 20 January 2019, https://www.huffingtonpost.com/entry/oxfam-report-wealth-inequality-poverty-tax_us_5c408586e4b027c3bbbeb91d:

A new economic system is needed to tackle rampant inequality, says a new Oxfam report.

The gap between rich and poor is fracturing society, poisoning politics and fueling public anger, according to a new report from anti-poverty nonprofit Oxfam, which found that last year just 26 people owned the same amount of wealth as the poorest 3.8 billion people. This figure is down from 43 the year before.

The *Public Good or Private Wealth?* report, published Sunday, found that the wealth of billionaires has increased by $900 billion in the last year, or $2.5 billion a day. This bonanza has not been felt by the poorest half of the world, which saw its wealth decline by 11 percent.

Since the 2008 financial crisis, the number of billionaires has doubled, according to the report, and the very rich along with corporations are paying lower taxes than they have in decades. At the same time, 3.4 billion people are living in poverty on less than $5.50 a day, and women are often hardest hit. Men hold 50 percent more of the world's wealth than women, according to the report….

… Unfair tax regimes are one of the core problems highlighted by Oxfam. In wealthy countries, average top personal income tax rates fell from 62 percent in 1970 to 38 percent in 2013, according to the nongovernmental organization's report.

"People generally are beginning to realize that they have been sold a bad bill of goods," said O'Brien. "Today, 262 million kids are going to stay home because there is no funding for their education, 10,000 people today will die because they don't have access to basic health care that could easily be funded through proper fiscal systems."

While talk of poverty and inequality often focuses on the developing world, rich nations are far from immune. A report published this week by the Institute for Policy Studies, a left- leaning Washington, D.C., think tank, found that the <u>400 richest Americans own more wealth than all black households</u> and a quarter of Latino households. And <u>social mobility in America is falling</u>. Yet Donald Trump's administration has slashed taxes for the wealthiest. The 2017 tax bill, trumpeted as a break for the middle class, in reality was found <u>primarily to benefit the wealthiest 1 percent</u>.

In its report, Oxfam calls for a new economic model, a "human economy" where tax systems for corporations and the super-rich are overhauled to eliminate tax avoidance and evasion, and to increase tax revenues. This money would then be plowed into providing universal public services like education and healthcare as key to tackling inequality and poverty. "Inequality is not inevitable," the report says, "it's a political choice."

Key Information: Max Lawson et al., *Public good or private wealth?* Oxford: Oxfam GB. Brief. 20 January 2019, <u>https://www.oxfamamerica.org/static/media/files/bp-public-good-or-private-wealth-210119-en.pdf</u>:

Boomtime for the world's billionaires

It is 10 years since the financial crisis that shook our world and caused enormous suffering. In that time, the fortunes of the richest have risen dramatically:

- In the 10 years since the financial crisis, the number of billionaires has nearly doubled.
- The wealth of the world's billionaires increased by $900bn in the last year alone, or $2.5bn a day. Meanwhile the wealth of the

poorest half of humanity, 3.8 billion people, fell by 11%.

- Billionaires now have more wealth than ever before. Between 2017 and 2018, a new billionaire was created every two days.
- Wealth is becoming even more concentrated – last year 26 people owned the same as the 3.8 billion people who make up the poorest half of humanity, down from 43 people the year before.
- The world's richest man, Jeff Bezos, owner of Amazon, saw his fortune increase to $112bn. Just 1% of his fortune is the equivalent to the whole health budget for Ethiopia, a country of 105 million people.
- If all the unpaid care work done by women across the globe was carried out by a single company, it would have an annual turnover of $10 trillion– 43 times that of Apple.

While the richest continue to enjoy booming fortunes, they are also enjoying some of the lowest levels of tax in decades – as are the corporations that they own:

- Wealth is particularly undertaxed. Only 4 cents in every dollar of tax revenue comes from taxes on wealth.
- In rich countries, the average top rate of personal income tax fell from 62% in 1970 to 38% in 2013.31 In developing countries, the average top rate of personal income tax is 28%.
- In some countries like Brazil and the UK, the poorest 10% are now paying a higher

proportion of their incomes in tax than the richest 10%.

- Governments should focus their efforts on raising more from the very wealthy to help fight inequality. For example, getting the richest to pay just 0.5% extra tax on their wealth could raise more money than it would cost to educate all 262 million children out of school and provide healthcare that would save the lives of 3.3 million people.
- The super-rich are hiding $7.6 trillion from the tax authorities. Corporates also hide large amounts offshore. Together this deprives developing countries of $170bn a year.

[*Citations have been removed—refer to the original document*]

Key Information: Rebecca Ratcliffe, "Record private jet flights into Davos as leaders arrive for climate talk." *The Guardian.* 22 January 2019, https://www.theguardian.com/global-development/2019/jan/22/record-private-jet-flights-davos-leaders-climate-talk?CMP=twt_gu:

David Attenborough might have urged world leaders at Davos to take urgent action on climate change, but it appears no one was listening. As he spoke, experts predicted up to 1,500 individual private jets will fly to and from airfields serving the Swiss ski resort this week.

Political and business leaders and lobbyists are opting for bigger, more expensive aircrafts, according to analysis by the Air Charter Service, which found the number of private jet flights grew by 11% last year.

"There appears to be a trend towards larger aircraft, with expensive heavy jets the aircraft of choice, with Gulfstream GVs and Global Expresses both being used more than 100 times each last year," said Andy Christie, private jets director at the ACS.

This is partly due to the long distances travelled, he said, "but also possibly due to business rivals not wanting to be seen to be outdone by one another". Last year, more than 1,300 aircraft flights were recorded at the conference, the highest number since ACS began recording private jet activity in 2013.

Countries with the highest number of arrivals and departures out of the local airports over the past five years included Germany, France, UK, US, Russia and the United Arab Emirates, according to ACS…

Key Information: Jo Confino, "Americans Have Lost Faith In Their Ability To Move From Poverty To Riches." *The Huffington Post.* 21 January 2019, https://www.huffingtonpost.com/entry/american-dream-world-econo...rum-pollus5c4583b7e4b027c3bbc33c48?ncid=engmodush pmg00000006:

More than two-thirds said it's no longer commonplace for hard work to be a path from poverty to wealth, according to a new World Economic Forum poll.

DAVOS, Switzerland – People in the United States and other developed countries are losing faith in the capitalist system to improve their lives, according to a new global poll commissioned by the World Economic Forum, published on the eve of its annual meeting in Davos, Switzerland.

Almost two-thirds of U.S. respondents said it was no longer commonplace for hard work to be a sure path from poverty to riches, with only 10 percent saying it was extremely common.

The lack of faith in the current system to deliver upward mobility was even more marked in Western

Europe, where only a fifth of respondents said it was common to be able to start poor and become wealthy through hard work.…

… The WEF points to <u>an analysis in Harvard Business Review</u> that found that almost half of American workers surveyed said they are "often or always exhausted due to work" — up by a third in 20 years…

… The WEF emphasizes the importance of considering well- being rather than profit and growth at any cost. It warns that if we continue as we are, "beyond the economic risks, there are potential political and societal implications. For example, a world of increasingly angry people would be likely to generate volatile electoral results and to increase the risk of social unrest."…

Key Information: SAP + Qualtrics, *GLOBALIZATION 4.0: The Human Experience.* Presented to the World Economic Forum. 18 January 2019, <u>http://www3.weforum.org/docs/WEF_globalization4_Jan18.pdf</u>:

Significant variation across countries suggests more belief in social mobility in developing countries.

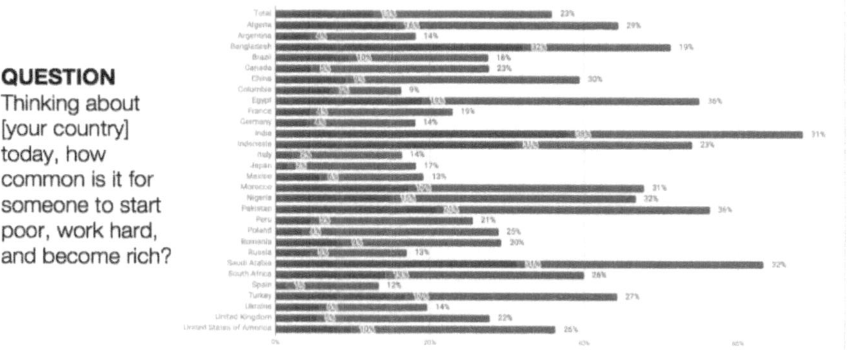

Respondents in Eastern Europe/Central Asia, Latin America, and Western Europe see upward mobility as elusive in their country.

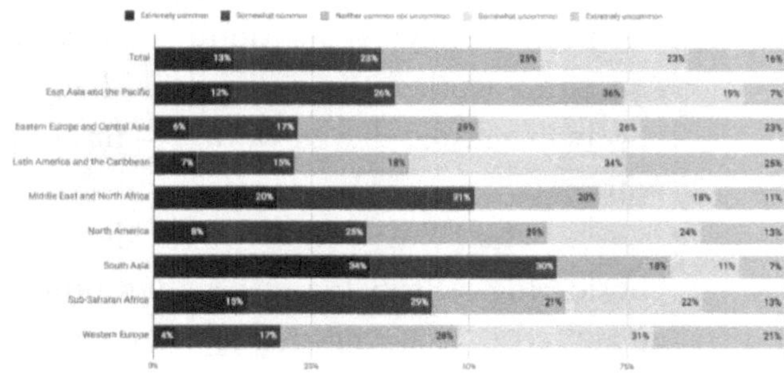

Who: The global rich and poor with an increasingly smaller middle class segment within Western societies and a rising—yet stunted middle class—emerging in developing countries.

What: Rising inequality around the world as a component of increasing predatory capitalism, as a post-modern form of dark (deviant) globalization. *Laissez-faire* capitalism—the invisible hand—free of state-moderation resulting in the failure of the liberal-democratic order by allowing vast sums of wealth to be concentrated within smaller and smaller segments of humanity.

When: The present; January 2019.

Where: A global phenomena; with key information focusing on Davos, Switzerland, the perceptions of the poor in the United States, and national tax policies throughout the globe. These elite super rich are found not only within democratic societies but also within authoritarian ones.

Why: Increasing wealth polarization between the world's elites (roughly +2,200 billionaires and their families) and the rest of humanity.[2]

Analysis: Three interrelated themes are covered in this plutocratic insurgency note. The major takeaway from the Oxfam report—addressing the initial theme of increasing global wealth concentration—is that "Wealth is becoming even more concentrated – last year 26 people owned the same as the 3.8 billion people who make up the poorest half of humanity, down from 43 people the year before."[3] Within the last year, the wealth of the world's billionaires has increased by $900 billion while the world's poorest 50% saw their wealth decline by 11%.[4] This concentration of wealth at the top is due to a recovering global economy benefiting the rich and their multinational (i.e. stateless) corporations which are pulling in record breaking profits as well as shielding more and more revenues via a) falling tax rates for the highest income brackets (in both the developed and developing world) and b) the extensive use of tax havens with some '$7.6 trillion' being sheltered from sovereign taxing entities.[5] Hence, this finely tuned extractive capacity of the super rich (directed at the global masses) and their ability to achieve impunity from governmental (i.e. public goods directed) taxation represents a global economic insurgent strategy benefiting the plutocracy.

The second theme focuses on private jetliner records being broken at the annual Davos, Switzerland World Economic Forum (WEF) focusing on the state of the world—which also serves as a 'behind the scenes' ultra rich deal cutting conclave. It is closely linked to the Fourth Industrial Revolution project which seeks to 'maximize the benefits of science and technology for society'[6], with Davos corporate executive attendance fees beginning at 60,000 francs (€53,000; $60,000).[7] This year, 1,500 private jets were expected to fly in for the WEF as contrasted with the 1,300 estimated to have flown in last year. Further, heavier expensive jets are increasingly being seen as a component of conspicuous consumption and plutocratic one-upmanship behaviors.[8] This significant increase in privatized elite transport is representative of wealth concentration amongst WEF attendees and the value that they place in attending the yearly Davos meeting for global elite networking—facilitating both corporate and family advancement—purposes.

The third and final theme in this note focuses on the present perceptions and mindset of the poor within American society. According to a section of the new SAP + Qualtrics poll commissioned by WEF, "Almost two-thirds of U.S. respondents said it was no longer commonplace for hard work to be a sure path from poverty to riches, with only 10 percent saying it was extremely common."[9][10] This perception of the poor in the United States—along with the acknowledgement that their (and their children's) chances for social mobility within America is severely limited[11]—is reflective of their disenfranchisement with 21st century *Laissez-faire* capitalism. It signifies the demise of the American dream linked to the Horatio Alger 'hard work and integrity will result in your success' mythos underpinning our belief in the fairness of our economic system and the potential to pull oneself up by one's bootstraps to rise from rags to riches. These shifting perceptions are very dangerous from a societal cohesion perspective because they indicate that a widening perceptual—and actual according to numerous indicators—firebreak is emerging in our country between the economic elite (the plutocrats) and the masses.[12] Such increasing gulfs between the haves and have nots, if left to fester, may result in increased levels of criminality as well as street protests and other forms of civil unrest directed at what is considered to be unjust governance and a rigged economic system exploiting those on the lower socio-economic rungs of American society.

Sources

Jo Confino, "Americans Have Lost Faith In Their Ability To Move From Poverty To Riches." *The Huffington Post.* 21 January 2019, https://www.huffingtonpost.com/entry/american-dream-world-econo...rum-poll_us_5c4583b7e4b027c3bbc33c48?ncid=engmodushpmg00000006.

Max Lawson et al., *Public good or private wealth?* Oxford: Oxfam GB. Brief. 20 January 2019, https://www.oxfamamerica.org/static/media/files/bp-public-good-or-private-wealth-210119-en.pdf.

Laura Paddison, "26 Billionaires Own The Same Wealth As The Poorest 3.8 Billion People." *Huffington Post.* 20 January 2019, https://www.huffingtonpost.com/entry/oxfam-report-wealth-inequality-poverty-tax_us_5c408586e4b027c3bbbeb91d.

Rebecca Ratcliffe, "Record private jet flights into Davos as leaders arrive for climate talk." *The Guardian*. 22 January 2019, https://www. theguardian.com/global-development/2019/jan/22/record-private-jet-flights-davos-leaders-climate-talk?CMP=twt_gu.

SAP + Qualtrics, *GLOBALIZATION 4.0: The Human Experience*. Presented to the World Economic Forum. 18 January 2019, http://www3.weforum.org/docs/WEF_globalization4_Jan18.pdf.

Notes

All opinions are strictly those of the authors and in no way reflect the viewpoints of any U.S. Governmental, academic, or corporate entity.

1. https://smallwarsjournal.com/jrnl/art/plutocratic-insurgency-note-10-increasing-global-wealth-concentration-record-private-jets.
2. Catherine Clifford, "There are a record 2,208 billionaires in the world, according to Forbes' 2018 rich list." *CNBC*. 7 March 2018, https://www.cnbc.com/2018/03/07/forbes-there-are-a-record-2208-billionaires-in-the-world.html.
3. Max Lawson et al., *Public good or private wealth?* Oxford: Oxfam GB. Brief. 20 January 2019, https://www.oxfamamerica.org/static/media/files/bp-public-good-or-private-wealth-210119-en.pdf.
4. Ibid.
5. Ibid.
6. World Economic Forum, Centre for the Fourth Industrial Revolution. 2019, https://www.weforum.org/centre-for-the-fourth-industrial-revolution.
7. "Davos 2019: What you need to know about 'the world's most exclusive business bash.'" *The Local/AFP*. 21 January 2019, https://www.thelocal.ch/20190121/davos-2019-what-you-need-to-know-about-the-worlds-biggest-business-bash-switzerland-wef.
8. Rebecca Ratcliffe, "Record private jet flights into Davos as leaders arrive for climate talk." *The Guardian*. 22 January 2019, https://www.theguardian.com/global-development/2019/jan/22/record-private-jet-flights-davos-leaders-climate-talk?CMP=twt_gu.
9. Jo Confino, "Americans Have Lost Faith In Their Ability To Move From Poverty To Riches." *The Huffington Post*. 21 January 2019, https://www.huffingtonpost.com/entry/american-dream-world-econo...rum-poll_us_5c4583b7e4b027c3bbc33c48?ncid=engmodushpmg00000006.

10. SAP + Qualtrics, *GLOBALIZATION 4.0: The Human Experience.* Presented to the World Economic Forum. 18 January 2019, http://www3.weforum.org/docs/WEF_globalization4_Jan18.pdf.

11. Ibid.

12. See these recent wealth polarization statistics: "About 172,000 U.S. households have net worths of at least $25 million, Spectrem estimated last year. That's up from 84,000 in 2008." and "Even as more young people entered the top 0.1 percent, most of their Millennial and Generation X compatriots were struggling. Americans 75 and older are the only age group whose median net worth rose from 2007 to 2016, according to the Federal Reserve Survey of Consumer of Finances released in July 2018. Typical Americans age 35 to 54 saw their wealth—heavily concentrated in housing—plunge by more than 41 percent in that time frame." Ben Steverman, "Super Rich Americans Are Getting Younger and Multiplying." *Bloomberg.* 23 January 2019, https://www.bloomberg.com/news/articles/2019-01-23/super-rich-americans-are-getting-younger-and-multiplying.

Further Reading

Jake Bernstein, *Secrecy World: Inside the Panama Papers Investigation of Illicit Money Networks and the Global Elite*. New York: Henry Holt and Co., 2017.

Anand Giridharadas, *Winners Take All: The Elite Charade of Changing the World*. New York: Alfred A. Knopf, 2018.

Brooke Harrington, *Capital without Borders: Wealth Managers and the One Percent.* Cambridge, MA: Harvard University Press, 2016.

Paul Kennedy, *Vampire Capitalism: Fractured Societies and Alternative Futures*. New York: Palgrave Macmillan, 2017.

David Rothkopf, *Superclass: The Global Power Elite and the World They Are Making*. New York: Farrar, Straus and Giroux, 2009.

Reading 27

Plutocratic Insurgency Note 11: Low-Paid, Part-Time, "Gig Economy" as a New Involuntary Labor Model

Pamela Ligouri Bunker and Robert J. Bunker

First Published in Small Wars Journal on 16 February 2019 [1]

A modern miracle related to the effects of the globalized economy upon the United States and the United Kingdom is the fact that we are now witnessing the lowest levels of unemployment seen in almost a generation in the U.S. (since 2001) and two generations in the UK (since 1971).[2] On the surface, while such low levels of unemployment may appear to represent the triumph of unfettered capitalism and the belief in the benefits of a globalized—and supranational—liberal economic order, something far more ominous for the Western middle classes is taking place. Full-time jobs with benefits and secure retirement packages are increasingly being replaced with low-paid and part-time "gig economy" positions as a new involuntary labor model. This labor model not only benefits predatory (i.e. hyper efficient extractive) capitalism but may also be considered a component of the larger transition to human worker replacement by robotic automation and artificial intelligence

(AI) systems and the continued hollowing out of the Western welfare state by the plutocratic class.[3][4]

Key Information: Jim Edwards, "Unemployment is low only because 'involuntary' part-time work is high." *Business Insider.* 27 January 2019, https://www.businessinsider.com/unemployment-vs-involuntary-part-time-work-underemployment-2019-1:

- Unemployment is at record lows in both the UK and the US.
- But "involuntary" part-time work is at least 40% higher in both countries than it was 10 years ago.
- The structure of the labour market has fundamentally changed, and what we used to think of as "unemployment" has been replaced by mass part-time work, much of it unwanted.
- "Gig economy" jobs are to blame, according to Rob Valletta of the San Francisco Fed.

Britain just notched up yet another record-breaking low for unemployment, according to the government. Unemployment stayed at just 4%, while the number of people with jobs rose to 32.54 million, or 75.8%, "the highest since comparable estimates began in 1971," according to the UK's Office for National Statistics.

But once again, the monthly jobs tally eclipsed how that miracle was achieved. "Headline" unemployment is only at a record low because of a *42% increase in the number of people who are in "involuntary" part-time work.*

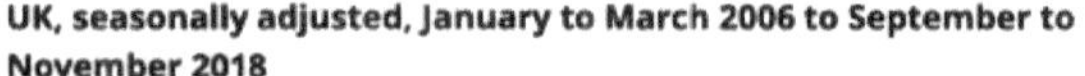

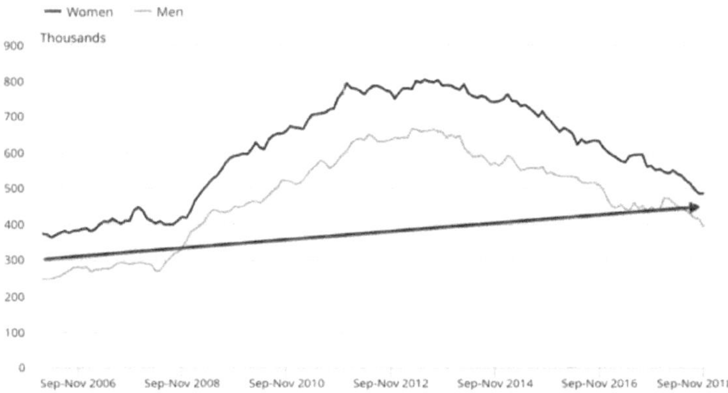

Since 2006, the number of people in "involuntary" part-time work has risen from 620,000 to 881,000 today—an increase of 42%. ONS

"Involuntary" means they're only working part-time because they cannot get a full-time job…

Here is the situation in America.

Involuntary part-time work is probably 40% higher than "normal" in the US.

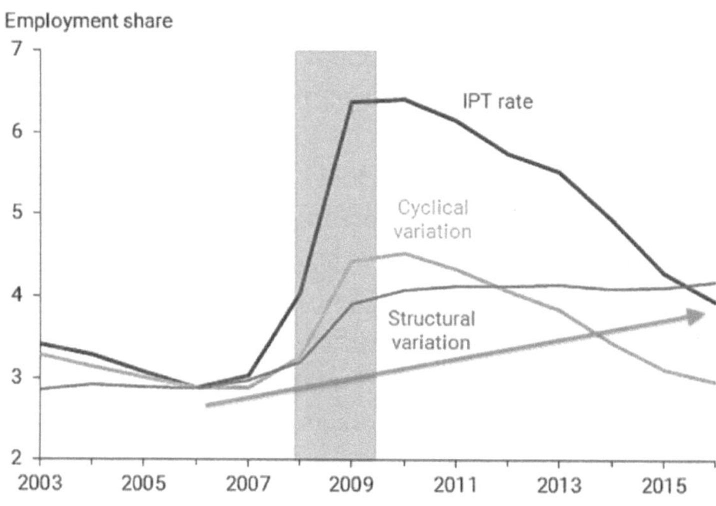

"During early 2018, involuntary part-time work was running nearly a percentage point higher than its level the last time the unemployment rate was 4.1%, in August 2000," according to Rob Valletta, a vice president in the Economic Research Department of the Federal Reserve Bank of San Francisco. "This represents about 1.4 million additional individuals who are stuck in part-time jobs. These numbers imply that the level of IPT work is about 40% higher than would normally be expected at this point in the economic expansion."

Mass unemployment — the historic kind, with dole queues, unemployment benefits, and idle workers on street corners — has been replaced by low-paid, part-time, "gig economy" or "zero-hours" contract work…

Key Information: Macy Bayern, "How the gig economy will change in 2019." *TechRepublic*. 12 December 2018, https://www.techrepublic.com/article/how-the-gig-economy-will-change-in-2019/:

The gig economy is type of employment made up of independent workers, who typically engage in short-term job positions. Freelancers, Uber drivers, Airbnb hosts, and more, make up this new wave of employment, one in which employees are free to make their own schedules, be their own bosses, and work where they want.

More than one-third (36%) of US workers are a part of the gig economy, totaling to about 57 million people, according to Forbes (https://www.forbes.com/sites/tjmccue/2018/08/31/57-million-u-s-workers-are-part-of-the-gig-economy/#4e5c48567118). While the gig economy used to be a way to make ends meet in-between traditional jobs, workers are starting to morph the gig economy into full-time professions.

"People realize that the dynamics, when it comes to the workforce, are changing. In the next 10 years, 25% of the jobs will not exist anymore," said Marcos Jacober (http://marcosjacober.com/), CEO of Life Hacks Wealth. "At first, people saw that as an opportunity to make a side gig, but it actually came and replaced the old part-time job. People realized that this is actually kind of cool, not to have a boss. I can be managing my own hours, I can make extra cash. So they migrate to that, and it is now the new trend for 2019. This is a very lucrative business."

This way of work is especially popular with younger crowds, said Matthew Guarini, research director serving CIO professionals at Forrester. Nearly half (46%) (https://www.techrepublic.com/article/how-the-gig-economy-is-fundamentally-changing-the-next-generation-of-work/) of Generation Z workers are freelancers, a number that is only expected to grow as nearly 61 million Gen Zers come into the workforce in the next couple years.

However, the gig economy has the potential to change even more as more people adopt the gig mindset, said Jacober. And more companies are going to start catering to gig employees, added Guarini.

Here are the three biggest shifts the gig economy will see in 2019:

1. *More companies will jump on the gig economy bandwagon…*
2. *Positions will target selective problems…*
3. *A change in mentality…*

Key Information: Nicole Torres, "Are There Good Jobs in the Gig Economy?" *Harvard Business Review*. July-August 2018 Issue, https://hbr.org/2018/07/are-there-good-jobs-in-the-gig-economy:

There's no denying the growth of the gig economy. Economists estimate that the portion of U.S. workers earning a living as independent contractors, freelancers, temps, and on-call employees jumped from 10% in 2005 to nearly 16% in 2015, and the trend shows little sign of slowing. Advocates of these "alternative work arrangements"—many of which are enabled by sharing or on-demand apps such as Uber and TaskRabbit—bill them as a way to trade unemployment, burnout, or hating one's job for freedom, flexibility, and financial gains. Skeptics, meanwhile, point to the costly trade-offs: unstable earnings, few or no benefits, reduced job security, and stalled career advancement.

But what do the gig workers themselves say? *Gigged*, a new book by Sarah Kessler, an editor at Quartz, focuses on their perspective. In profiling a variety of people in contingent jobs—from a 28-year-old waiter and Uber driver in Kansas City, to a 24-year-old programmer who quit his New York office job to join Gigster, to a 30-something mother in Canada who is earning money through Mechanical Turk—Kessler illuminates a great divide: For people with desirable skills, the gig economy often permits a more engaging, entrepreneurial lifestyle; but for the unskilled who turn to such work out of necessity, it's merely "the best of bad options."

Financial insecurity is a big and ever-present concern. So is the lack of human connection: When you're managed by an algorithm that sends notifications to your phone, it becomes harder to build relationships with bosses or even fellow employees—relationships that can help you advocate for better working conditions. Kessler writes, "I don't think Silicon Valley was wrong to attempt to restructure the job. Our current model wasn't working, and the startup spirit of experimentation was necessary. But attempting to tackle the problems of the job…without fixing the support structures around it can't quite count as progress, and it certainly doesn't look like innovation."

That tension is also a central theme of *Temp*, a forthcoming book that explains our new world of work. Author Louis Hyman, a Cornell professor and economic historian, notes that in America traditional organizations began moving away from offers of full-time employment and toward more-flexible short-term staffing jobs as a result of both new management ideas (such as the Lean Revolution) and changing values (such as prioritizing short-term profits). This restructuring of the workforce was facilitated, he emphasizes, by management consultants, who believed that "the long hours, the tensions, the uncertainty were all a perfectly reasonable way to work," and by temp agencies, which created pools of standby, on-demand labor. By the 1980s temps were providing not emergency help but cyclical replacement.

Hyman's stats are striking: By 1988 about nine-tenths of businesses were using temp labor; since 1991 every economic downturn has meant a permanent loss of jobs; by 1995, 85% of companies were "outsourcing all or part of at least one business function." And, Hyman notes, most of the affected employees fall on the wrong side of the divide Kessler describes: They became temps and "gig workers" owing to events beyond their control, such as elimination of full-time positions—with their secure paychecks and perks.

Although Hyman does seem to hold out hope for this new era of employment—"The gig economy might have the best of both worlds: the autonomy and independence of an economy before wage labor, but with individuals possessed of the productive capacity of an industrial economy"—he also argues that the only sustainable path forward is to somehow reconnect temp workers to the support they once got from full-time jobs. That could come through either portable benefits (which he thinks are feasible) or a universal benefits system (which he thinks is not). "Americans need life security," he writes, "not job security."

Another new book offers a similar message but begins in a very different place. In *Bullshit Jobs*, David Graeber, a professor of anthropology at the London School of Economics, lambastes today's corporations for engaging in "ruthless downsizing…layoffs and speed-ups," which "invariably fall on that class of people who are actually making, moving, fixing, and maintaining things." Even worse: As the doers among us are pushed into tenuous, low-paid, benefit-less gig work, somehow "the number of salaried paper pushers ultimately seems to expand." …

Key Information: Abha Bhattarai, "Now hiring, for a one-day job: the gig economy hits retail." *The Washington Post*. 4 May 2018, https://www.washingtonpost.com/business/economy/now-hiring-for-a-...d3c-4257-11e8-ad8f-27a8c409298b_story.html?utm_term=.ce8ffdba8e70:

…The gig economy is clocking in to retailers and restaurants.

The unemployment rate is at a 17-year low, but stagnant wages, chronic underemployment and growing inequality are leading more Americans to take on so-called side hustles. Some want to supplement their incomes. Others are just trying to eke out a living. Nearly 1 in 4 Americans now earn money from the digital "platform economy," according to the Pew Research Center. Most of that work is for domestic tasks, such as housecleaning and repairs, or driving for companies such as Uber.

By moving into shops and cafes, on-demand work stands to reshape a broader slice of the U.S. economy. There are implications for low-wage workers, too, as a new class of employers fills its labor pool with on-call temp workers. Retail and hospitality — which accounts for 20 percent of U.S. positions, according to the Bureau of Labor Statistics — is the on-ramp for many employees to better jobs. But the sector is also pinched by rising minimum wages and health-care costs, and employers are seeking more flexible work arrangements that respond to the ebbs and flows of their businesses.

But labor experts say companies such as Snag Work could set a dangerous precedent. Employers are already wary of hiring full- time employees because of overtime and health-care costs, they say, and having a pool of potential gig workers at the ready could make matters worse for those seeking the stability, benefits and protections that come with full-time work.

"We're seeing only one trend here, which is that the gig economy is big and getting bigger," said Diane Mulcahy, a lecturer at Babson College and author of "The Gig Economy." "Companies will do just about anything to avoid hiring full-time employees. Add to that the fact that there is no job security anymore, and workers are increasingly aware that they need to work differently if they want to create any sort of stability for themselves."

Snag Work and other new platforms are the go-betweens, allowing users to pick up open shifts from retailers, restaurants and hotels that have gaps in their schedules. Wonolo, which bills itself as 40 percent cheaper than traditional temporary staffing companies, counts Coca-Cola, McDonald's and Papa John's Pizza among its clients. Other start-ups include AllWork and Coople...

Key Information: Patrick Gillespie, "America's part-time worker problem is permanent, San Francisco Fed says." *CNN.* 11 April 2018, https://money.cnn.com/2018/04/11/news/economy/part-time-unemployment/index.html:

The US job market is one of the bright spots in the global economy. America has millions of new jobs, falling unemployment and even some nascent signs of growing paychecks.

One problem persists: A historically high number of Americans have part-time jobs, but want full-time positions.

Economists long argued that the trend, known as "involuntary part-time," was temporary. But it now appears to be a permanent problem, according to a blog post published Wednesday by the San Francisco Federal Reserve.

"In the absence of public policies aimed directly at altering work schedules, it looks like higher rates of involuntary part-time work are here to stay," San Francisco Fed economist Rob Valletta wrote.

Related: US job growth slowed in March

With the current unemployment rate of 4.1%, the number of involuntary part-timers should be much lower. But it's 40% higher now than it was when unemployment was last that low in 2000. That group does not include people who work part-time because they want to.

Nearly nine years after the Great Recession ended, there are still more involuntary part-time workers than there were before the crisis began, according to the Labor Department.

Some experts outside the Fed call it "<u>hidden unemployment</u>" because the extra hours workers want go unpaid. Workers <u>describe the jobs</u> as "dead ends" with high demands from employers and low pay.

A surge of job growth in recent years at restaurants, bars, retail stores and freelance gigs has pushed more Americans into part-time work, according to Valletta.

There were 5 million involuntary part-timers in March. In 2006, despite a higher unemployment rate than today, there were a million fewer part-timers...

Who: Labor (human workers) in the United States and the United Kingdom unable to get full-time employment positions with benefits that allow for upward economic mobility.

What: The replacement of full-time workers enjoying higher wages, medical and retirement benefits, and job security with part-time (temporary or "gig") workers who are lower paid, have no benefits, and have no job security. This can be considered a new involuntary labor model which has turned American and United Kingdom workers into 'disposable commodities' that can be utilized as needed and then abandoned.

When: An upward trend since the 1980s with temporary workers shifting from emergency labor to cyclical labor to a permanent condition—with the elimination of more and more full-time positions— over the course of the last thirty-five years. This trend has steadily increased over the last decade.

Where: Principally seen within the United States and the United Kingdom but this new labor model is spreading to other post-industrial Western states.

Why: By eliminating full-time positions, corporations do not have to pay higher salaried wages and benefits and can hire and fire employees at will which gives them fast market reaction versatility allowing for business costs to be lowered, profits to be increased, and new opportunities to be maximized. While the use of temporary workers is also said to allow corporations to better utilize 'high maintenance'

Generation Zers who have been socialized to work as freelancers but this socialization process was originally a result of corporate practices themselves as a component of their own 'just-in-time' efficiency methods. Just as only enough inventory is kept on hand by corporations to aggressively minimize costs so too does at will contract labor (human workers).

Analysis: The part-time work force in America is said to have reached over one third of US workers according to an August 2018 *Forbes* article:

> More than one third (36 percent) of U.S. workers
> are in the gig economy, which works out to a very large
> number of approximately 57 million people.[5]

This part-time employment trending in the UK is not so nearly as advanced but has seen a 42% increase to 881,000 workers from March 2006—enough to change the UK unemployment levels from 4% to 7% if underemployment levels are figured into this statistic.[6]

US underemployment levels are striking the younger Generation Z workers the hardest with nearly half of them (46%) working in the 'gig economy'.[7] Such "involuntary part-time" employment has become recognized as a permanent problem—rather than a temporary one—per a Federal Reserve Bank of San Francisco post in April 2018.[8]

Part-time ("gig") contract workers provide corporations and their well-heeled plutocratic shareholders with numerous economic advantages over full-time benefit workers from a predatory capitalist perspective. Such 'throw-away labor' is ultimately utilized to maximize the profit line of corporations in the United States, and increasingly the United Kingdom, within the larger and hyper-competitive globalized economy. Rather than being a stand-alone trending data point, it should be considered to exist within the larger context of evolving Western economic phases and labor models (See Table 1).

Table 1. Western Economic Phases and Labor Models

ECONOMIC PHASE	TIME PERIOD	LABOR MODEL	PHASE ATTRIBUTES
Industrial Welfare State	Post-World War II through 1970s	• Full-Time Employment (Benefits & Retirement) • Strong Labor Unions • High Taxation of Economic Elites	• State Moderated Capitalism • Robust Middle Class • Strong Political Parties • Political Insurgencies
Industrial Deconstruction/ Informational Transition	1980s through 2010s	• Increasing Part-Time Employment (No Benefits) • Weak Labor Unions • Low Taxation of Economic Elites	• Globalized Economy • Thinning of the Middle Class • Wealth Polarization • Political Party Fragmentation • Predatory Capitalism • Religious & Commercial Insurgencies (Criminal & Plutocratic)
Informational/ Market State	2020s+	• Increasing Robotic Automation and AI Systems • *Part-Time Employment Levels Will Further Increase*	• *The preceding phase attributes as initial status quo trajectory futures* • *US Third Party Potentials* • *Authoritarian Insurgency*

Italics—Speculative Futures

Two contemporary economic and labor phases can be said to have existed for the US and the UK since post World War II—with an emergent phase now in the offing. The initial phase beginning in roughly 1945 and extending into the 1970s can generally be considered the heyday of the modern industrial welfare state. Full-time employment of blue and increasingly white-collar workers with health and retirement benefits represented the archetype supported by strong labor unions. Economic elites were kept in check by high levels of taxation for societal redistribution purposes—a lesson learned from the extreme measure of political influence and economic excesses which took place during the earlier Gilded Age and well into the late 1920s which contributed to a global depression. This labor model existed within the context of the prevailing form of state moderated capitalism that was in play which resulted in the rise of a robust middle class in the US and the UK. Strong democratic representation was the order of the day with the Tories and Labour in the UK and Republicans and Democrats in the US not always ideologically agreeing on policies but able to mutually enact centrist legislation that keep the majority of their citizenry relatively franchised. The dominant insurgency form of this era was politically based and Maoist in its revolutionary tradition.[9]

The second contemporary economic and labor phase—that of industrial deconstruction and informational transition—roughly spans the 1980s through the 2010s; the recent here and now. This phase has witnessed the rise of the part-time (no benefits or job security) worker employment model. Along with this deconstruction process—which saw the emergence of rust belts and communities within these states—came the decline in the strength (and political influence) of labor unions. This shifting labor model has taken place within the greater context of the ongoing compression of the middle class structure in both America and the United Kingdom with the loss of living wage blue and white-collar jobs. The accelerating forces of globalization have also resulted in a 'winner take all' form of predatory capitalism emerging in the West (and in fact globally) that has increasingly polarized wealth between the economic haves and have nots.[10] With the loss of the socio-economic middle class buffer, political fragmentation of the dominant party structures in both the US and the UK has taken place. One component of this fragmentation has been the election of the populist Trump administration in the US that is the antithesis of many Republication party values—a party that merely served as an expedient political vessel for its ascendancy. During this era, the dominant types of insurgency have shifted away from the political (e.g. Maoist revolutionary) to religious (e.g. spiritual, primarily radical Islamist) and commercial (criminal and plutocratic variant) forms.[11]

The emergent economic and labor phase of the 2020s and beyond is still relatively opaque, however, one component of it is already clear. Robotics and AI systems are increasingly being utilized in economic production with the projection that more and more human jobs will be replaced by these advanced technologies and manufacturing processes[12] This will result in the loss of full time jobs as a cost saving measure by corporations seeking to squeeze out more profits. In all likelihood, part-time employment levels will further increase as a result, only serving to further cull the middle class in America and the United Kingdom.[13] What is more speculative are the attributes of this emergent phase. From a status quo perspective, the pre-existing ones will initially extend along their present trajectories, however, they will then begin to deviate as new governmental and non-state actor policies and economic and social class structures begin to form. For instance, increasing wealth polarization in the Western states—along with high levels of public and private mass citizenry debt—is unsustainable[14] and will either result in the creation of new top down national governmental policies and/or bottom up street level societal protest and unrest in response. Some sort of 3rd party political realignment in the US may also be expected with independent voters—representing a 'void party'—now becoming the largest political bloc. Additionally, concern exists that an authoritarian insurgent form (representative of a fusion of plutocratic and criminal insurgency components) will develop with China, and potentially Russia, utilizing it to further undermine the Western liberal democracies and their allies.

In retrospect, the increasing permanent use of part-time employees in the US and UK to the detriment of full time employee positions should on its own be cause for consternation. However, when considered within the larger context of broader economic and class structure changes taking place in the West, these changes portend the increasing compression of the middle class and the ascendancy of plutocratic interests within Western states as they further transition from industrial to post-industrial (informational) based economic production. The burning question now is whether the middle class citizenry of the US and the UK go quietly into the night or if they will begin to flex what electoral influence they still retain in order to enact more fair and equitable national wealth redistributive policies vis-à-vis the growing power and influence of the plutocratic class.

Sources

Macy Bayern, "How the gig economy will change in 2019." *TechRepublic*. 12 December 2018, https://www.techrepublic.com/article/how-the-gig-economy-will-change-in-2019/.

Abha Bhattarai, "Now hiring, for a one-day job: the gig economy hits retail." *The Washington Post*. 4 May 2018, https://www.washingtonpost.com/business/economy/now-hiring-for-a-...d3c-4257-11e8-ad8f-27a8c409298b_story.html?utm_term=.ce8ffdba8e70.

Jim Edwards, "Unemployment is low only because 'involuntary' part-time work is high." *Business Insider*. 27 January 2019, https://www.businessinsider.com/unemployment-vs-involuntary-part-time-work-underemployment-2019-1.

Patrick Gillespie, "America's part-time worker problem is permanent, San Francisco Fed says." *CNN*. 11 April 2018, https://money.cnn.com/2018/04/11/news/economy/part-time-unemployment/index.html.

Nicole Torres, "Are There Good Jobs in the Gig Economy?" *Harvard Business Review*. July-August 2018 Issue, https://hbr.org/2018/07/are-there-good-jobs-in-the-gig-economy.

Notes

1. https://smallwarsjournal.com/jrnl/art/plutocratic-insurgency-note-11-low-paid-part-time-gig-economy-new-involuntary-labor-model.
2. Jim Edwards, "Unemployment is low only because 'involuntary' part-time work is high." *Business Insider*. 27 January 2019, https://www.businessinsider.com/unemployment-vs-involuntary-part-time-work-underemployment-2019-1 and Abha Bhattarai, "Now hiring, for a one-day job: the gig economy hits retail."

The Washington Post. 4 May 2018, https://www.washingtonpost.com/business/economy/now-hiring-for-a-...d3c-4257-11e8-ad8f-27a8c409298b_story.html?utm_term=.ce8ffdba8e70.

3. Robert J. Bunker and Pamela Ligouri Bunker, "Plutocratic Insurgency Note No. 3: No Shoring: Job Obsolescence Via Artificial Intelligence (AI) and Robotics." *Small Wars Journal*. 22 February 2017, https://smallwarsjournal.com/index.php/jrnl/art/plutocratic-insurgency-note-no-3-no-shoring-job-obsolescence-via-artificial-intelligence-ai.

4. John Robb, "Onward to a Hollow State." *Global Guerrillas*. 22 September 2008, https://globalguerrillas.typepad.com/globalguerrillas/2008/09/onward-to-a-hol.html and his follow on "Hollow State" writings.

5. T.J. McCue, "57 Million U.S. Workers Are Part Of The Gig Economy." *Forbes*. 31 August 2018, https://www.forbes.com/sites/tjmccue/2018/08/31/57-million-u-s-workers-are-part-of-the-gig-economy/#125816aa7118. Still determining such part-time employment numbers can be problematic. Economists of one 2016 study had to downgrade their findings. See Lydia DePillis, "There are fewer gig jobs than you think. Economists walk back study that showed huge increase." *CNN*. 10 January 2019, https://www.cnn.com/2019/01/07/economy/gig-economy-katz-krueger/index.html.

6. Jim Edwards, "Unemployment is low only because 'involuntary' part-time work is high." *Business Insider*.

7. Marc Bayern, "How the gig economy is fundamentally changing the next generation of work." *TechRepublic*. 28 September 2018, https://www.techrepublic.com/article/how-the-gig-economy-is-fundamentally-changing-the-next-generation-of-work/.

8. Federal Reserve Bank of San Francisco, "Involuntary Part-Time Work: Yes, It's Here to Stay." *SF Fed Blog*. 11 April 2018, https://www.frbsf.org/our-district/about/sf-fed-blog/involuntary-part-time-work-here-to-stay/.

9. Mao Zedong, *On Guerrilla Warfare*. Translated by Samuel Griffith. Champaign, IL: Illinois University Press, 2000 (1937 Original Chinese publication).

10. See, for instance, Mark Abadi, "Income Inequality Is Growing Across the U.S. — Here's How Bad it Is In Every State." *Money*. 21 March 2018, http://money.com/money/5207987/income-inequality-every-state/ and Matt Egan, "Record inequality: The top 1% controls 38.6% of America's wealth." *CNN*. 27 September 2017, https://money.cnn.com/2017/09/27/news/economy/inequality-record-top-1-percent-wealth/index.html.

11. For the basis of the commercial and spiritual insurgency projections, see Steven Metz, *The Future of Insurgency*. Carlisle, PA: Strategic Studies Institute, US Army War College, 1 December 1993, https://ssi.armywarcollege.edu/pubs/display.cfm?pubID=344.

12. Courtney Connley, "Robots may replace 800 million workers by 2030. These

skills will keep you employed." *CNBC*. 30 November 2017, https://www.cnbc.com/2017/11/30/robots-may-replace-up-to-800-million-workers-by-2030.html. A more recent study suggests this trend may take place at a slower pace than initially projected. See Suzie Dundas, "Robots Replacing Humans In Manufacturing? Not So Fast, New Study Says." *Forbes*. 12 November 2018, https://www.forbes.com/sites/suziedundas/2018/11/12/robots-replacing-humans-in-manufacturing-not-so-fast-new-study-says/#f570e207fb16.

13. See, for instance, Liz Alderman, "Europe's Middle Class Is Shrinking. Spain Bears Much of the Pain." *The New York Times*. 14 February 2019, https://www.nytimes.com/2019/02/14/business/spain-europe-middle-class.html and Carlos Vacas-Soriano and Enrique Fernández-Macías, "Europe's shrinking middle class." *Eurofound*. 23 Juni 2017, https://www.eurofound.europa.eu/de/publications/blog/europes-shrinking-middle-class.

14. The US national debt is now $22 trillion; Bill Chappell, "U.S. National Debt Hits Record $22 Trillion." *NPR*. 13 February 2019, https://www.npr.org/2019/02/13/694199256/u-s-national-debt-hits-22-trillion-a-new-record-thats-predicted-to-fall and the UK "General government gross debt was £1,763.8 billion at the end of the financial year ending March 2018, equivalent to 85.4% of gross domestic product (GDP)"; "UK government debt and deficit: September 2018." Office for National Standards. 17 January 2019, https://www.ons.gov.uk/economy/governmentpublicsectorandtaxes/publicspending/bulletins/ukgovernmentdebtanddeficitforeurostatmaast/september2018. Concerning US private debt; "U.S. household debt rises to $13.3 trillion in second quarter." *Reuters*. 14 August 2018, https://www.reuters.com/article/us-usa-fed-debt/u-s-household-debt-rises-to-13-3-trillion-in-second-quarter-idUSKBN1KZ1QZ.

Further Reading

Anand Giridharadas, *Winners Take All: The Elite Charade of Changing the World*. New York: Knopf, 2018.

David Graeber, *Bullshit Jobs: A Theory*. New York: Simon & Schuster, 2018.

Louis Hyman, *Temp: How American Work, American Business, and the American Dream Became Temporary*. New York: Viking, 2018.

Sarah Kessler, *Gigged: The End of the Job and the Future of Work*. New York: Saint Martin's Press, 2018.

Alissa Quart, *Squeezed: Why Our Families Can't Afford America*. New York: Ecco, 2018.

Andrew Yang, *The War on Normal People: The Truth About America's Disappearing Jobs and Why Universal Basic Income Is Our Future*. New York: Hachette Books, 2018.

All opinions are strictly those of the authors and in no way reflect the viewpoints of any U.S. Governmental, academic, or corporate entity.

Postscript

Wealth and Power in the Hands of the Few

George Thomas

Overland Park, KS

February 2019

My first encounter with the term "plutocratic insurgency" came from reading the series of articles on the subject published by Robert J. Bunker and Pamela Ligouri Bunker on the *Small Wars Journal* website. It was clear to me that their work was of momentous significance. It seemed to me that some kind of breakthrough in conflict theory had been achieved. Many writers, of course, have commented on the tremendous wealth inequalities of modern society. The topic has been discussed with varying degrees of alarm for many years. Yet the Bunkers took matters one step further: they identified the unrelenting aggregation of wealth and influence into the hands of a few *as a new form of insurgent warfare*. As far as I am aware, no one else had made this critical connection.

And yet the evidence was there, right before our eyes. The systematic effort of the elites to reshape all sectors of society for their benefit—a convenient definition of the term "plutocratic insurgency"—penetrated nearly every aspect of modern life. It went far beyond the mere hoarding of wealth. It stretched into aspects of society that the plutocrats of ages past could never have hoped to control: information and public education, health care, land use and planning, artificial intelligence, even genetic engineering.

There was no way to avoid the conclusion that this was a form of insurgent warfare. The fact that it was taking place slowly and in the shadows made it that much more disturbing. And it was a new kind of insurgency. Unlike the insurgencies of old, it did not work from the "bottom up;" rather, it was waged from the "top down." The insurgents were not jungle-dwelling guerrillas with automatic rifles. They were suited economic and political elites who sought to restructure all of human life for their sole benefit. I did what I could to amplify the Bunkers' work with my own articles and podcasts on the subject. Yet the topic remains mostly off-limits for the mainstream media. The reasons for this are not difficult to understand. The rise and progress of the plutocratic insurgency are evidence of an unforgivable betrayal by political leaders of the public they were sworn to serve and protect.

The cyclic concentration of wealth and power in the hands of the few is a familiar theme in history. The Athenian statesman Solon (c. 638 B.C.—c. 558 B.C.) was confronted with a situation during his archonship where his city-state's wealth and land was controlled by a very few. The debt burden on the citizenry became crushing, and there was talk of open revolt. Solon's wise reforms included the reduction of personal debt, the control of usurious interest, the calibration of income tax to make the rich pay at a rate twelve times that of the poor, and thorough reforms of a court system that had favored the plutocracy. The rich were furious, and called these measures confiscation, but it soon became clear that Solon's foresight had saved Athens from civil breakdown.

Rome took a different course. When the landed aristocracy's control over Roman economic life began to throttle commerce and impoverish its citizens, cries for reform became louder. The Gracchus brothers—Tiberius and then Caius—set out to introduce desperately needed corrective legislation. Tiberius Gracchus proposed to limit land ownership to 333 acres per person (thereby breaking up Italy's huge landed estates, called *latifundia*), and tried to enlist the public to support his projects. The Roman senate, controlled by the rich, dug in its heels and refused to take action; Tiberius himself was killed in 133 B.C. after a campaign of incitement against him. His brother Caius sought to complete his brother's work, but was himself maligned and finally slain in 121 B.C. Social reform never really took place, and Rome suffered thereafter from protracted civil wars and domestic turbulence.

Another example is provided by Renaissance Italy. The city-state of Florence in the late 13th century suffered from an imbalance of political and economic power. In its hands the nobility had concentrated vast powers to the detriment of common citizens, who were either ignored or deliberately disenfranchised. Political leaders functioned as the hand-puppets of powerful families—the medieval equivalent of the modern corporate conglomerate or "special interest" group—who pulled the strings from behind the scenes. Demagogues, ever-ready to prey on the innocence or gullibility of the masses, promised what they never intended to deliver; and when they could not deliver, they contented themselves with distracting the populace with frights, amusements, or foreign military adventures.

Into this picture stepped the figure of Giano Della Bella (1240–1305). Like many great reformers in history, he himself was a noble who grew disgusted with the avarice and lack of public feeling displayed by his class. The historian Leonardo Bruni called him *claris quidem maioribus ortus, sed ipse modicus civis et apprime popularis*, which means "born of illustrious ancestors, but a citizen both moderate and very much popular in his inclinations." Giano was outraged by both the arrogance of the nobility, as well as the blind inertia of the people, who were willing to sit in silence in the face of shameful servitude. He took to warning the people of Florence that their fates were all linked together and that, if the nobility were successful in pitting one group or faction against another, it would be successful in denying the people their rights. The historian Bruni states:

> He thought it was extremely foolish to believe
> that violence would not eventually come to each man
> personally. When the first opponents were successfully

subdued [by the nobility], such violence would then leap to each man's roof, spreading like a conflagration. Something had to be done now, so the growth of the evil was not simply allowed in silence. The evil had spread somewhat, to be sure; but it had not yet become so strong that it could not be remedied. But if they [the citizens] neglected their responsibilities any longer, and watched for one man or another to do something, they would in vain be looking for help against a debilitating pestilence (*frustra tandem auxilium contra inveteratam pestem optaturos*).[1]

Florentines were aroused by Giano's uncompromising talk, the likes of which they had never before heard. Eventually, a body of laws called the Ordinances of Justice was passed. These ordinances targeted about thirty-eight powerful families who controlled the industry and economic life in Florence; the nobility was hit hard by the laws, and the good of the public began to replace what had previously been the good of a small minority. Giano himself was elevated to political power.

Giano's reforms naturally aroused extreme anger with the nobility, who screamed (as they do now) about "confiscation" and "unfairness." He was not helped by the short memory of the people, which is inclined to forget that hard-won reforms can vanish as quickly as the morning mist if money and power are allowed once again to concentrate in the hands of a few. Giano began to be blamed for riots he had not instigated. The poor wanted him to go farther than he did; the rich, less than he had. The result was that he was criticized by both extremes of society; factionalism gathered strength and bided its time. But here Giano proved he was the greater man. Not wishing to be blamed as the spark that touched off a civil war, he agreed to go into exile. "I cede to the slanders of my enemies, and permit a place for their jealousies." (*Cedamus potius inimicorum calumniis, et locum invidiae permittamus*). It was a cruel ending for a man who had done so much for his republic.

Similar examples of reform to check the power of plutocracies can be found in the twentieth-century American political careers of

Theodore Roosevelt and Franklin D. Roosevelt. These presidents were willing to confront the entrenched power of the railroad and banking industries when it became clear that their monopolies threatened the national health. The picture that emerges from all these examples is that hyperconcentration of wealth is a historical tendency that must be alleviated by periodic social reform. Some societies succeed in carrying out such reforms, and some do not. "The student of insurgency and practitioner of counterinsurgency," says the US Army's *Counterinsurgency Field Manual* (FM 3-24), "must begin by understanding the specific circumstances of their particular situation; while studying the history of this mode of warfare, they must also understand how varied it can be."[2] This is certainly true. Bold, courageous leadership must be willing to confront entrenched plutocracies and fight them with the same weapons they deploy against the public.

It is hoped that the seminal work appearing in this volume increases the public's awareness of the insurgency directed against it. We must have the courage to examine what is happening in our society, rather than retreat into delusions or platitudes. We must see the situation as it exists, rather than how we wish it to be. We must free ourselves of outmoded ways of thinking, and take bold measures when necessary. During another terrible time in our nation's history, Abraham Lincoln said in a message to Congress on December 1, 1862 that "The dogmas of the quiet past are inadequate to the stormy present. The occasion is piled high with difficulty, and we must rise with the occasion. As our case is new, so we must think anew, and act anew."

Few things are inevitable in history. We must take heart in knowing that social trends are not necessarily irreversible. Determined action and bold leadership can move mountains when the right conditions are present. For if it is true that the plutocratic insurgency exists—which it undoubtedly does—then it must also be true that a counterinsurgency strategy exists. The broad outlines of such a strategy are provided by some of the historical examples cited above. But it will be the task of future generations, animated by a spirit of public duty and fortified by an iron determination, to inscribe the historical record with the specific details.

Notes

1. Author's translation of the Latin text appearing in James Hankins, Editor, *Leonardo Bruni: History of the Florentine People*. Cambridge, MA: Harvard University Press, 2001: 360.
2. Headquarters, Department of the Army, *Counterinsurgency Field Manual* (FM 3-24). Washington, DC: December 2006: 1-3, https://www.hsdl.org/?view&did=468442.

Afterword

Plutocratic Insurgency and the
Rise of Authoritarian States

John P. Sullivan

Los Angeles, CA

June 2019

Politics can be viewed as a battle for the spoils (power, wealth, prestige) that allows the winners to control their destiny. Of course in the contemporary world, politics is largely seen as a function of distributing power within and among states. Yet, the nature of states has changed over time and all power is not concentrated in states.[1] As this *Plutocratic Insurgency Reader* comes to press, liberal democracy, as the dominant form of political organization among states, is being severely challenged. Russian President Vladimir Putin, in an interview at the end of the G20 summit in Osaka in June 2019, said that 'liberalism' and multiculturalism are obsolete and have "outlived their purpose," while suggesting that nationalist populist movements represent the future of political organization.[2][3] This crisis of liberal democracy is at the core of multiple social, political, and economic challenges tearing at the foundations and legitimacy of modern states—in what Manuel Castells calls 'Rupture.'[4]

What is the source of this crisis of liberal democracy?

The fragmentation of political stability leading to new—as yet, still to be determined—political relationships is the defining characteristic of our 'post-modern' age. Indeed, Robert Bunker identified the social shifts facing us today as an 'epochal change' where war would be waged over new forms of social and political organization.[5] These new wars often challenge existing conceptions of identity.[6] As Nils Gilman noted in the preface to this collection, "We are reaching the end of the Westphalian-modernist system."[7]

The challenges to the legitimacy of the 'Westphalian state' became acutely visible after the global financial crisis of 2007-2009. Disillusion, apathy, and social division leading to a crisis of legitimacy followed in the wake of the uneven harm caused by the financial crisis. Coggan describes the implosion of the welfare state and the corruption of the political system caused by the extreme distribution of wealth (stemming from plutocratic influence).[8] For Castells, the "malignant winds" challenging us are comprised of "multiple crises" including labor insecurity and low wages, terrorism waged by fanatics that fuels fear, "fractures coexistence" and stimulates "restrictions on liberty in the name of security."[9] This leads to the rise of securitization and state surveillance. Together, these factors contribute to a crisis of governance (and state legitimacy): "the rupture of the relationship between those who govern and the governed."[10] It also leads to a lack of trust, delegitimizes political institutions and a search for new frameworks of representation. The interim result is chaos and conflict. Pretenders for governance arise and compete for control. Economic stresses lead to inequality and the rise of criminal challengers to the state.

Economic Inequality

Economic inequality is a major source of discontent and both a source and result of 'plutocratic insurgency.' Thomas Picketty, the French economist, describes the critical situation of global income inequality in his work *Capital in the Twenty-Fist Century* (also referred to as *C21*).[11] For Piketty, the rate of return on capital is greater than the rate of economic growth, leading to the concentration of wealth and unequal wealth distribution. Piketty's work questions the capital-labor split and the dynamics of the interactions between capital and income and specifically, for our purposes, inequality and the concentration of wealth. Extreme income inequality is essentially a destabilizing force in both national and global contexts.

In the United States, Piketty demonstrated that income inequality basically followed a 'U shaped curve' with the share of overall income held by the top ten percent of households climbing steeply in the 'Roaring Twenties,' falling sharply in the decade following 1929's 'Great Crash,' and then steadily rising to top the pre-Depression levels by 2007.[12] These figures rose again by 2012 to show real income growth by the top 1% between 1993-2012 at 86.1% while the bottom 99% only experienced real growth of 6.6% with the top 1% capturing 68% of total income growth. In the post-financial crisis recovery (2009-2012), these figures show an even starker picture with real income growth of the top 1% at 31.4% compared to a 0.4% real income growth for the bottom 99%; that is, the top 1% captured 95% of the growth during that 'recovery.'[13] The income distribution of the top 1% echoes the shape of the inequality curve with the top 15% gaining the bulk of the benefit as a result of the concentration of capital in their hands.[14]

Unequal income distribution is a serious concern. In the United States, the richest 10% of households now account for 70% of all wealth. Indeed, as has long been stated, the gaps between the have and have-nots are deepening.[15] This stark income inequality drives the growth of the illicit global political economy (illicit flows and deviant globalization) as criminal cartels, mafias, and gangs fill the void in state legitimacy left by legitimate political actors ceding their roles to criminals and plutocrats.[16] As a consequence, states lose capacity and legitimacy, eroding their own solvency. Corruption (and impunity) become the new currency of power and plunder.[17] For Castells, Russia was at the forefront of the deviant global economy. Crime, business, and politics merged to forge a new networked 'criminal-counterpower' amassing power and profit.[18] This corrupt nexus threatens global security according to Sarah Chayes.[19]

Plutocratic Insurgency and State Change

The conceptualization of 'plutocratic insurgency' as a driver of state change is at first glance controversial. For many, 'insurgency' is merely an uprising directed toward changing the government of a state. In that formulation, rebels and guerrillas wage civil war to capture the reins of the state and govern. That is one—albeit, I would argue a narrow and outdated—view. It certainly captures much of the revolutionary warfare of the 19th-20th Century, but misses the current and emerging conflicts in much of the Global South where criminal bands wage war to gain (or retain) freedom of movement and change the nature of states by dominating the illicit flows of the global criminal political economy, corrupt and co-opt states, exercise territorial control, and become the *de facto* rulers of large territorial spaces.

'Criminal insurgencies' and 'crime wars' are altering the nature of sovereignty and governance.[20] The result is potentially 'mafia' or 'narco' states.[21] The traditional view is one where 'insurgency' is seen as 'hard' insurgency where there is overt conflict seeking state change rather than 'soft' insurgency where a range of tools (including kinetic and cyber conflict) contribute to state change. Here we see Joseph S. Nye's distinction between "hard' and 'soft' power playing out.[22] A range of insurgent actors are able to exploit both types of power as seen in the 'twin' criminal and 'plutocratic' insurgencies. Criminal insurgencies come from below where the global disenfranchised (criminal cartels and gangs) resist, co-opt, and avoid states to enrich themselves and challenge incumbent political actors while, from the top, globalized elites elude national obligations and responsibilities, like taxes, to enrich themselves. Both seek power and freedom from state constraints on their economic activity.[23]

While some see both the criminal and plutocratic insurgent constructs as a variety of organized crime or kleptocracy rather than an insurgent driver of state change, this collection asserts that 'plutocratic insurgency' goes beyond merely corrupt rulers extracting resources for personal gain as seen in the classic case of Gaius Verres, the corrupt governor of Sicily[24] but instead their quest for power and profit benefits a small 'plutocratic' class that subverts legitimate political economy to the point that it changes the nature of the state. The result, as we are seeing, is a trend toward authoritarian regimes that erode democracy in a pattern similar to the 'Putinization' of the Russian state (and now the Chinese 'surveillance' state).[25][26]

Conclusion

The interim result of 'plutocratic insurgency' is a 'new Gilded Age.' As Paul Krugman observed, we are experiencing a second Gilded Age— or in Piketty's words a second *Belle Époque* characterized by the incredible rise of the one percent.[27] Now, income inequality must be viewed as a potential contributor to political instability and change. Capital is largely seen as the economic driver of growth, while labor and workers are deemphasized. The losers are the middle and working classes. In the short-term, populist sentiment is on the rise as dissatisfaction is vented on the neoliberal state. Yet, in the long-term, it is expected that the failed promises of the plutocratic movement will continue to fuel additional instability and ultimately economic and political conflict.

As Piketty observed in *C21*, "Capitalism automatically generates arbitrary and unsustainable inequalities that radically undermine the meritocratic values on which democratic societies are built."[28] While Picketty implicitly acknowledges the political component of capital, his discussion of broader politics with the political economy of capital is scant. As Jacobs notes in her critique of *C21*, much of his implied political theory is apparently rooted in faith in deliberative democracy's power.[29] This power, however, is diminished when the rich (plutocrats and oligarchs) gain an amplified voice due to the access to power (or the corridors of power) that money allows.

Both rich individuals and corporations acting through lobbyists and powerful political action groups can skew the democratic allocation of power and, in turn, erode the rule of law through the corrosive power of corruption. This corrosive effect of corruption applies to both plutocratic and criminal power (and combinations of both). The essays contained in this collection help frame the discussion for the political dimensions of plutocratic insurgency as it erodes democratic foundations and interacts with criminal insurgencies to amplify its corrosive reach though these 'twin insurgencies'.

This text explores the dimensions and dynamics of the concentration of wealth, income inequality, corruption, and the erosion of state legitimacy and democratic precepts. The rise of state challengers is anticipated. Their exact form remains to be seen: will it be a deviant variation of the market state (as envisioned by Bobbitt),[30] a criminal or market state (as envisioned by Moisés Naím),[31] a dystopian variant of the network state (as envisioned by Castells),[32] or a 'nexus-state' (as described by Ronfeldt).[33] In the interim, authoritarian potentials appear to be ascendant.[34] Further analysis is needed to see which of these major state variants (or hybrids among them) is likely to emerge. This collection provides some of the raw material needed to conduct that assessment.

Notes

1. See Philip Bobbitt, *The Shield of Achilles: War, Peace and the Course of History*. New York: Alfred Knopf, 2002; and Martin van Creveld, *The Rise and Decline of the State*. Cambridge: Cambridge University Press, 1999, for salient discussions of state transformation over time.
2. "Putin: Russian president says liberalism 'obsolete'," *BBC News*, 28 June 2019, https://www.bbc.com/news/world-europe-48795764 and Lionel Barber, Henry Foy, and Alex Barker, "Vladimir Putin says liberalism has

'become obsolete'," *Financial Times*, 27 June 2019, https://www.ft.com/content/670039ec-98f3-11e9-9573-ee5cbb98ed36.

3. When asked about Putin's comments about 'Western Liberalism' being in decline, US President Trump, who espouses nationalist populist views—either not understanding the concept or obfuscating his position—launched into a criticism of domestic 'liberals,' who he sees as opponents to his agenda, in Los Angeles and San Francisco. David Nakamura, "In Japan, Trump calls Jimmy Carter a 'terrible president' and says Kamala Harris got 'too much credit' in debate." *Washington Post*, 29 June 2019, https://www.washingtonpost.com/politics/in-japan-trump-calls-jimmy-carter-a-terrible-president-and-says-kamala-d-harris-got-too-much-credit-in-debate/2019/06/29/27969022-9a46-11e9-830a-21b9b36b64ad_story.html?utm_term=.1dd75626aae7.

4. Manuel Castells (Rosie Marteau, Trans.), *Rupture: The Crisis of Liberal Democracy*. Cambridge: Polity Press, 2019, 3.

5. See Robert J. Bunker, "Epochal Change: War over Social and Political Organization." *Parameters*, 27.2 (1997): 15-25.

6. Michael Vlahos, *Fighting Identity: Sacred War and World Change*. Westport, CT: Praeger Security, 2009.

7. Nils Gilman, "Preface" to this work. The Westphalian system is the foundation of the states system where states have sovereignty over their own territory. This 'sovereignty' is challenged from many fronts ranging from international organizations, like the United Nations, supra-national organizations, like the European Union, and criminal challengers like drug cartels and warlords from below.

8. Philip Coggan, *The Last Vote: The Threats to Western Democracy*. London: Allen Lane (Penguin), 2013.

9. Ibid, see note 4.

10. Ibid, see note 4.

11. Thomas Piketty (Arthur Goldhammer, Trans.), *Capital in the Twenty-First Century*. Cambridge, MA: Belknap Press (Harvard University), 2014.

12. See John Cassidy, "Piketty's Inequality Story in Six Charts," *The New Yorker*, 26 March 2014, https://www.newyorker.com/news/john-cassidy/pikettys-inequality-story-in-six-charts. In addition, Picketty's main findings are reviewed in John Cassidy, "Forces of Divergence," *The New Yorker*, 24 March 2104, https://www.newyorker.com/magazine/2014/03/31/forces-of-divergence.

13. Emmanuel Saez, "Striking it Richer: The Evolution of Top Incomes in the United States (Updated with 2012 preliminary estimates). Working paper. Berkeley: University of California, Berkeley, 3 September 2013, https://eml.berkeley.edu//~saez/saez-UStopincomes-2012.pdf.

14. Ibid, notes 11 and 12. The same increases in the updated 2012 figures referenced in note 12 are found in the share of income held (or should we say taken) by the

top 1%. These are the highest since 1928.

15. Mark DeCambre, "The richest 10% of households now represent 70% of all U.S. wealth," *MarketWatch*, 31 May 2019, https://www.marketwatch.com/story/the-richest-10-of-households-now-represent-70-of-all-us-wealth-2019-05-24.

16. Noah Raford and Andrew Trablusi (Eds.), *Warlords, Inc.: Black Markets, Broken States, and the Rise of the Warlord Entrepreneur*. Berkeley: North Atlantic Books, 2015.

17. See Nils Gilman, Jesse Goldhammer, and Steven Webber, *Deviant Globalization: Black Market Economy in the 21ˢᵗ Century*. London & New York: Continuum, 2011. and John P. Sullivan, "How Illicit Networks Impact Sovereignty," (Chapter 10) in Michael Miklaucic and Jacqueline Brewer (Eds.), *Convergence: Illicit Networks and national Security in the Age of Globalization*. Washington, DC: National Defense University Press, 2013, 171-188.

18. Manuel Castells, "The Perverse Connection: The Global Criminal Economy," (Chapter 3) in *End of Millennium, The Information Age: Economy, Society and Culture (Vol. III)*. Oxford: Blackwell, 2000.

19. Sarah Chayes, *Thieves of States: Why Corruption Threatens Global Security*. New York: W.W. Norton & Company, 2015.

20. See John P. Sullivan, "From Drug Wars to Criminal Insurgency: Mexican Cartels, Criminal Enclaves and Criminal Insurgency in Mexico and Central America. Implications for Global Security." Paris: Fondation Maison des sciences de l'homme. FMSH-WP-2012-09, April 2012, https://halshs.archives-ouvertes.fr/halshs-00694083/document; John P. Sullivan and Robert J. Bunker, "Rethinking insurgency: criminality, spirituality and societal warfare in the Americas." Robert J. Bunker, (Ed.), *Criminal Insurgencies in Mexico and the Americas: The Gangs and Cartels Wage War*. London: Routledge, 2012: 742-762; and Robert Muggah and John P. Sullivan, "The Coming Crime Wars." *Foreign Policy*, 21 September 2018, https://foreignpolicy.com/2018/09/21/the-coming-crime-wars/.

21. John P. Sullivan and Robert J. Bunker (Eds.), *The Rise of the Narcostate (Mafia States)—A Small Wars Journal-El Centro Anthology*. Bloomington: Xlibris, 2018, https://www.amazon.com/Rise-Narcostate-John-P-Sullivan/dp/198454392X.

22. See Joseph S. Nye, Jr. *The Future of Power*. New York: Public Affairs, 2011 for a discussion of the varieties of power in modern state competition.

23. Nils Gilman, "The Twin Insurgency." *The American Interest*. Vol.9, No. 6, 15, June 2014, https://www.the-american-interest.com/2014/06/15/the-twin-insurgency/.

24. See Marcus Tullius Cicero, *In Verrem*. Rome (70 BC). References at "The Trial of Gaius Verres: Selected Links & Bibliography," *Famous Trials*, https://www.famous-trials.com/gaius-verres/71-links.

25. Putinization is shorthand for the erosion of the state and shift from liberal democracies to an authoritarian state(s) that is tightly coupled with organized

crime and criminal oligarchs.

26. The Chinese surveillance state uses technology and oppression as dual means of social control See Michael Barbaro, Andy Mills, Alexandra Leigh Young, Jessica, Cheung, Luke Vander Ploeg, and Lisa Tobin, "The Chinese Surveillance State, Part I." *New York Times* ("The Daily" Podcast), 6 May 2019, https://www.nytimes.com/2019/05/06/podcasts/the-daily/china-surveillance-uighurs.html.

27. See Paul Krugman, "Why We're in a New Gilded Age," (Chapter Three) in Heather Boushey, J. Bradford DeLong, and Marshall Steinbaum (Eds.). *After Piketty: The Agenda for Economics and Inequality.* Cambridge, MA: Harvard University Press, 2017, 60-74.

28. Piketty, *Capital (C21).* 1.

29. Elizabeth Jacobs, "Everywhere and Nowhere: Politics in C21,: (Chapter Twenty-One) in Heather Boushey. J. Bradford Delong, and Marshall Steinbaum (Eds.). *After Piketty: The Agenda for Economics and Inequality,* 512-540.

30. On Bobbitt's analysis on alternative forms of the market state, see note 1.

31. Naím's conception of mafia States is discussed in "Mafia States: Organized Crime Takes Office," *Foreign Policy,* May/June 2012, https://www.foreignaffairs.com/articles/2012-04-20/mafia-states. He also discusses criminal states with Michael Miklaucic in Michael Miklaucic and Moisés Naím, "The Criminal State," (Chapter 9) in Michael Miklaucic and Jacqueline Brewer (Eds.), *Convergence: Illicit Networks and national Security in the Age of Globalization.* Washington, DC: National Defense University Press, 2013, 149-170.

32. For Castells, the 'network state' or power arrangements where states interact in multilayered processes to allocate power become central. See Manuel Castells, *Communication Power.* Oxford: Oxford University Press, 2009 and John P. Sullivan and Adam Elkus, "Security in the network-state." *openDemocracy,* 6 October 2009, https://www.opendemocracy.net/en/state-change-sovereignty-and-global-security/.

33. David Ronfeldt provides a variant to Castells's network power dynamics in his concept of the nexus-state, see David Ronfeldt and Danielle Varda, "The Prospects for Cyberocracy (Revisited)." 1 December 2009. Available at SSRN: https://papers.ssrn.com/sol3/papers.cfm?abstract_id=1325809.

34. See Sullivan and Bunker, *The Rise of the Narcostate*; especially the Introduction by Sullivan and Bunker and the Afterword: "The Rise of the Oligarchs" by Robert Killebrew.

Appendix I

The Future of Insurgency—
Commercial Insurgency Excerpts

Steven Metz

*First Published 10 December 1993 at Strategic Studies Institute,
US Army War College* [1] Reprinted with permission
of the Strategic Studies Institute and U.S. Army
War College Press, U.S. Army War College.

Analysts of insurgency have long recognized that ideological rhetoric provides a poor tool for categorizing and understanding insurgency. In response, they crafted other analytical frameworks. Most of these relied on one of two variables: the goals of the insurgency, or its strategy. More sophisticated schemas combined the two.[2] But both of these variables generate analytical problems. Frameworks based on the goals of insurgents assume a Western, linear, and proto-Marxist notion of development. A revolutionary insurgency is thus one seeking socialism; a reactionary opposes the Western model of development. This means that a framework based on this variable is only as valid as the model of development it assumes. Using the insurgents' strategy is equally problematic, in large part because the strategy reflects the external training and sponsors of the insurgent leadership.

In an attempt to bypass this Western bias and understand insurgency the way its proponents do rather than the way we would if we were in their position, this study examines insurgency using an essentially psychological framework. I assume that it is not a particular social, political, and economic system or condition that sparks insurgency, but a particular way of understanding this system or condition. Phrased differently, it is not repression, poverty or misery as we define it that inspires insurgency, but as the insurgents define it. Psychological factors rather than structural ones are preeminent.

Using this psychological approach, then, what forms will insurgency take in the post-cold war international system? Of course every insurgency will be unique, reflecting the history, geography, and culture of the society in which it occurs. Still, there are likely to be two dominant forms. One can be called spiritual insurgency. This is the descendant of the cold war-era revolutionary insurgency. It will be driven by the problems of modernization, especially anomie, the search for meaning, and the pursuit of justice. The other form will be commercial insurgency. This will be driven less by the desire for justice than wealth. Its psychological foundation is a warped translation of Western popular culture which equates wealth, personal meaning, and power.

***

Commercial Insurgency and the Search for Wealth. In the pursuit of personal meaning in the developing world, there is an alternative to violent nativism or other forms of spiritual insurgency. When the discontented define personal meaning by material possessions rather than psychic fulfillment, they create the environment for commercial insurgency. This was made possible when Western materialism penetrated nearly every corner of the Third World via electronic communications and widespread travel. Commercial insurgency is a quasi-political distortion of materialism. When relatively unsophisticated and discontented audiences (whether in the Third World or the inner cities of the West) are bombarded with Western or Western-style advertising, it is easy for them to associate the personal satisfaction evident among the actors and models who populate the commercials, television programs, and movies with their material possessions. Personal meaning is thus defined as owning a flashy car, clothes, and audio and video equipment. When the citizens of the Third World contrast this artificial image of Western life with their daily existence, the result is frustration and discontent. This can inflame the revolutionary impulse when the poor of the Third World recognize that the lives of their own indigenous elites appear closer to the idealized Western lifestyle than to their own, and when they expect their government to ameliorate the ensuing frustration.

The quickest and easiest path to material possessions and the satisfaction they appear to bring is crime. And, since the discontented of the Third World feel little attachment to the dominant system of values in their societies anyway, moral restraints on criminal activity are limited. In situations of perceived deprivation and frustration— and again this holds for American inner cities as well as the Third World—the possession of wealth and power is more important than the techniques used to acquire them. In this psychological context, commercial insurgency is essentially widespread and sustained criminal activity with a proto-political dimension that challenges the security of the state. In the modern world, its most common manifestation is narco-insurgency, although it may also be based on other forms of crime, especially smuggling. The defining feature is expansion of the criminal activity into a security threat, especially in the hinterlands where government control is limited.

This has a very long history. Its antecedents are the eternal problems of banditry and piracy. Despite contemporary arguments that the "war on drugs" is not an appropriate conflict for modern militaries, it is likely that armies and navies throughout history have spent more time fighting banditry and piracy than any other kind of security threat. Banditry and piracy were traditionally seen as security threats not only because of the tangible danger they posed to commerce and public order, but also because of what they might become. As Eric Hobsbawm pointed out in his classic work on social banditry, it often served as a precursor for revolution by illustrating the weakness of the regime and galvanizing discontent.[3] And, according to Desai and Eckstein, "The line between the criminal activity of rural bandits (who defy established authority) and their political mobilization (in attempts to alter or destroy such authority) has always been thin and has often been crossed."[4]

The same relationship holds in modern developing societies. Organized criminals find that in order to mobilize sufficient power to resist the state, they must move their organizations beyond pure criminalism with its limited appeal to most citizens and add elements of political protest. In this way, they legitimize their activities in the eyes of many people not otherwise inclined to support them but who are frustrated by the existing politico-economic system. From Robin Hood through "Pretty Boy" Floyd to Carlos Lehder and Pablo Escobar, criminals have swathed themselves in vaguely populist, anti-establishment political rhetoric to generate sympathy or outright support. Their immediate followers find personal meaning through wealth, and their sympathizers find fulfillment though seeing the regime made to look impotent and helpless.

Today, a number of Third World regimes face severe security threats from commercial insurgencies or, as in Peru and Colombia, from the marriage of spiritual and commercial insurgencies. Given their vast wealth, commercial insurgents are often able to match the technological sophistication of the government's counterinsurgent forces as they purchase items such as rocket propelled grenades and night vision goggles. They also weaken governments through bribes and corruption. Furthermore, they have developed extensive international linkages, making them an even more persistent and formidable foe. While commercial insurgents may not seek the outright capture of political power like traditional revolutionary insurgents, they can pose serious security threats. Just as simple illnesses such as mumps or measles can kill someone already stricken with another disease, commercial insurgency can prove deadly to regimes weakened by other forces.

*****

…By contrast, commercial insurgency will largely be determined by geography. For organized crime to grow to the point that it poses a security threat rather than simply a challenge to law and order, there often is some sort of geographic factor which allows the accumulation of extensive wealth by the criminal organization. Additional preconditions include weak legal and criminal justice systems, security apparatuses which do not consider commercial insurgency a security threat, and a tradition of both organized crime and political violence. The geographic factor may be a climate amenable to the production of drugs as in Peru's Upper Huallaga Valley or Southeast Asia's Golden Triangle, or location on a logical route for drugs. The geographic factor may also be a location and topography that contribute to nondrug related criminal activity such as smuggling. This geographic limitation, however, is not absolute. Some forms of criminal activity which can support commercial insurgency such as arms trafficking can occur almost anywhere, especially in the electronic age when the need for local communications and banking centers is limited.

***

The preeminent task of those who would use insurgency as a roadway to power is mobilization of support. It takes a powerful incentive for people to place themselves in serious danger, whether as active participants in an insurgency or passive supporters. In the modern world, this incentive is often discontent and frustration born of a failed search for personal meaning. When large numbers of people define personal meaning through psychic fulfillment, the outcome may be spiritual insurgency. When people define personal meaning materially, the outcome may be commercial insurgency.

The end of the cold war changed the normative structure of international politics. The United Nations and the values it represents are experiencing a renaissance. This has eroded the international support network for insurgency, and thus made it less likely to actually overthrow a regime. In addition, most Third World regimes appear stronger than in previous decades and their security forces more effective.

The democratic revolution in the Third World deflated a number of insurgencies and, so long as it lasts, helps forestall the emergence of new ones. But trends indicate that Third World regimes will face escalating challenges. As they fail to meet these challenges, insurgencies will appear. The most likely result is a spate of stalemates as regimes are unable to prevent the rise of insurgencies or to fully defeat them once they appear, but insurgents are unable to seize power without external support or the internal collapse of the regime.

All this could change if insurgent movements are able to find external sponsors and to cooperate as they did during the cold war. This will be difficult given the nativistic nature of many forthcoming insurgencies, but not impossible. International politics occasionally spawns unusual, even bizarre alliances. It is possible, then, that insurgency may again become part of interstate conflict, a form of indirect aggression made attractive by the inability of states to use conventional military power. The proliferation of weapons of mass destruction may be the trend that leads to this. In a nuclearized world, indirect aggression—including the creation and sponsorship of insurgencies—would be infinitely safer for aggressive states than more conventional uses of military force.

Frustration and discontent will persist and even increase in the Third World. So will the physical equipment and skills needed to make insurgencies. What the counterinsurgent strategists of the world must now do is recognize that much of their understanding of insurgency is dated and rapidly approaching obsolescence. After all, insurgency itself will continue to change. It is not difficult to imagine additional forms emerging further in the future. For example, what can be called "neo-inclusionist" movements could arise in opposition to exclusionist governments based on ethnic, tribal, or religious identities. The evolution of insurgency thus demands great mental flexibility on the part of those who oppose it. New forms require new mental constructs. To date, these have not appeared.

Notes

The views expressed in this report are those of the author and do not necessarily reflect the official policy or position of the Department of the Army, the Department of Defense, or the U.S. Government. This report is approved for public release; distribution is unlimited.

1. https://ssi.armywarcollege.edu/pubs/display.cfm?pubID=344.
2. For example, Bard E. O'Neill, *Insurgency and Terrorism: Inside Modern Revolutionary Warfare*, Washington: Brassey's, 1990.
3. Eric Hobsbawm, *Bandits*, n.p.: Delacorte, 1969, p. 21.
4. Raj Desai and Harry Eckstein, "Insurgency: The Transformation of Peasant Rebellion," *World Politics*, Vol. 42, No. 4, July 1990, p. 452.

Appendix II

Onward to a Hollow State

John Robb

First Published 22 September 2008 at Global Guerrillas [1]
Reprinted with permission of *Global Guerrillas.*

The modern nation-state is in a secular decline, made inevitable by the rise of a global market system. Even developed nations, like the US, are not immune to this process. The decline is at first gradual but then it suddenly accelerates until it reaches a final end-point: a hollow state. The hollow state has the trappings of a modern nation-state ("leaders", membership in international organizations, regulations, laws, and a bureaucracy) but it lacks any of the legitimacy, services, and control of its historical counter-part. It is merely a shell that has some influence over the spoils of the economy. The real power rests in the hands of corporations and criminal/guerrilla groups that vie with each other for control of sectors of wealth production. For the individual living within this state, life goes on, but it is debased in a myriad of ways.

The shift from a marginally functional nation-state in manageable decline to a hollow state often comes suddenly, through a financial crisis. This crisis typically has the following features:

- Corporations and connected individuals systematically loot the nation-state of financial assets and natural resources through a series of insider/no cost deals. These deals are made to "save" the nation's economy or financial system from collapse.
- Once the full measure of the crisis is known, the nation-state's currency falls precipitously, it's debt becomes expensive, and it is forced to submit to international oversight/rules.
- The services the state provides rapidly evaporate as its bureaucracy is starved for cash/financing. This opens up a window for the corruption of government employees unused to deprivation.

The Dynamic of Primary Loyalties

The decline from a functional nation-state to a hollow state appears sudden to observers. For individuals, the experience is a sustained decline in the standard of living. Over time, critical items and services become increasingly inaccessible—healthcare to housing. Small business disappear, or become prey to connected companies/individuals with access to the remaining coercive power of the nation-state. As the deprivation becomes commonplace, people turn to primary loyalties for support and services—loyalties to a corporation, tribe, gang, family, or community. These groups, energized by new levels of loyalty but deeply obligated to reciprocate this loyalty with support, become extremely aggressive in pursuit of their survival. Once this shift in loyalty is made, a self-generating cycle of violence, crime, and corruption (fueled in large part through connections to the global market system) becomes entrenched. The nation-state, at that point, becomes irretrievably hollow.

The Looting

It's instructive to view the US Treasury's plans for a bail-out of the global financial system through the lens of the hollow state. By this measure, the bailout as it stands today, is a form of financial looting of the US Treasury (it isn't socialism, since the government isn't nationalizing the financial system). Trillions of dollars in government monies ($700 billion to begin with) will be infused directly into the coffers of corporations and wealthy individuals (via hedge funds). Specifically, the plan buys toxic assets at inflated prices and sells them back for nearly nothing—no equity or assets of real value are provided in exchange for the purchase. The national debt will likely grow 20-30% in a single year, with obligations extended to many trillions more in guarantees.

Given this, one potential next step forward is a decline the credit rating of US debt (which radically increases the costs of US borrowing), a collapse in the dollar relative to more stable global currencies, and a rapid decline in government services. Other scenarios achieve the same result with different timing. Regardless, our (the US and the UK) journey to a hollow state has officially begun.

NOTE: <u>Philip Bobbitt</u> got it wrong in his book, "The Shield of Achilles." The prosperous market-state he envisioned through constitutional reform isn't possible. The REAL market-state, the form of governance that that has truly embraced the global market system, is hollow. In effect, a state that doesn't place any barriers between itself and the global marketplace. As a result, the only real opportunities created by the emergence of the market-state are opportunities to steal extreme wealth.

Notes

1. <u>https://globalguerrillas.typepad.com/globalguerrillas/2008/09/onward-to-a-hol.</u>
   <u>html</u>.

Appendix III

Deviant Globalization— Introduction and Conclusion Excerpts

Nils Gilman, Jesse Goldhammer, and Steven Weber, Editors

First Published in 2011 in Deviant Globalization:
Black Market Economy in the 21ˢᵗ Century. New
York: Continuum, 2011: 9-13, 274-278.
Reprint permission granted by the publisher.

The following excerpts have been drawn from the introduction and conclusion of the work and focus on the deviant globalization construct and the challenge it represents to the state and to liberal (read liberal-democratic) views of globalization. Plutocratic insurgency in retrospect exploits the deviant economic 'doppelgänger effect' within globalization by leveraging illicit (black) and sovereign-free markets for global elite impunity from sovereign rights and prerogatives.

What is Deviant Globalization?

Our goal is to add the concept of deviant globalization to the center of the ongoing debate about the dynamics and implications of global economic activity. In contrast to how deviant globalization practices and activities have been framed in the mainstream globalization debates, we consider deviant globalization more than just an annoyance or just another form of exploitation. Rather, it is a different category of economic action. What makes these value-additive processes deviant and distinctive is that they violate noneconomic, conventional, "Western" norms expressed in terms of human rights, modalities of violence and health, and even notions of the sacred.[1]

Deviant globalization is an economic concept, and also a legal and moral one. It cannot, however, be reduced merely to economic activities that violate the law, however the law is codified. On the one hand, some expressions of deviant globalization are perfectly legal, such as the journeys of American pedophiles to Canada, where the legal age of consent was fourteen (until 2008, when it was raised to 16, in order to "harmonize" with U.S. laws).[2] On the other hand, some illegal economic activities, such as monopolistic pricing, are not deviant in the sense that they offend conventional moral sensibilities. Even some of the damaging, but perfectly legal, effects of globalization are not deviant per se. The loss of unskilled jobs in Lincoln, Nebraska, to off-shore call-centers in Bangalore, India, is a distributional problem of globalization that helps some and hurts others, but it is not an example of moral arbitrage, regardless of the debate over its impact on aggregate wealth.

In contrast, here's something deviant, by our definition: Exporting toxic waste from junked European cell-phones and burying that waste in African landfills next to populated urban slums where the next generation of children will ingest high levels of mercury from landfill runoff water.[3] This example is not just a redistribution of the cost of a waste stream from one part of the world to another; it is a deviant globalization flow, for it violates what the waste-exporting players would conventionally claim are their own norms about human health. And here's another: Americans who fly to Southeast Asia to have paid sex with local young women. This transaction is not just about the exploitation of labor, but specifically about *the knowing economic exploitation of the differences in morality between the two cultures;* if those men could get the same services back home, most of them probably wouldn't pay to join the global flow of sex tourists.

Because deviant globalization operates on globalization's infrastructural backbones, we find it useful to think of it in terms of global flows of goods, services, information, people, animals, and microbes around the world.[4] What determines the pathways of deviant flows is not just border security and state authority but also the particular factor endowments that generate comparative advantage for deviant globalization processes. For instance, Romania is a hotbed of hacker activity focused on economic scams thanks to the availability of technical education, good broadband connectivity, and the relative paucity of information technology jobs that might otherwise absorb young, gifted coders into the mainstream economy.[5] Deviant flows also move through and to places that have robust demand and/or supply of particular goods and services that make up these flows—drugs, antiquities, some minerals and stones, exotic wildlife, human organs, sex, oil, highly enriched uranium, toxic wastes, and so on.

In contrast to some mainstream theories of globalization, which depict it as a process that annihilates differences across space,[6] the concept of deviant globalization highlights the continued importance of spatial differences in the structure of the global economy. Appreciating the geographic particularities of deviant flows is therefore crucial. Deviant flows move through cities—in a de facto archipelago that runs from the inner metropolitan cities of the United States to the *favelas* of Rio de Janeiro to the *banlieues* of Paris to the almost continuous urban slum belt that girds the Gulf of Guinea from Abidjan to Lagos. They move through towns and villages—along the cocaine supply route that links the mountains of Columbia to São Paulo and the waterways of West Africa to noses in the Netherlands. And they move through the "global nodes" that make up the world's financial infrastructure—from Wall Street to the City of London to Tokyo's Nihombashi District. In sum, it is possible to find manifestations of deviant globalization in almost every city, every household, every shipping lane and port, as well as almost every IP address connected to the global economy.

This broad scope is also not new. Like mainstream globalization, deviant globalization has a long historical record of geographic scope. Consider piracy, a phenomenon as old as sea-based navigation and commerce itself. Consider the eighteenth-century transatlantic slave trade, with its interconnected system of trade in human beings as well as addictive substances: sugar, alcohol, and tobacco. Consider the Victorian-era drug trade and what was de facto the British East India Company's war with the Qing Dynasty in China over trade in opium, which the company produced mainly on its colonial plantations in India.[7]

Globalization, then, has always had a deviant component. But here's where an element of conventional wisdom is actually quite correct: the scale, speed, scope, and impacts of deviant globalization have increased dramatically in the past twenty years. The articles in this book demonstrate four reasons for this acceleration, whose significance varies depending on the particular activity.

The first two reasons for this acceleration we have already discussed, because they are also the principal drivers of early twenty-first century mainstream globalization. That is, technology has compressed space and time in ways that were previously unimaginable, and the end of the Cold War opened up massive new geographies and populations, which—although not entirely disconnected from deviant globalization flows in the previous era—were suddenly liberated from structural constraints that complicated their ability to engage. The third reason is new: Ascendant neoliberal ideology allowed the disciples of privatization and marketization to spread eastward and southward—most visibly to China—and in doing so set up conditions for the disruption of traditional economic relationships and the formation of radically new ones. With all these changes came an explosion of opportunities for initiative, innovation, and entrepreneurship, not all of which rest in mainstream and licit economic action.

These three drivers of change are exactly what one would find in almost any mainstream political-economy analysis of globalization. There's a fourth dimension that sits apart from and modulates the relationships between the first three. And that is simply "power," in all its own dimensions, including most importantly the ability to define the principles and norms that make some things sanctioned and others not. In this respect, globalization and deviant globalization are no different from other socially embedded human processes, which always depend on some source of power to separate acceptable from aberrant, normal from deviant, legitimate from illegitimate behavior and action.[8]

Let's put it plainly: What enables globalization, enables deviant globalization as well. But, whereas globalization reinforces the power structures that enable it, deviant globalization works against those very sources of power. Our collective fascination with globalization's wonders can blind us to the ways in which this "good news" story is itself generating an important and powerful counternarrative. Here are some obvious but poignant examples of how deviant processes connect to, are enabled by, intersect with, or synergize around globalization:

Mainstream Globalization	Deviant Globalization
Companies like Walmart are using extraordinary supply-chain technologies to revolutionize logistics; this generates jobs for workers in developing countries and brings much cheaper mass-consumption goods to the global middle classes.	The same supply chain technologies are used to tune up the efficiency of the global supply chain for counterfeit goods. Many of the inputs for the factories that make counterfeits are competitively sourced on global markets at minimum price, and the products are transported with new efficiency to consumers.
The Internet facilitates the global distribution of information, collective production of knowledge goods, and enhances freedom to speak and to listen.	The Internet has become the easiest entry point to global systems for hostile and exploitative technologies (malware); social exploits (scams and spam); the identification of remote targets for pederasts; and the dissemination of radical ideologies that oppose or negate freedoms.
Capital mobility across national borders improves the efficiency with which the global economy allocates investment and should thereby enhance productivity immediately and, in particular, over the long term.	Capital mobility makes all kinds of finance for illegal activities, including crime and terrorism, as well as the laundering of money from other illicit activities far easier and much more challenging for political authorities.
The spreading ideology of privatization and market allocation released an historic burst of entrepreneurial energy, and raised on the order of a billion people out of abject poverty in less than a generation.	The same ideologies have lent legitimacy to the concept of "everything for sale" including human beings (both whole and in pieces). Privatization ideologies in particular have led to the collapse in public goods provision—for example, by dumping waste and garbage "elsewhere."

Although this chart draws a firm line between mainstream and deviant globalization, in practice deviant globalization operates without clear boundaries. Rather, it stretches and integrates: from the licit to the illicit, from the visible to the hidden, and from the conventional to the rogue. As the stories in this book show, the transplant doctors who arrange dubiously brokered organs for clients are also doing perfectly aboveboard transplant surgeries; the Mafiosi who traffic drugs and counterfeit goods into Europe are also running perfectly legitimate bakeries, laundromats, and farms; the companies that dump toxic waste in the Global South are listed on stock exchanges in London and New York and receive investment from pension funds that pay the healthcare benefits for retired American workers.

Seen from another perspective, it's also apparent that virtually every mainstream industry is shadowed by a deviant doppelgänger. Prescription painkillers and psychotropic medicines have their deviant counterpart in illegal narcotics; recreational travel includes sex tourism; collecting antiques fuels archaeological theft and grave-robbing; military procurement supply chains also furnish weapons to warlords; software finds its counterpart in malware; financial services mirrors money laundering; and so on. All of which is simply to say that the deviant and the mainstream are inseparable. Which is precisely why enabling mainstream globalization inevitably also enables deviant globalization.

Challenging the State

Why does this matter? Even if one grants that state-led development has mostly failed (with a few very large but still exceptional exceptions) and been widely replaced or at least back-filled by illiberal forms of self-empowerment, does that matter for the larger geopolitical system? We have pointed several times to the argument that deviant globalization is just an annoying side effect of mainstream globalization, one that saps a small amount of blood from each of these mainstream processes as a kind of persistent tax, but which doesn't affect the larger functioning of the system. From this perspective, deviant globalization might be worth commenting on, but not worth taking all that seriously, compared to the big things that "really matter" in international politics.

We disagree. Our argument is that deviant globalization has profound geopolitical implications because it is degrading state power, eroding state capacity, corroding state legitimacy, and, ultimately, undermining the foundations of mainstream globalization. More specifically, deviant globalization is creating a new type of political actor whose geopolitical importance will only grow in the coming decades. What makes these political actors unique is the fact that they thrive in weak-state environments, and their activities reinforce the conditions of this weakness. In his essay in this volume, John Robb refers to these new players as "global guerrillas."

Deviant entrepreneurs wield political power in three distinct ways. First, they have money. As we have seen, deviant entrepreneurs control huge, growing swathes of the global economy, operating most prominently in places where the state is hollowed or hollowing out. State corruption fueled by drug money on both sides of the US-Mexico border exemplifies this point. Second, many deviant entrepreneurs control and deploy a significant quota of violence—an occupational hazard for people working in extra-legal industries, who cannot count on the state to adjudicate their contractual disputes. This use of violence brings deviant entrepreneurs into primal conflict with one of the state's central sources of legitimacy, namely its monopoly (in principle) over the socially sanctioned use of force. Finally, and most controversially, these deviant entrepreneurs in some cases are also emerging as private providers of security, health care, and infrastructure—that is, precisely the kind of goods that functional states are supposed to provide to the public. Hezbollah in Lebanon, the MEND in Nigeria, the narco-traffickers in Mexico, the criminal syndicates in the favelas of Brazil—all are deviant entrepreneurs who not only have demonstrated that they can shut down their host states' basic functional capacity, thereby upsetting global markets half a world away, but who are also increasingly providing social services to local constituencies.

Deviant entrepreneurs generally do not start out as political actors, in the sense of actors who wish to control or usurp the state. In the first iteration, as we saw in the last section, deviant globalization represents a response to the failure of development and the hollowing out of the state. Once these deviant industries take off, however, they begin to take on a political life of their own. The state weakness that was a condition of deviant globalization's initial local emergence becomes something that the now empowered deviant entrepreneurs seek to perpetuate and even exacerbate. They siphon off money, loyalty, and sometimes territory; they increase corruption; and they undermine the rule of law. They also force well-functioning states in the global system to spend an inordinate amount of time, energy, and attention trying to control what comes in and out of their borders. Although deviant globalization may initially have flowered as a result of state hollowing out, as it develops, it becomes a positive feedback loop, in much the same way that many successful animal and plant species, as they invade a natural ecosystem, reshape their ecosystem in ways that improve their ability to exclude competitors.[9]

What's new in this dynamic is that many of these "political actors" only rarely develop an interest in actually taking control of the formal institutions of the state. Deviant entrepreneurs have developed market niches in which extractable returns are more profitable, and frankly easier, than anything they could get by "owning" enough of the state functions to extract rents from those instead. Organizations such as the First Command of the Capital in Brazil, the 'Ndrangheta in Italy, or the drug cartels in Mexico have no interest in taking over the states in which they operate. Why would they want that? This would only mean that they would be expected to provide a much broader and less selective menu of services to everyone, including ungrateful and low-profit clients, those so-called citizens. None of these organizations plan to declare sovereign independence and file for membership of the United Nations. What they want, simply, is to carve out autonomous spaces where they can do their business without state intervention. This underscores a crucial point about deviant globalization: it does not thrive in truly "failed" states—that is, in places where the state has completely disappeared—but rather in weak but well-connected states, in which the deviant entrepreneur can establish a zone of autonomy while continuing to rely on the state for some of the vestigial services it continues to furnish.[10]

Alas, states and deviant entrepreneurs are unlikely to find a sustainable equilibrium. On the one hand, the more deviant industries grow, the more damage they do to the political legitimacy of the states within which the deviant entrepreneurs operate, thus undermining the capacity of the state to provide the infrastructure and services that the deviant entrepreneurs want to catch a free-ride on. On the other hand, the people living in the semi-autonomous zones controlled by deviant entrepreneurs increasingly recognize those entrepreneurs rather than the hollowed out state as the real source of local power and authority—if for no other reason than the recognition that if you can't beat them, you should join them. As these groups take over functions that would have been expected of the state, their stakeholders increasingly lose interest in the hollowed-out formal state institutions.[11] Thus, even though deviant entrepreneurs hardly want to kill their host state, they may end up precipitating a process whereby the state implodes catastrophically. Something like this took place in Colombia in the 1980s, in Zaire/Congo since the 1990s, and may be taking place in Mexico today.

Challenging Liberal Views of Globalization

The foregoing claims may be a tough pill for some cheerleaders of globalization to swallow.[12] It's not so much that they question the deleterious effects of globalization on the state; it's more that the most avid advocates of mainstream globalization don't judge those effects to be a problem on balance. In fact, they almost welcome them in their promotion of mainstream globalization, for weakening states that routinely promote national interests—such as excess taxation and trade restrictions—are a net positive for the global economy. The problem is that this argument makes sense only if one believes, first, in a zero-sum game between states and markets and, second, that what the state loses, globalization wins. It's an extreme position, hard to justify in historical terms, and blind to the important synergies between states and markets.

Even for more nuanced proponents of globalization—those who recognize the importance of public goods and the role that the state plays in regulating the excesses of the market—deviant globalization is something of a nightmare. When deviant globalization comes to the fore, it calls into question sixty years of liberal economic development in the Global South and painfully replaces it with an version of unfettered economics and exploitation that causes dry rot in states. This is no longer a world in which states and markets find a tense but nonetheless functional balance of power. Rather, it is one in which the optimism that global economic integration will lift all boats is forced to confront the fact that deviant industries represent torpedoes aimed at these rising boats—torpedoes guided by deviant entrepreneurs who are as adaptable, ruthless, and consequential as their mainstream counterparts. Metropolitan observers and state leaders have failed to recognize that the existence of deviant globalization makes them less able to determine winners and losers in the global political economy. That loss of control is discomforting, but it is real. It is also a more nuanced and yet more challenging threat to conventional, policy than the one that proponents of the "failed-states" language usually recognize. In other words, the problem is not simply that states are "failing"—a phrase that implies they can and want to get "fixed." Rather, it is that the synergy between weak states and strong deviant entrepreneurs creates—sometimes involving personal political connections at a very high level—a self-reinforcing dynamic that continually reinforces and extends the scope of deviant globalization.

All of this underscores the extent to which the liberalism that supports the idea of a wholly integrated global market is a fragile, contradiction-ridden ideology, especially when it attempts to encompass communities and institutions that aren't themselves imbued with liberal values. Deviant globalization is a product of this ideological and institutional stretch. And, paradoxically, these same illiberal groups in fact often participate in the global market from an ultra-liberal economic perspective. They are free-market entrepreneurs unburdened by the moral qualms and regulatory cuffs that confine the value-added processes of liberals in wealthier nations. It's really not a question of whether participants in mainstream globalization will let these deviant entrepreneurs into the tent. They're in. And because they're in, all of us face an important and challenging question: is it really possible to be a global liberal in the early decades of the twenty-first century?

Notes

1. Our concept of "deviance" is partly a serious nod to classic sociological theories of social deviance (which derive from the seminal work of Emile Durkheim and Sigmund Freud), which stress that social deviance is, as Kai Erikson put it, "a normal product of stable institutions, a vital resource which guarded and preserved by forces found in all human organizations"; and partly an ironic nod to the fact that it is the uncritical social construction of deviance—that is, of socially unacceptable behavior—which makes possible both the opportunities and the horrors described in this volume. See Kai Erikson, "Notes on the Sociology of Deviance," *Social Problems* 9:4 (1962).
2. "Low age of consent luring pedophiles to Canada," *CBC News* (19 December 2006).
3. "Europe's e-waste in Africa," *Ghana Business News* (5 September 2009); Jon Mooallem, "The Afterlife of Cellphones," *New York Times* (13 January 2008).
4. Alternately, deviant commodities can also be thought of as "hopping" rather than "flowing" from place to place—in the sense that they skip certain locales and distribute themselves unevenly. See James Ferguson, *Global Shadows: Africa in the Neoliberal World Order* (Durham: Duke University Press, 2006).
5. Christopher Condon and Scott Morrison, "Phishing, pharming and fraud: how hackers' prying eyes threaten confidence in online commerce," *Financial Times* (9 March 2005); Nils Gilman, "Hacking Goes Pro," *Engineering and Technology* 4:3 (2009).
6. Cultural analyses of mainstream globalization tend to highlight this "deterritorializing" aspect of globalization; see for example John Tomlinson, *Globalization and Culture* (Chicago: University of Chicago Press, 1999); Nikos Papastergiadis, *The Turbulence of Migration: Globalization, Deterritorialization and Hybridity* (New York: Wiley, 2000).
7. David Courtwright, *Forces of Habit: Drugs and the Making of the Modern World* (Cambridge: Harvard University Press, 2004); Alan Karras, *Smuggling: Contraband and Corruption in World History* (London: Rowman & Littlefield, 2009).
8. In other words, we are asking the same questions of deviant globalization that Foucaultians ask of mainstream markets: how does the regulation of customs,

norms and values give rise to deviant globalization and how, in turn, do deviant flows and processes impact and undermine the more traditional notions of power associated with sovereignty? See Michel Foucault, *Discipline and Punish: The Birth of the Prison* (New York: Vintage Books, 1995) and *"Society Must Be Defended": Lectures at the College de France, 1975-1976* (New York: Picador, 2003).

9. John P. Sullivan and Robert J. Bunker, "Drug Cartels, Street Gangs, and Warlords," *Small Wars & Insurgencies* 13:2 (2002); Max G. Manwaring, "Street Gangs: The New Urban Insurgency," Strategic Studies Institute (2005); Enrique Desmond Arias, "The Dynamics of Criminal Governance: Networks and Social Order in Rio de Janeiro," *Journal of Latin American Studies* 38:2 (2006).

10. One critical misconception promoted by the liberal enthusiasts of globalization, most prominently by Thomas P. M. Barnett in *The Pentagon's New Map: War and Peace in the Twenty-First Century* (New York: Putnam, 2005), is that the cause of poverty and insecurity and ultimately state failure is "disconnectedness" from the world economy. In fact, all of the most seriously "failed" states—Congo, Somalia, Afghanistan—are deeply connected to the global economy, albeit in ways that are hard to see clearly from London, New York, or Washington. While it is true that they remain weakly connected to the *formal* and *legal* parts of the global economy, such places are in fact highly *deviantly* connected—via the illicit trade in minerals, via piracy, or via the global drug trade, and so on. The crucial issue, in other words, is not connectedness or disconnectedness, but rather what kind of connectedness. Everyone gets their globalization, the only question is what kind.

11. Diane E. Davis, "Irregular armed forces, shifting patterns of commitment, and fragmented sovereignty in the developing world," *Theory and Society* 39:3-4 (2010). It is worth noting here that, paradoxically, globalization in undermining national political institutions identities is not producing a "global" political identity, as the "cosmopolitical" dreamers have hoped, but rather more localized identities rooted in clan, sect, ethnicity, and gang.

12. Kenichi Ohmae, *The End of the Nation-State: The Rise of Regional Economies* (New York: Free Press, 1995) articulated the paradigmatic version of this "hyperglobalist" view from a neoliberal perspective. But hyperglobalism can also be celebrated from a leftish, "cosmopolitan," perspective; see for example: Pheng Cheah and Bruce Robbins, eds., *Cosmopolitics: Thinking and Feeling beyond the Nation* (Minneapolis: University of Minnesota Press, 1999) and Daniele Archibugi, ed., *Debating Cosmopolitics* (London: Verso, 2003).

Appendix IV

Old and New Insurgency Forms—Commercial, Twin, and Plutocratic Insurgency Excerpts

Robert J. Bunker

First Published 15 March 2016 at Strategic Studies Institute, US Army War College [1] Reprinted with permission of the Strategic Studies Institute and U.S. Army War College Press, U.S. Army War College.

This historical review of post-Cold War insurgency typologies will begin with the seminal 1993 work by Steven Metz titled, *The Future of Insurgency.* In about a half- dozen or so pages within that work Metz lays out the conceptual basis of both *commercial* and *spiritual* insurgency projections. These insurgency forms are highlighted below via direct quotes from Metz's paper.[2] Commercial insurgency is described as follows:

> When the discontented define personal meaning by material possessions rather than psychic fulfillment, they create the environment for commercial insurgency.

Commercial insurgency is a quasi-political distortion of materialism.

The quickest and easiest path to material possessions and the satisfaction they appear to bring is crime. And, since the discontented of the Third World feel little attachment to the dominant system of values in their societies anyway, moral restraints on criminal activity are limited.

In this psychological context, commercial insurgency is essentially widespread and sustained criminal activity with a proto-political dimension that challenges the security of the state. In the modern word, its most common manifestation is narco-insurgency, although it may also be based on other forms of crime, especially smuggling. The defining feature is expansion of the criminal activity into a security threat, especially in the hinterlands where government control is limited.[3]

The core regions in which this form of insurgency may arise are Latin America with its endemic organized crime related to narcotics trafficking and smuggling and the Golden Triangle area of Myanmar, Thailand, and Laos based on narcotics production.

***

Robert Bunker, in 2011, then developed the *plutocratic* insurgency form as a variation of Metz's *commercial* insurgency articulation and a post-modern counterpart to Sullivan's concept of *criminal* insurgency. It is also related to John Robb's view on the hollowing out of the state (2008), the *Deviant Globalization* (2011) work of Nils Gilman *et al.,* and the extensive literature on the growing disparity of income between the 1% (to the .001%) and the rest of the Western social classes.[4] Theoretically, this represented a missing component of epochal change model elements focusing on state deinstitutionalization during the transition to the post-modern era. This insurgency form may be contentious due to the fact that ". . . it involves global elites and lacks the traditional trappings of an insurgency (i.e., an armed struggle)."[5] As an insider threat to the Westphalian state system, however, it leverages "the coercive force of the state" via the use of lawyers, lobbyists, and campaign donations to create national laws and policies favorable to its global capitalism needs. This places it an odds with state moderated forms of capitalism, older middle class based socio-economic patterns, and allows for the suppression of protests and dissent of the governed by means of captured domestic policing and court structures. In a 2015 essay on this insurgency form, Bunker identified such predatory capitalist activities as follows:

- Stress profit and equity gain at all costs;
- Follow the principles of hyper-rationalism;
- Show no loyalty to workers, supplies, customers, or even nations;
- Increasingly operate within a sovereign free economy;
- Utilize corruption, co-option, and coercive force as required; and,
- Have a willingness to profit from the informal, and even illicit, economy.[6]

In that essay, Bunker went on to highlight the growing power of multinational corporations and global elites, to better define plutocratic insurgency elements, and discussed the ongoing "public looting for private gain" of what is becoming a new class of supra-bourgeoisie transnational elites.

***

Nils Gilman, in fact, in a 2015 foreword to a work focusing on both the *criminal* and *plutocratic* insurgency forms, went on to highlight their interaction within "The Twin Insurgency" construct tied to epochal change and deviant globalization strategic perceptions. The piece discusses the failures of social modernism, the revolts of mainstream globalization's winners (the plutocrats) and deviant globalization's winners (the criminals) compressing the modern state form between them, and the enclavization of micro-sovereignties and the end of the middle class.[7]

***

Plutocratic (2008). Of all of the insurgency forms offered in this monograph, this may be one of the most contentious. It specifically views the rise of globalized capital devoid of any ties to the state—in essence, representative of an emerging form of 21st century postmodern capitalism—in direct conflict with earlier forms of 20th century state moderated capitalism promoted by liberal democratic governments. It views the rise of stateless multinational corporations, and the global elites (.001% to 1%) they serve as the major stakeholders, as insider insurgent threats to the international order. This insurgent form serves as a corollary to the preceding *criminal* form and represents another variant to Metz's (1993) *commercial* articulation postulated by Bunker (2011). In this case, however, rather than being promoted by criminal outsiders and have nots, this form is being promoted by the winners of globalization to maximize their profits even more. It utilizes subversion and corruption by means of lawyers and lobbyists aimed at democratically elected officials and coercive force based on co-opted elements of the state to shut down protests backed up by private security forces serving as private enclave protective details. It may ultimately result in making the social contract between the citizen and the state as meaningless as it has become between the citizen and their private employer. Business risk and future costs are increasingly being placed on the employee who is being stripped of medical and retirement benefits and are being utilized increasingly in contract and part- time positions. Trending toward this form began with the Reagan-Thatcher revolution in the 1980s, but had not become clear until 2008 with the global nature of the *plutocratic* insurgency—as seen with the ensuing stock market crashes and bank bailouts—unmasking it.[8] An outcome of this insurgency form is the compression of the American middle class and an increasing bifurcation of the haves and have nots within American society. Gilman's "Twin Insurgency" construct later served to illustrate the interaction of this insurgency form and the *criminal* one to the detriment of Westphalian sovereignty and Western democratic peoples.

***

Plutocratic (2008). Strategic implications: None presently. The U.S. military has no current role in the response to the rise of predatory global capitalism and the emerging "sovereign free" entities engaging in it. Rather, varying governmental agencies with a legalistic and economic mandate will be required to promote state moderated capitalist values and laws. Federal law enforcement agencies will be tasked to support such efforts as they relate to financial crimes, tax avoidance, and related offenses.

Notes

The views expressed in this report are those of the author and do not necessarily reflect the official policy or position of the Department of the Army, the Department of Defense, or the U.S. Government. Authors of Strategic Studies Institute (SSI) and U.S. Army War College (USAWC) Press publications enjoy full academic freedom, provided they do not disclose classified information, jeopardize operations security, or misrepresent of official U.S. policy. Such academic freedom empowers them to offer new and sometimes controversial perspectives in the interest of furthering debate on key issues. This report is cleared for public release; distribution is unlimited.

1. https://ssi.armywarcollege.edu/pubs/display.cfm?pubID=1313.
2. A more in depth analysis of these two insurgency forms can be found in John P. Sullivan and Robert J. Bunker, "Rethinking insurgency: criminality, spirituality, and societal warfare in the Americas," in Robert J. Bunker, ed., *Criminal Insurgencies in Mexico and the Americas,* London: Routledge, 2013, pp. 29-50.
3. Steven Metz, *The Future of Insurgency*, Carlisle, PA: Strategic Studies Institute, U.S. Army War College, December 10, 1993, available from http://publications. armywarcollege.edu/pubs/2382.pdf.
4. John Robb, "Onward to a Hollow State," *Global Guerrillas*, September 22, 2008,

available from https://globalguerrillas.typepad.com/globalguerrillas/2008/09/onward-to-a-hol.html; Nils Gilman, Jesse Goldhammer, and Steven Weber, eds., *Deviant Globalization: Black Market Economy in the 21ˢᵗ Century*, New York: Bloomsbury Academic, 2011; David Rothkopf, *Superclass: The Global Power Elite and the World They Are Making*, New York: Farrar, Strauss, and Giroux, 2008; and Chrystia Freeland, *Plutocrats: The Rise of the New Global Super-Rich and the Fall of Everyone Else*, New York: Penguin Books, 2012.

5. Robert J. Bunker, "Plutocratic Insurgency," *Small Wars Journal*, September 6, 2012, available from http://smallwarsjournal.com/blog/plutocratic-insurgency.

6. Robert J. Bunker, "Chapter 6: Public looting for private gain: Predatory capitalism, MNCs and global elites, and plutocratic insurgency," in Robert J. Bunker and Pamela Ligouri Bunker, eds., *Global Criminal and Sovereign Free Economies and the Demise of the Western Democracies: Dark Renaissance*, London: Routledge, 2015, pp. 137-139.

7. Nils Gilman, "Foreword: The twin insurgency—facing plutocrats and criminals," in Robert J. Bunker and Pamela Ligouri Bunker, eds., *Global Criminal and Sovereign Free Economies and the Demise of the Western Democracies: Dark Renaissance*, London: Routledge, 2015, pp. 1-17. This foreword was released while the book was going to publication. See Nils Gilman, "The Twin Insurgency," *The American Interest*, Vol. 9, No. 6, June 15, 2014, available https://www.the-american-interest.com/2014/06/15/the-twin-insurgency/.

8. Author's email correspondence with Nils Gilman, July 13, 2015.

Curated Plutocracy Bibliography

Joel Bakan, _The Corporation: The Pathological Pursuit of Profit and Power_. New York: Simon & Schuster, 2005.

Larry M. Bartels, _Unequal Democracy: The Political Economy of the New Gilded Age_. Princeton: Princeton University Press, 2016.

Jake Bernstein, _Secrecy World: Inside the Panama Papers Investigation of Illicit Money Networks and the Global Elite_. New York, Henry Holt and Co, 2017.

Heather Boushey, J. Bradford DeLong, and Marshall Steinbaum, Eds., _After Piketty: The Agenda for Economics and Inequality_. Cambridge: Harvard University Press, 2017

Robert J. Bunker and Pamela Ligouri Bunker, Eds., _Global Criminal and Sovereign Free Economies and the Demise of the Western Democracies: Dark Renaissance_. London: Routledge, 2015.

Steven Clifford, _The CEO Pay Machine_. New York: Blue Rider Press, 2017.

Chuck Collins, _99 to 1: How Wealth Inequality Is Wrecking the World and What We Can Do about It_. San Francisco: Berrett-Koehler Publishers, 2012.

Mike Davis and Daniel Bertrand Monk, Eds., _Evil Paradises: Dreamworlds of Neoliberalism_. New York: The New Press, 2008.

G. William Domhoff, _Who Rules America? The Triumph of the Corporate Rich_. New York: McGraw-Hill, 2009.

Jeff Faux, *The Global Class War: How America's Bipartisan Elite Lost Our Future - and What It Will Take to Win It Back*. Hoboken: John Wiley & Sons, Inc., 2006.

Jeff Faux, *The Servant Economy: Where America's Elite is Sending the Middle Class*. Hoboken: John Wiley & Sons, Inc., 2012.

Ronald P. Formisano, *Plutocracy in America*. Baltimore: Johns Hopkins University Press, 2015.

Ronald P. Formisano, *American Oligarchy*. Urbana: University of Illinois Press, 2017.

Chrystia Freeland, *Plutocrats*. New York: The Penguin Press, 2012.

Denis L. Gilbert, *The American Class Structure in an Age of Growing Inequality*. Thousand Oaks: Sage Publications, 2014.

Nils Gilman, Jesse Goldhammer, and Steven Weber, Eds., *Deviant Globalization: Black Market Economy in the 21st Century*. New York: Continuum, 2011.

Anand Giridharadas, *Winners Take All: The Elite Charade of Changing the World*. New York: Alfred A. Knopf, 2018.

David Graeber, *Bullshit Jobs: A Theory*. New York: Simon & Schuster, 2018.

David Grusky and Tamar Kricheli-Katz, Eds., *The New Gilded Age*. Stanford: Stanford University Press, 2012.

Brooke Harrington, *Capital without Borders: Wealth Managers and the One Percent.* Cambridge, MA: Harvard University Press, 2016.

Nigar Hashimzade and Yuliya Epifantseva, Eds., *The Routledge Companion to Tax Avoidance Research*. Abingdon: Routledge, 2017.

Noreena Hertz, *The Silent Takeover: Global Capitalism and the Death of Democracy*. New York: The Free Press, 2001.

Louis Hyman, *Temp: How American Work, American Business, and the American Dream Became Temporary*. New York: Viking, 2018.

Paul Kennedy, *Vampire Capitalism: Fractured Societies and Alternative Futures*. New York: Palgrave Macmillan, 2017.

Sarah Kessler, *Gigged: The End of the Job and the Future of Work*. New York: Saint Martin's Press, 2018.

Naomi Klein, *The Shock Doctrine: The Rise of Disaster Capitalism*. New York: Metropolitan Books, 2007.

Margaret Kohn, *Brave New Neighborhoods: The Privatization of Public Space*. London: Routledge, 2004.

David C. Korten, *When Corporations Rule the World*. San Francisco: Berrett-Koehler Publishers, 2001.

Isaac William Martin, *Rich People's Movements: Grassroots Campaigns to Untax the One Percent*. Oxford: Oxford University Press, 2013.

Walter Mattli, *Darkness by Design: The Hidden Power in Global Capital Markets*. Princeton: Princeton University Press, 2019.

Peter Philips, *Giants: The Global Power Elite*. New York: Seven Stories Press, 2018.

Thomas Piketty (Arthur Goldhammer, Trans.), *Capital in the Twenty-First Century*. Harvard: Belknap Press, 2014.

Thomas Piketty (Arthur Goldhammer, Trans.), *The Economics of Inequality*. Harvard: Belknap Press, 2015.

Sam Pizzigati, *The Rich Don't Always Win: The Forgotten Triumph Over Plutocracy that Created the American Middle Class, 1900-1970*. New York: Seven Stories Press, 2012.

Alissa Quart, *Squeezed: Why Our Families Can't Afford America*. New York: Ecco, 2018.

Dani Rodrik, *The Globalization Paradox: Democracy and the Future of the World Economy*. New York: W. W. Norton & Company, 2012.

David Rothkopf, *Superclass: The Global Power Elite and the World They Are Making*. New York: Farrar, Straus, and Giroux, 2008.

David Rothkopf, *Power, Inc.*, New York: Farrar, Straus, and Giroux, 2012.

Kay Lehman Schlozman, Henry E. Brady, and Sidney Verba, *Unequal and Unrepresented: Political Inequality and the People's Voice in the New Gilded Age*. Princeton: Princeton University Press, 2018.

Joseph E. Stiglitz, *The Price of Inequality: How Today's Divided Society Endangers Our Future*. New York: W.W. Norton & Company, 2013.

Joseph E. Stiglitz, *The Great Divide: Unequal Societies and What We Can Do About Them*. New York, NY: W. W. Norton and Company, 2016.

David Stockman, *The Great Deformation: The Corruption of Capitalism in America*. New York: Public Affairs, 2013.

Tim Wu, *The Curse of Bigness: Antitrust in the New Gilded Age*. New York: Columbia Global Reports, 2018.

Andrew Yang, *The War on Normal People: The Truth About America's Disappearing Jobs and Why Universal Basic Income Is Our Future*. New York: Hachette Books, 2018.

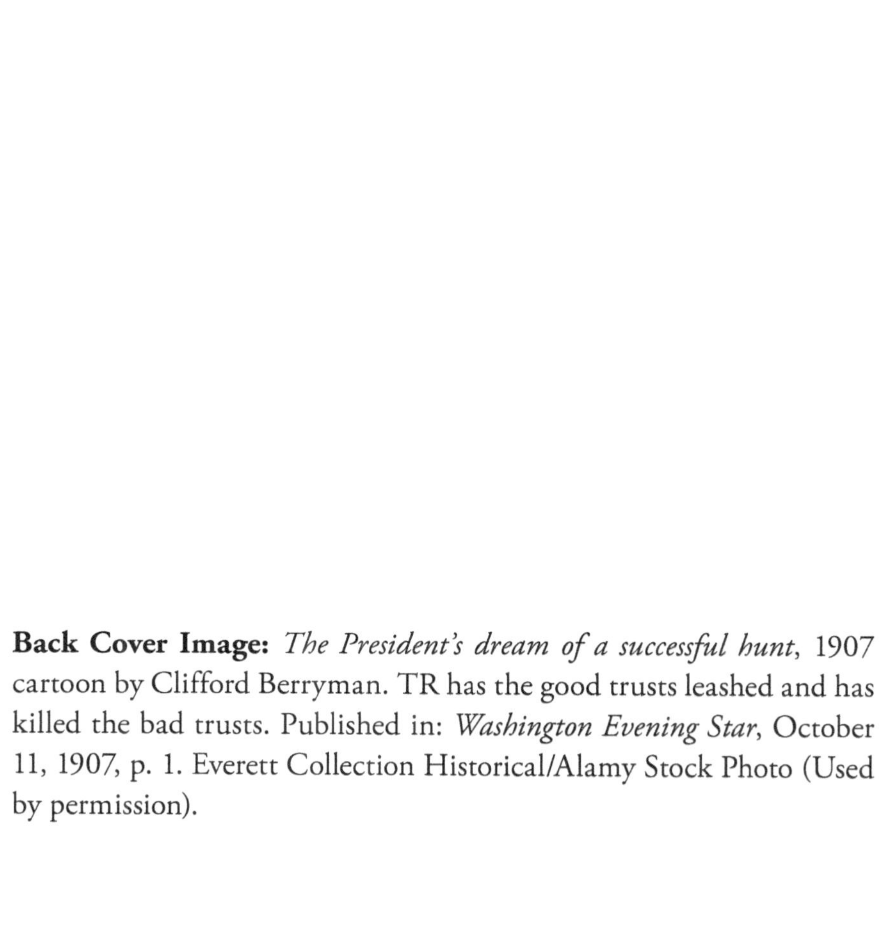

Back Cover Image: *The President's dream of a successful hunt,* 1907 cartoon by Clifford Berryman. TR has the good trusts leashed and has killed the bad trusts. Published in: *Washington Evening Star,* October 11, 1907, p. 1. Everett Collection Historical/Alamy Stock Photo (Used by permission).